The Foundations of Personality

Abraham Myerson

The Foundations of Personality

Contact:
IndoEuropeanPublishing@gmail.com

The present edition is a reproduction of 1931 publication of this work, produced in the current edition with completely new, easy to read format by Indo-European Publishing.

For an authentic reading experience, the Spelling, punctuation, and capitalization have been retained from the original text.

Cover Design by Indo-European Design Team

ISBN: 978-1-60444-732-3

IndoEuropean
Publishing.com
Los Angeles, CA, USA

CONTENTS

INTRODUCTION

Man's interest in character is founded on an intensely practical need. In whatsoever relationship we deal with our fellows, we base our intercourse largely on our understanding of their characters. The trader asks concerning his customer, "Is he honest?" and the teacher asks about the pupil, "Is he earnest?" The friend bases his friendship on his good opinion of his friend; the foe seeks to know the weak points in the hated one's make-up; and the maiden yearning for her lover whispers to, herself, "Is he true?" Upon our success in reading the character of others, upon our understanding of ourselves hangs a good deal of our life's success or failure.

Because the feelings are in part mirrored on the face and body, the experience of mankind has become crystallized in beliefs, opinions and systems of character reading which are based on physiognomy, shape of head, lines of hand, gait and even the method of dress and the handwriting. Some of these all men believe in, at least in part. For example, every one judges character to a certain extent by facial expression, manner, carriage and dress. A few of the methods used have become organized into specialties, such as the study of the head or phrenology, and the study of the hand or palmistry. All of these systems are really "materialistic" in that they postulate so close a union of mind and body as to make them inseparable.

But there are grave difficulties in the way of character-judging by these methods. Take, for example, the study of the physiognomy as a means to character understanding. All the physiognomists, as well as the average man, look upon the high, wide brow as related to great intelligence. And so it is—sometimes. But it is also found in connection with disease of the brain, as in hydrocephalus, and in old cases of rickets. You may step into hospitals for the feeble-minded or for the insane and find here and there a high, noble brow. Conversely you may attend a scientific convention and find that the finest paper of the meeting will be read not by some Olympian-browed member, but by a man with a low, receding forehead, who nevertheless possesses a high-grade intellect.

So for centuries men have recognized in the large aquiline nose a sign of power and ability. Napoleon's famous dictum that no man with this type of proboscis is a fool has been accepted by many, most of whom, like Napoleon probably, have large aquiline noses. The number of failures with this facial peculiarity has never been studied, nor has any one remarked that many a highly successful man has a snub nose. And in fact the only kind of a nose that has a real character value is the one presenting no obstruction to breathing. The assigned value given to a "pretty" nose has no relation to character, except as its owner is vain because of it.

1

One might go on indefinitely discussing the various features of the face and discovering that only a vague relationship to character existed. The thick, moist lower lip is the sensual lip, say the physiognomists, but there are saints with sensual lips and chaste thoughts. Squinty eyes may indicate a shifty character, but more often they indicate conjunctivitis or some defect of the optical apparatus. A square jaw indicates determination and courage, but a study of the faces of men who won medals in war for heroism does not reveal a preponderance of square jaws. In fact, man is a mosaic of characters, and a fine nature in one direction may be injured by a defect in another; even if one part of the face really did mean something definite, no one could figure out its character value because of the influence of other features—contradictory, inconsistent, supplementary. Just as the wisest man of his day took bribes as Lord Chancellor, so the finest face may be invalidated by some disharmony, and a fatal weakness may disintegrate a splendid character. Moreover, no one really studies faces disinterestedly, impartially, without prejudice. We like or dislike too readily, we are blinded by the race, sex and age of the one studied, and, most fatal of all, we judge by standards of beauty that are totally misleading. The sweetest face may hide the most arrant egoist, for facial beauty has very little to do with the nature behind the face. In fact, facial make-up is more influenced by diet, disease and racial tendency than by character.

It would be idle to take up in any detail the claims of phrenologist and palmist. The former had a very respectable start in the work of Broca and Gall [1] in that the localization of function in the various parts of the brain made at least partly logical the belief that the conformation of the head also indicated functions of character. But there are two fatal flaws in the system of phrenological claims. First, even if there were an exact cerebral localization of powers, which there is not, it would by no means follow that the shape of the head outlined the brain. In fact, it does not, for the long-headed are not long-brained, nor are the short-headed short-brained. Second, the size and disposal of the sinuses, the state of nutrition in childhood have far more to do with the "bumps" of the head than brain or character. The bump of philoprogenitiveness has in my experience more often been the result of rickets than a sign of parental love.

Without meaning to pun, we may dismiss the claims of palmistry offhand. Normally the lines of the hand do not change from birth to death, but character does change. The hand, its shape and its texture are markedly influenced by illness, [2] toil and care. And gait, carriage, clothes

---

[1] It is to be remembered that phrenology had a good standing at one time, though it has since lapsed into quackdom. This is the history of many a "short cut" into knowledge. Thus the wisest men of past centuries believed in astrology. Paracelsus, who gave to the world the use of Hg in therapeutics, relied in large part for his diagnosis and cures upon alchemy and astrology.

[2] Notably is the shape of the hand changed by chronic heart and lung disease and by arthritis. But the influence of the endocrinal secretions is very great.

and the dozen and one details by which we judge our fellows indicate health, strength, training and culture, all of which are components of character, or rather are characters of importance but give no clue to the deeper-lying traits.

As a matter of fact, judgment of character will never be attained through the study of face, form or hand. As language is a means not only of expressing truth but of disguising it, so these surface phenomena are as often masks as guides. Any sober-minded student of life, intent on knowing himself or his fellows, will seek no royal road to this knowledge, but will endeavor to understand the fundamental forces of character, will strive to trace the threads of conduct back to their origins in motive, intelligence, instinct and emotion.

We have emphasized the practical value of some sort of character analysis in dealing with others. But to know himself has a hugely practical value to every man, since upon that knowledge depends self-correction. For "man is the only animal that deliberately undertakes while reshaping his outer world to reshape himself also." [3] Moreover, man is the only seeker of perfection; he is a deep, intense critic of himself. To reach nobility of character is not a practical aim, but is held to be an end sufficient in itself. So man constantly probes into himself—"Are my purposes good; is my will strong—how can I strengthen my control, how make righteous my instincts and emotions?" It is true that there is a worship—and always has been—of efficiency and success as against character; that man has tended to ask more often, "What has he done?" or, "What has he got?" rather than, "What is he?" and that therefore man in his self-analysis has often asked, "How shall I get?" or, "How shall I do?" In the largest sense these questions are also questions of character, for even if we discard as inadequate the psychology which considers behavior alone as important, conduct is the fruit of character, without which it is sterile.

This book does not aim at any short cuts by which man may know himself or his neighbor. It seeks to analyze the fundamentals of personality, avoiding metaphysics as the plague. It does not define character or seek to separate it from mind and personality. Written by a neurologist, a physician in the active practice of his profession, it cannot fail to bear more of the imprint of medicine, of neurology, than of psychology and philosophy. Yet it has also laid under contribution these fields of human effort. Mainly it will, I hope, bear the marks of everyday experience, of contact with the world and with men and women and children as brother, husband, father, son, lover, hater, citizen, doer and observer. For it is this plurality of contact that vitalizes, and he who has not drawn his universals of character out of the particulars of everyday life is a cloistered theorist, aloof from reality.

---

[3] Hocking.

CHAPTER I

THE ORGANIC BASIS OF CHARACTER

The history of Man's thought is the real history of mankind. Back of all the events of history are the curious systems of beliefs for which men have lived and died. Struggling to understand himself, Man has built up and discarded superstitions, theologies and sciences.

Early in this strange and fascinating history he divided himself into two parts—a body and a mind. Working together with body, mind somehow was of different stuff and origin than body and had only a mysterious connection with it. Theology supported this belief; metaphysics and philosophy debated it with an acumen that was practically sterile of usefulness. Mind and body "interacted" in some mysterious way; mind and body were "parallel" and so set that thought-processes and brain-processes ran side by side without really having anything to do with one another. [4] With the development of modern anatomy, physiology and psychology, the time is ripe for men boldly to say that applying the principle of causation in a practical manner leaves no doubt that mind and character are organic, are functions of the organism and do not exist independently of it. I emphasize "practical" in relation to causation because it would be idle for us here to enter into the philosophy of cause and effect. Such discussion is not taken seriously by the very philosophers who most earnestly enter into it.

The statement that mind is a function of the organism is not necessarily "materialistic." The body is a living thing and as such is as "spiritualistic" as life itself. Enzymes, internal secretions, nervous activities

---

[4] William James in Volume 1 of his "Psychology" gives an interesting resume of the theories that consider the relationship of mind (thought and consciousness) to body. He quotes the "lucky" paragraph from Tyndall, "The passage from the physics of the brain to the corresponding facts of consciousness is unthinkable. Granted that a definite thought and a definite molecular action in the brain occur simultaneously; we do not possess the intellectual organ, or apparently any trace of the organ which would enable us to pass by a process of reasoning from one to the other." This is the "parallel" theory which postulates a hideous waste of energy in the universe and which throws out of count the same kind of reasoning by which Tyndall worked on light, heat, etc. We cannot understand the beginning and the end of motion, we cannot understand causation. Probably when Tyndall's thoughts came slowly and he was fatigued he said—"Well, a good cup of coffee will make me think faster." In conceding this practical connection between mind and body, every "spiritualist" philosopher gives away his case whenever he rests or eats.

are the products of cells whose powers are indeed drawn from the ocean of life.

To prove this statement, which is a cardinal thesis of this book, I shall adduce facts of scientific and facts of common knowledge. One might start with the statement that the death of the body brings about the abolition of mind and character, but this, of course, proves nothing, since it might well be that the body was a lever for the expression of mind and character, and with its disappearance as a functioning agent such expression was no longer possible.

It is convenient to divide our exposition into two parts, the first the dependence upon proper brain function and structure, and the second the dependence upon the proper health of other organs. For it is not true that mind and character are functions of the brain alone; they are functions of the entire organism. The brain is simply the largest and most active of the organs upon which the mental life depends; but there are minute organs, as we shall see, upon whose activity the brain absolutely depends.

Any injury to the brain may destroy or seriously impair the mentality of the individual. This is too well known to need detailed exposition. Yet some cases of this type are fundamental in the exquisite way they prove (if anything can be proven) the dependence of mind upon bodily structure.

In some cases of fracture of the skull, a piece of bone pressing upon the brain may profoundly alter memory, mood and character. Removal of the piece of bone restores the mind to normality. This is also true of brain tumor of certain types, for example, frontal endotheliomata, where early removal of the growth demonstrates first that a "physical" agent changes mind and character, and second that a "physical" agent, such as the knife of the surgeon, may act to reestablish mentality.

In cases of hydrocephalus (or water on the brain), where there is an abnormal secretion of cerebro-spinal fluid acting to increase the pressure on the brain, the simple expedient of withdrawing the fluid by lumbar puncture brings about normal mental life. As the fluid again collects, the mental life becomes cloudy, and the character alters (irritability, depressed mood, changed purpose, lowered will); another lumbar puncture and presto!—the individual is for a time made over more completely than conversion changes a sinner,—and more easily.

Take the case of the disease known as General Paresis, officially called Dementia Paralytica. This disease is caused by syphilis and is one of its late results. The pathological changes are widespread throughout the brain but may at the onset be confined mostly to the frontal lobes. The very first change may be—and usually is—a change in character! The man hitherto kind and gentle becomes irritable, perhaps even brutal. One whose sex morals have been of the most conventional kind, a loyal husband, suddenly becomes a profligate, reckless and debauched, perhaps even perverted. The man of firm purposes and indefatigable industry may lose his grip upon the ambitions and strivings of his lifetime and become an inert slacker, to the amazement of his associates. Many a fine character, many a splendid mind, has reached a lofty height and then crumbled before the assaults of this disease upon the brain. Philosopher, poet, artist, statesman, captain of industry, handicraftsman, peasant, courtesan and housewife,—all are lowered to the same level of dementia and destroyed character by the consequences of the thickened meninges, the altered blood vessels and the injured nerve cells.

Now and then one is fortunate enough to treat with success an early case of General Paresis. And then the reversed miracle takes place, unfortunately too rarely! The disordered mind, the altered character, leaps upward to its old place,—after being dosed by the marvelous drug Salvarsan, created by the German Jewish scientist, Paul Ehrlich.

Of extraordinary interest are the rare cases of loss of personal identity seen after brain injury, say in war. A man is knocked unconscious by a blow and upon restoration of consciousness is separated from that past in which his ego resides. He does not know his history or his name, and that continuity of the "self" so deeply prized and held by all religions to be part of his immortality is gone. Then after a little while, a few days or weeks, the disarranged neuronic pathways reestablish themselves as usual,—and the ego comes back to the man.

One might cite the feeble-mindedness that results from meningitis, brain tumor, brain abscess, brain wounds, etc., as further evidence of the dependence of mind upon brain, of its status as a function of brain. No philosopher seriously doubts that equilibrium and movement are functions of the brain, and yet to prove this there is no evidence of any other kind than that cited to prove the relationship of mind to brain. [5] And what applies to the intelligence applies as forcibly to character, for purpose, emotion, mood, instinct and will are altered with these diseases.

Interesting as is the relationship between mind and character and the brain, it is at the present overshadowed by the fascinating relationship between these psychical activities and the bodily organs. What I am about to cite from medicine and biology is part of the finest achievements of these sciences and hints at a future in which a true science of mind and character will appear.

Certain of the glands of the body are described as glands of internal secretions in that the products of their activity, their secretions, are poured into the blood stream rather than on the surface of the body or into the digestive tract. The most prominent of these glands, all of which are very small and extraordinarily active, are as follows:

---

[5] Except that equilibrium does not itself judge of its relationship to brain, whereas mind is the sole judge of its relationship and dependence on brain. Since everything in the world is a mental event, mentality cannot be dependent upon anything, and everything depends upon mind for its existence, or at least its recognition. But we get nowhere by such "logic" gone mad. Apply the same kind of reasoning to brain-mind, body-mind relationship which anatomists and physiologists apply to other functions, and one can no longer separate body and mind.

The Pituitary Body (Hypophysis)—a tiny structure which is situated at the base of the brain but is not a part of that organ.

The Pineal Body (Epiphysis)—a still smaller structure, located within the brain substance, having, however, no relationship to the brain. This gland has only lately acquired a significance. Descartes thought it the seat of the soul because it is situated in the middle of the brain.

The Thyroid gland, a somewhat larger body, situated in the front of the neck, just beneath the larynx. We shall deal with this in some detail later on.

The Parathyroids, minute organs, four in number, just behind the thyroid.

The Thymus, a gland placed just within the thorax, which reaches its maximum size at birth and then gradually recedes until at twenty it has almost disappeared.

The Adrenal glands, one on each side of the body, above and adjacent to the kidney. These glands, which are each made up of two opposing structures, stand in intimate relation to the sympathetic nervous system and secrete a substance called adrenalin.

The Sex organs, the ovary in the female and the testicle in the male, in addition to producing the female egg (ovum) and the male seed (sperm), respectively, produce substances of unknown character that have hugely important roles in the establishment of mind, temperament and sex character.

Without going into the details of the functions of the endocrine glands, one may say that they are "the managers of the human body." Every individual, from the time he is born until the time he dies, is under the influence of these many different kinds of elements,—some of them having to do with the development of the bones and teeth, some with the development of the body and nervous system, some with the development of the mind, etc. (and character), and later on with reproduction. These glands are not independent of one another but interact in a marvelous manner so that under or overaction of any one of them upsets a balance that exists between them, and thus produces a disorder that is quite generalized in its effects. The work on this subject is a tribute to medicine and one pauses in respect and admiration before the names and labors of Brown, Sequard, Addison, Graves and Basedow, Horsley, King, Schiff, Schafer, Takamine, Marie, Cushing, Kendal, Sajous and others of equal insight and patient endeavor.

But let us pass over to the specific instances that bear on our thesis, to wit, that mind and character are functions of the organism and have their seat not only in the brain but in the entire organism.

How do the endocrines prove this? As well as they prove that physical growth and the growth of the secondary sex characters are dependent on these glands. Take diseases of the thyroid gland as the first and shining example.

The thyroid secretes a substance which substantially is an "iodized globulin,"—and which can be separated from the gland products. This secretion has the main effect of "activating metabolism" (Vassale and Generali); in ordinary phrase it acts to increase the discharge of energy of the cells of the body. In all living things there is a twofold process constantly going on: first the building up of energy by means of the foodstuffs, air and water taken in, and second a discharge of energy in the form of heat, motion and—in my belief —emotion and thought itself, though this would be denied by many psychologists. Yet how escape this conclusion from the following facts?

There is a congenital disease called cretinism which essentially is due to a lack of thyroid secretion. This disease is particularly prevalent in Southern France, Spain, Upper Italy and Switzerland. It is characterized mainly by marked dwarfism and imbecility, so that the adult untreated cretin remains about as large as a three or four-year-old child and has the mental level about that of a child of the same age. But, this comparison as to intelligence is a gross injustice to the child, for it leaves out the difference in character between the child and the cretin. The latter has none of the curiosity, the seeking for experience, the active interest, the pliant expanding will, the sweet capacity for affection, friendship and love present in the average child. The cretin is a travesty on the human being in body, mind and character.

But feed him thyroid gland. Mind you, the dried substance of the glands, not of human beings, but of mere sheep. The cretin begins to grow mentally and physically and loses to a large extent the grotesqueness of his appearance. He grows taller; his tongue no longer lolls in his mouth; the hair becomes finer, the hands less coarse, and the patient exhibits more normal human emotions, purposes, intelligence. True, he does not reach normality, but that is because other defects beside the thyroid defect exist and are not altered by the thyroid feeding.

There is a much more spectacular disease to be cited, —a relatively infrequent but well-understood condition called myxoedema, which occurs mainly in women and is also due to a deficiency in the thyroid secretion. As a result the patient, who may have been a bright, capable, energetic person, full of the eager purposes and emotions of life, gradually becomes dull, stupid, apathetic, without fear, anger, love, joy or sorrow, and without purpose or striving. In addition the body changes, the hair becomes coarse and scanty, the skin thick and swollen (hence the name of the disease) and various changes take place in the sweat secretion, the heart action, etc.

Then, having made the diagnosis, work the great miracle! Obtain the dried thyroid glands of the sheep, prepared by the great drug houses as a by-product of the butcher business, and feed this poor, transformed creature with these glands! No fairy waving a magical wand ever worked a greater enchantment, for with the first dose the patient improves and in a relatively short time is restored to normal in skin, hair, sweat, etc., and MIND and character! To every physician who has seen this happen under his own eyes and by his direction there comes a conviction that mind and character have their seat in the organic activities of the body,—and nowhere else.

An interesting confirmation of this is that when the thyroid is overactive, a condition called hyperthyroidism, the patient becomes very restless and thin, shows excessive emotionality, sleeplessness, has a rapid heart action, tremor and many other signs not necessary to detail here. The thyroid in these cases is usually swollen. One of the methods used to treat the disease is to remove some of the gland surgically. In the early days an operator would occasionally remove too, much gland and then the symptoms, of myxoedema would occur. This necessitated the artificial feeding of thyroid the rest of the patient's life! With the proper dosage of the gland substance the patient remains normal; with too little she becomes dull and stupid; with too much she becomes unstable and emotional!

There are plenty of other examples of the influence of the endocrines on mind, character and personality. I here briefly mention a few of these.

In the disease called acromegaly, which is due to a change in the pituitary gland, amongst other things are noted "melancholic tendencies, loss of memory and mental and physical torpor."

A very profound effect on character and personality, exclusive of intelligence, is that of the sex glands. One need not accept the Freudian extravagances regarding the way in which the sex feelings and impulses enter into our thoughts, emotions, purposes and acts. No unbiased observer of himself or his fellows but knows that the satisfaction or non-satisfaction of the sex feeling, its excitation or its suppression are of great importance in the destinies of character. Further, man as herdsman and man as tyrant have carried on huge experiments to show how necessary to normal character the sex glands are.

As herdsman he has castrated his male Bos and obtained the ox. And the ox is the symbol of patience, docility, steady labor, without lust or passion,—and the very opposite of his non-castrated brother, the bull. The bull is the symbol of irritability and unteachableness, who will not be easily yoked or led and who is the incarnation of lust and passion. One is the male transformed into neuter gender; and the other is rampant with the fierceness of his sex.

Compare the eunuch and the normal man. If the eunuch state be imposed in infancy, the shape of the body, its hairiness, the quality of the voice and the character are altered in characteristic manner. The eunuch essentially is neither man nor woman, but a repelling Something intermediate.

Enough has been said to show that mind and character are dependent upon the health of the brain and the glands of the body; that somewhere in the interaction of tissues, in the chemistry of life, arises thought, purpose, emotion, conduct and deed. But we need not go so far afield as pathology to show this, for common experience demonstrates it as well.

If character is control of emotions, firmness of purpose, cheerfulness of outlook and vigor of thought and memory, then the tired

9

man, worn out by work or a long vigil, is changed in character. Such a person in the majority of cases is irritable, showing lack of control and emotion; he slackens in his life's purposes, loses cheerfulness and outlook and finds it difficult to concentrate his thoughts or to recall his memories. Though this change is temporary and disappears with rest, the essential fact is not altered, namely, fatigue alters character. It is also true that not all persons show this vulnerability to fatigue in equal measure. For that matter, neither do they show an equal liability to infectious diseases, equal reaction to alcohol or injury. The feeling of vigor which rest gives changes the expression of personality to a marked degree. It is true that we are not apt to think of the tired man as changed in character; yet we must admit on reflection that he has undergone transformation.

Even a loaded bowel may, as is well known, alter the reaction to life. Among men who are coarse in their language there is a salutation more pertinent than elegant that inquires into the state of the bowels. [6] The famous story of Voltaire and the Englishman, in which the sage agreed to suicide because life was not worth living when his digestion was disordered and who broke his agreement when he purged himself, illustrates how closely mood is related to the intestinal tract. And mood is the background of the psychic life, upon which depends the direction of our thoughts, cheerful or otherwise, the vigor of our will and purpose. Mood itself arises in part from the influences that stream into the muscles, joints, heart, lungs, liver, spleen, kidneys, digestive tract and all the organs and tissues by way of the afferent nerves (sympathetic and cerebro-spinal). Mood is thus in part a reflection of the health and proper working of the organism; it is the most important aspect of the subconsciousness, and upon it rests the structure of character and personality.

This does not mean that only the healthy are cheerful, or that the sick are discouraged. To affirm the dependence of mind upon body is not to deny that one may build up faith, hope, courage, through example and precept, or that one may not inherit a cheerfulness and courage (or the reverse). "There are men," says James, "who are born under a cloud." But exceptional individuals aside, the mass of mankind generates its mood either in the tissues of the body or in the circumstances of life.

Children, because they have not built up standards of thought, mood and act, demonstrate in a remarkable manner the dependence of their character upon health.

A child shows the onset of an illness by a complete change in character. I remember one sociable, amiable lad of two, rich in the curiosity and expanding friendliness of that time of life, who became sick with diphtheria. All his basic moods became altered, and all his wholesome

---

[6] What is called coarse is frequently crudely true. Thus, in the streets, in the workshops, and where men untrammeled by niceties engage in personalities the one who believes the other to be a "crank" informs him in crude language that he has intestinal stasis (to put the diagnosis in medical language) and advises him accordingly to "take a pill."

reactions to life disappeared. He was cross and contrary, he had no interest in people or in things, he acted very much as do those patients in an insane hospital who suffer from Dementia Praecox. What is character if it is not interest and curiosity, friendliness and love, obedience and trust, cheerfulness and courage? Yet a sick child, especially if very young, loses all these and takes on the reverse characters. The little lad spoken of became "himself" again when the fever and the pain lifted. Yet for a long time afterward he showed a greater liability to fear than before, and it was not until six months or more had repaired the more subtle damage to his organism that he became the hardy little adventurer in life that he had been before the illness.

There is plenty of chemical proof of this thesis as here set forth. Men have from time immemorial put things "in their bellies to steal their brains away." The chemical substance known as ethyl alcohol has been an artificial basis of good fellowship the world over, as well as furnishing a very fair share of the tragedy, the misery and the humor of the world. This is because, when ingested in any amount, its absorption produces changes in the flow of thought, in the attitude toward life, in the mood, the emotions, the purposes, the conduct,—in a word, in character. One sees the austere man, when drunk, become ribald; the repressed, close-fisted become open-mouthed and open-hearted; the kindly, perhaps brutal; the controlled, uncontrolled. In the change of character it effects is the regret over its passing and the greatest reason for prohibition.

Alcohol causes several well-defined mental diseases as well as mere drunkenness. In Delirium Tremens there is an acute delirium, with confusion, excitement and auditory and visual hallucinations of all kinds. The latter symptom is so prominent as to give the reason for the popular name of the "snakes." In alcoholic hallucinosis the patient has delusions of persecution and hears voices accusing him of all kinds of wrong-doing. Very frequently, as all the medical writers note, these voices are "conscience exteriorized"; that is, the voices say of him just what he has been saying of himself in the struggle against drink. Then there is Alcoholic Paranoia, a disease in which the main change is a delusion of jealousy directed against the mate, who is accused of infidelity. It is interesting that in the last two diseases the patient is "clear-headed"; memory and orientation are good; the patient speaks well and gives no gross signs of his trouble. As the effects of the alcohol wear away, the patient recovers,—i.e., his character returns to its normal.

It becomes necessary at this point to take up a reverse side of our study, namely, what is often called the influence of "mind over matter." Such cures of disease as seem to follow prayer and faith are cited; such incidents as the great strength of men under emotion or the disturbances of the body by ideas are listed as examples. This is not the place to discuss cures by faith. It suffices to say this: that in the first place most of such cures relate to hysteria, a disease we shall discuss later but which is characterized by symptoms that appear and disappear like magic. I have seen "cured" (and have "cured") such patients, affected with paralysis, deafness, dumbness, blindness, etc., with reasoning, electricity, bitter tonics, fake electrodes, hypnotism, and in one case by a forcible slap upon a prominent and naked part of the body. Hysteria has been the basis of many a saint's reputation and likewise has aided many a physician into affluence.

Nor is the effect of coincidence taken into account in estimating cures, whether by faith or by drugs. Many a physician has owed his start to the fact that he was called in on some obscure case just when the patient was on the turn towards recovery. He then receives the credit that belonged to Nature. Medical men understand this,—that many diseases are "self-limited" and pass through a cycle influenced but little by treatment. But faith curists do not so understand, and neither does the mass of people, so that neither one nor the other separates "post hoc" from "propter hoc." If the truth were told, most of the miracle and faith cures that are not of hysterical origin are due to coincidence. Faith curists report in detail their successes, but we have no statistics whatever of their failures.

If thought is a product of the brain activated by the rest of the organism, it would be perfectly natural to expect that thought would influence the organism. That thought is intimately associated with impulses to action is well known. This action largely takes place in the speech muscles but also it irradiates into the rest of the organism. Especially is this true if the thought is associated with some emotion. Emotion, as we shall discuss it later, is at least in large part a bodily reaction, a disturbance in heart, lungs, abdominal organs, blood vessels, sympathetic nervous system, endocrines, etc. The effect of thought and emotion upon the body, whether to heighten its activity or to lower its activity, is, from my point of view, merely the effect of one function of the organism upon others. We are not surprised if digestion affects thinking and mood, and we need not be surprised if thought and mood disturb or improve digestion. And we may substitute for digestion any other organic function.

As a working basis, substantiated by the kind of proof we use in our daily lives in laboratories and machine shops, we may state that mind, character and personality are organic in their origin and are functions of the entire organism. What a man thinks, does and feels (or perhaps we should reverse this order) is the result of environmental forces playing upon a marvelously intricate organism in which every part reacts on every other part, in which nervous energy influences digestion and digestion influences nervous energy, in which enzymes, hormones, and endocrines engage in an extraordinary game of checks and balance, which in the normal course of events make for the individual's welfare. What a man thinks, does, and feels influences the fate of his organism from one end of life to the other.

We have not adduced in favor of the organic nature of mind, character and personality the facts of heredity. This is a most important set of facts, for if the egg and the sperm carry mentality and personality, they may be presumed to carry them in some organic form, as organic potentialities, just as they carry size, [7] color, sex, etc. That abnormal mind is inherited is shown in family insanity in the second, third and fourth generation cases of mental disease. Certain types of feeble-mindedness surely are transmitted from generation to generation, as witness the case of the famous (or infamous) Jukes family. In this group vagabondage, crime, immorality and other character abnormalities appeared linked with the feeble-mindedness. But there is plenty of evidence to show that normal character qualities are inherited as well as the abnormal. [8] Galton, the father of eugenics, collected facts from the history of successful families to prove this. It is true that he failed to take into account the facts of SOCIAL heredity, in that a gifted man establishes a place for himself and a tradition for his family that is of great help to his son. Nevertheless, musical ability runs in families and races, as does athletic ability, high temper, passion, etc. In short, at least the potentialities, the capacities for character, are transmitted together with other qualities as part of the capital of heredity.

This means that in studying character and personality, we must start with an analysis of the physical make-up of the individual. We are not yet at the point in science where we can easily get at the activities of the endocrinal glands in normal mentality. We are able to recognize certain fundamental types, but more we cannot do; nor are we able to measure nervous energy except in relatively crude ways, but these crude ways have great value under certain conditions.

When there has been a change in personality, the question of bodily disease is always paramount. The first questions to be asked under such circumstances are, "Is this person sick?" "Is the brain involved?" "Are endocrinal glands involved?" "Is there disease of some organ of the body, acting to lower the feeling of well-being, acting to slacken the purposes and the will or to obscure the intelligence?"

There are other important questions of this type to answer, some of which may be deferred for the time. Meanwhile, the next equally fundamental thesis is on the effect of the environment upon mind, character and personality.

---

[7] I have collected and published from the records and wards of the State Hospital at Taunton, Mass., many such cases. The whole subject is to be reviewed in a following book on the transmission of mental disease, but no one seriously doubts that there is a transference of "insane" character from generation to generation. In fact, I believe that a little too much stress hag been laid on this aspect of mental disease and not enough on the fact that sickness may injure a family stock and cause the descendants to be insane. Any one who has seen a single case of congenital General Paresis, where a child has a mental disease due to the syphilis of a parent, and can doubt that character and mind are organic, simply is blinded by theological or metaphysical prejudice.

[8] See his book "Genius."

CHAPTER II
THE ENVIRONMENTAL BASIS OF CHARACTER

From the time any one of us is born into the world he is subject to the influences of forces that reach backwards to the earliest days of the race. The "dead hand" rules,—yes, and the dead thought, belief and custom continue to shape the lives and character of the living. The invention and development of speech and writing have brought into every man's career the mental life and character of all his own ancestors and the ancestors of every other man.

A child is not born merely to a father and a mother. He is born to a group, fiercely and definitely prejudiced in custom, belief and ideal, with ways of doing, feeling and thinking which it seeks to impose on each of its new members. Family, tribe, race and nation all demand of each accession that he accept their ideals, habits and beliefs on peril of disapproval and even of punishment. And man is so constituted that the approval and disapproval of his group mean more to him even than his life.

The social setting into which each one is born is his social heredity. "The heredity with which civilization is most supremely concerned," says Sir Edwin Ray Lankester, "is not that which is inborn in the individual. It is the SOCIAL inheritance which constitutes the dominant factor in human progress." [9] It is this social inheritance which shapes our characters, rough-hewn by nature. It is by the light of each person's social inheritance that we must also judge his character.

"Education," says Oliver Wendell Holmes, "is only second to nature. Imagine all the infants born this year in Boston and Timbuctoo to change places!" And education is merely social inheritance organized by parents and teachers for the sake of molding the scholar into usefulness and conformity to the group into which he is born. There may be in each individual an innate capacity for this ability or that, for expressing and controlling this or that emotion, for developing this or that purpose. Which ability will be developed, which emotion or purpose will be expressed, is a matter of the age in which a man is born, the country in which he lives, the

---

[9] The Eugenists fiercely contest this statement, and rightly, for it is extreme. Society is threatened at its roots by the present high birth rate of the low grade and the low birth rate of the high grade. Environment, culture, can do much, but they cannot make a silk purse out of a sow's ear. Neither can heredity make a silk purse out of silk; without culture and the environmental influences, without social heredity, the silk remains crude and with no special value. The aims of a rational society, which we are born a thousand years too soon to see would be twofold: to control marriage and birth so that the number of the unfit would be kept as low as possible, and then to bring fostering influences to bear on the fit.

family which claims him as its own. In a warrior age the fighting spirit chooses war as its vocation and develops a warlike character; in a peaceful time that same fighting spirit may seek to bring about such reforms as will do away with war. [10] When the world said that a man might and really ought now and then to beat his wife and rule her by force, the really conformable man did so, while his descendant, living in a time and country where woman is the domestic "boss," submits, humorously and otherwise, to a good-natured henpecking. And in the times where a woman had no vocation but that of housewife, the wife of larger ability merely became a discontented, futile woman; whereas in an age which opens up politics to her, the same type of person expands into a vigorous, dominating political leader. Though the force of the water remain the same, the nature of the land determines whether the water shall collect as a river, carrying the produce of the land to the sea, or as a stagnant lake in which idlers fish. Time, social circumstances, education and a thousand and one factors determine whether one shall be a "Village Hampden," quarreling in a petty way with a petty autocrat over some petty thing, or a national Hampden, whose defiance of a tyrannical king stirs a nation into revolt.

How conceptions of right and wrong, of proper and improper conduct, ideals and thoughts arise, it is not my function to treat in detail. That intelligence primarily uses the method of trial and error to learn is as true of groups as of individuals; and established methods of doing things—customs—are often enough temporary conclusions, though they last a thousand years. The feeling that such group customs are right and that to depart from them is wrong, is perhaps based on a specific instinct, the moral instinct; but much more likely, in my opinion, is it obedience to leadership, fear of social disapproval and punishment, conscience, imitation, suggestibility and sympathy, all of which are parts of that social cement substance, the social instinct. No child ever learns "what is right and wrong" except through teaching, but no child would ever conform, except through gross fear, unless he found himself urged by deep-seated instincts to be in conformity, in harmony and in sympathy with his group,—to be one with that group. Perhaps it is true, as Bergson suggests, as Galton [11] hints and as Samuel Butler boldly states, that there are no real individuals in life but we are merely different aspects of reality or, to phrase it materialistically, corpuscles in the blood stream of an organism too vast and complicated to be encompassed by our imagination. Just as a white blood cell obeys laws of which it can have no conception, fulfills purposes whose meaning transcends its own welfare, so we, with all our

---

[10] Indeed, a reformer is to-day called a crusader, though the knight of the twelfth century armed cap-a-pie for a joust with the Saracen would hardly recognize as his spiritual descendant a sedentary person preaching against rum. Yet to the student of character there is nothing anomalous in the transformation.

[11] For example, read what the hard-headed Galton says ("Hereditary Genius," p. 376):

self-consciousness and all the paraphernalia of individuality, are perhaps parts of a life we cannot understand.

"There is decidedly a solidarity as well as a separateness in all human and probably in all lives whatsoever, and this consideration goes far, I think, to establish an opinion that the constitution of the living universe is a pure theism and that its form of activity is what may he described as cooperative. It points to the conclusion that all life is single in its essence, but various, ever-varying and interactive in its manifestations, and that men and all other living animals are active workers and sharers in a vastly more extended system of cosmic action than any of ourselves, much less of them, can possibly comprehend. It also suggests that they may contribute, more or less unconsciously, to the manifestation of a far higher life than our own, somewhat as . . . the individual cells of one of the more complex animals contribute to the manifestations of its higher order of personality." Perhaps such a unity is the basis of instinct, of knowledge without teaching, of desire and wish that has not the individual welfare as its basis. No man can reject such phenomena as telepathy or thought transference merely because he cannot understand them on a basis of strict human individuality. To reject because one cannot understand is the arrogance of the "clerico-academic" type of William James.

No one can read the stories of travelers or the writings of anthropologists without concluding that codes of belief and action arise out of the efforts of groups to understand and to influence nature and that out of this practical effort AND seeking of a harmonious reality arises morality. "Man seeks the truth, a world that does not contradict itself, that does not deceive, that does not change; a real world,—a world in which there is no suffering. Contradiction, deception and variability are the causes of suffering. He does not doubt there is such a thing as, a world as it might be, and he would fain find a road to it." [12] But alas, intelligence and knowledge both are imperfect, and one group seeking a truth that will bring them good crops, fine families, victory over enemies, riches, power and fellowship, as well as a harmonious universe, finds it in idol worship and polygamy; another group seeking the same truth finds it in Christianity and monogamy. And the members of some groups are born to ideals, customs and habits that make it right for a member to sing obscene songs and to be obscene at certain periods, to kill and destroy the enemy, to sacrifice the unbeliever, to worship a clay image, to have as many wives as possible, and that make it WRONG to do otherwise. Indeed, he who wishes a child to believe absolutely in a code of morals would better postpone teaching him the customs and beliefs of other people until habit has made him adamant to new ideas.

It is with pleasure that I turn the attention of the reader to the work of Frazier in the growth of human belief, custom and institutions that he has incorporated into the stupendous series of books called "The Golden Bough." The things that influence us most in our lives are heritages, not

---

[12] Nietzsche.

much changed, from the beliefs of primitive societies. Believing that the forces of the world were animate, like himself, and that they might be moved, persuaded, cajoled and frightened into favorable action, undeveloped man based most of his customs on efforts to obtain some desired result from the gods. Out of these customs grew the majority of our institutions; out of these queer beliefs and superstitions, out of witchcraft, sympathetic magic, the "Old Man" idea, the primitive reaction to sleep, epilepsy and death grew medicine, science, religion, festivals, the kingship, the idea of soul and most of the other governing and directing ideas of our lives. It is true that the noble beliefs and sciences also grew from these rude seeds, but with them and permeating our social structure are crops of atrophied ideas, hampering customs, cramping ideals. Further, in every race in every country, in every family, there are somewhat different assortments of these directing traditional forces; and it is these social inheritances which are more responsible for difference in people than a native difference in stock.

Consider the difference that being born and brought up in Turkey and being born, let us say, in New York City, would make in two children of exactly the same disposition, mental caliber and physical structure. One would grow up a Turk and the other a New Yorker, and the mere fact that they had the same original capacity for thought, feeling and action would not alter the result that in character the two men would stand almost at opposite poles. One need not judge between them and say that one was superior to the other, for while I feel that the New Yorker might stand OUR inspection better, I am certain that the Turk would be more pleasing to Turkish ideas. The point is that they would be different and that the differences would result solely from the environmental forces of natural conditions and social inheritance.

Study the immigrant to the United States and his descendant, American born and bred. Compare Irishman and Irish-American, Russian Jew and his American-born descendant; compare Englishman and the Anglo-Saxon New England descendant. Here is a race, the Jew, which in the Ghetto and under circumstances that built up a tremendously powerful set of traditions and customs developed a very distinctive type of human being. Poor in physique, with little physical pugnacity, but worshiping, learning and reaching out for wealth and power in an unusually successful manner, the crucible of an adverse and hostile environment rendered him totally different in manners from his Gentile neighbors. With a high birth rate and an intensely close and pure family life, the Ghetto Jew lived and died shut off by the restrictions placed upon him and his own social heredity from the life of the country of his birth. Then came immigration to the United States through one cause or another,—and note the results.

With the old social heredity still at work, another set of customs, traditions and beliefs comes into open competition with it in the bosom of the American Jew. Nowhere is the struggle between the old and the new generations so intense as in the home of the Orthodox Jew. His descendant is clean-shaven and no longer observes (or observes only perfunctorily or with many a gross inconsistency) the dietary and household laws. He is a free spender and luxurious in his habits as compared with his economical, ascetic forefathers. He marries late and the birth rate drops with most astonishing rapidity, so that in one generation the children of parents who had eight or ten children have families of one or two or three children. He becomes a follower of sports, and with his love for scholarship still strong, as witness his production of scholars and scientists, the remarkable rise of the Jewish prize fighter stands out as a divergence from tradition that mocks at theories of inborn racial characters. And a third generation differs in customs, manners, ideals, purposes and physique but little from the social class of Americans in which the individual members move. The names become Anglicized; gone are the Abrahams and Isaacs and Jacobs, the Rachels and Leahs and Rebeccas, and in their place are Vernon, Mortimer, Winthrop, Alice, Helen and Elizabeth. And this change in name symbolizes the revolution in essential characters.

Has the racial stock changed in one generation or two? No. A new social heredity has overcome—or at least in part supplanted—an older social heredity and released and developed characters hitherto held in check. In every human being—and this is a theme we shall enlarge upon later—there are potential lines of development far outnumbering those that can be manifested, and each environment and tradition calls forth some and suppresses others. Every man is a garden planted with all kinds of seeds; tradition and teaching are the gardeners that allow only certain ones to come to bloom. In each age, each country and each family there is a different gardener at work, repressing certain trends in the individual, favoring and bringing to an exaggerated growth other trends.

That each family, or type of family, acts in this way is recognized in the value given to the home life. The home, because of its sequestration, allows for the growth of individual types better than would a community house where the same traditions and ideals governed the life of each child. In the home the parents seek to cultivate the specific type of character they favor. The home is par excellence the place where prejudice and social attitude are fostered. Though the mother and father seek to give broadmindedness and wide culture to the child, their efforts must largely be governed by their own attitudes and reactions,—in short, by their own character and the resultant examples and teaching. It is true that the native character of the child may make him resistant to the teachings of the parents or may even develop counter-prejudices, to react violently against the gardening. This is the case when the child is of an opposing temperament or when in the course of time he falls under the influence of ideals and traditions that are opposed to those of his home. Unless the home combines interest and freedom, together with teaching, certain children become violent rebels, and, seeking freedom and interest outside of the home, find themselves in a conflict, both with their home teaching and the home teachers, that shakes the unity and the happiness of parent and child. Like all civil wars this war between new and old generations reaches great bitterness.

In studying the cases of several hundred delinquent girls, as a consultant to the Parole Department of Massachusetts, it was found that the family life of the girls could be classified in two ways. The majority of the girls that reached the Reformatory came from bad homes,—homes in which drunkenness, prostitution, feeble-mindedness, and insanity were common traits of the parents. Or else the girls were orphans brought up by a stepmother or some careless foster mother. In any case, through either example, cruelty or neglect, they drifted into the streets.

And the streets! Only the poor child (or the child brought up over strictly) can know the lure of the streets. THERE is excitement, THERE is freedom from prohibitions and inhibitions. So the boy or girl finds a world without discipline, is without the restraints imposed on the sex instincts and comes under the influence of derelicts, sex-adventurers, thieves, vagabonds and the aimless of all sorts. Into this university of the vices most of the girls I am speaking of drifted, largely because the home influence either was of the street type or had no advantages to offer in competition with the street.

But the child on the streets is no more a solitary individual than the savage is, or for that matter the civilized man. He quickly forms part of a group, a roving group, called "The Gang." In the large cities gangs are usually composed of boys of one age or nearly so; in the small towns the gangs will consist of the boys of a neighborhood. In fact, regardless of whether they are street children or home children, boys form gangs spontaneously. The gang is the first voluntary organization of society, for the home, in so far as the child is concerned, is an involuntary organization. The gang has its leader or leaders, usually the strongest or the best fighter. At any rate, the best fighter is the nominal leader, though a shrewder lad may assume the real power. The gang has rules, it plays according to regulations, its quarrels are settled according to a code, property has a definite status and distribution. [13] The members of the gang are always quarreling with each other, but here, as in the larger aggregations of older human beings, "politics ends at the border," and the gang is a unit against foreign aggression. Indeed, gangs of a neighborhood may league against a group of other gangs, as did the quarreling cities of Greece against Persia.

For the student of mankind the gang is one of the most fascinating

---

[13] In the gang of which I was a member there was a ritual in the formation of partnership, an association within the association. Two boys, fond of each other and desiring to become partners, would link little fingers, while a third boy acting as a sort of priest—an elder of the gang—would raise his hand and strike the link, shouting, "Partners, partners, never break!" This ritual was a symbol of the unity of the pair, so that they fought for each other, shared all personal goods (such as candy, pocket money, etc.,) and were to be loyal and sympathetic throughout life. Alas, dear partner of my boyhood, most gallant of fighters and most generous of souls, where are you, and where is our friendship, now?

phenomena. Here the power of tradition, without the aid of records, is seen. Throughout America, in a mysterious way, all the boys start spinning tops at a certain season and then suddenly cease and begin, to play marbles. Without any standardization of a central type they have the same rules for their games, call them by the same names and use in their songs the same rhymes and airs. Every generation of children has the same jokes and trick games: "Eight and eight are sixteen, stick your nose in kerosene"—"A dead cat, I one it, you two it, I three it, you four it, I five it, you six it, I seven it, you eight it!" The fact is, of course, that there are no generations as distinct entities; there are always individuals of one age, and there is a mutual teaching and learning going on at all times, which is the basis of transmission of tradition. Children are usually more conservative and greater sticklers for form and propriety than even men are; only now and then a freer mind arises whose courage and pertinacity change things.

Therefore, in the understanding of character the influence of the environment becomes of as fundamental importance as the consideration of the organic make-up of the individual. The environment in the form of tradition, social ideal, social status, economic situation, race, religion, family, education is thus on the one hand the directing, guiding, eliciting factor in character and on the other is the repressing, inhibiting, limiting factor.

Putting the whole thing in another way: the organism is the Microcosmos, or little world, in which the potentialities of character are elaborated in the germ plasm we inherit from our ancestors, in the healthy interaction of brain with the rest of the body, especially the internal glands. The outside world is the Macrocosmos, or large world, and includes the physical conditions of existence (climate, altitude, plentiness of food, access to the sea) as well as the social conditions of existence (state of culture of times and race and family). The social conditions of existence are of especial interest in that they reach back ages before the individual was born so that the lives, thoughts, ideals of the dead may dominate the character of the living.

This macrocosmos both brings to light and stifles the character peculiarities of the microcosmos and the character of no man, as we see or know it, ever expresses in any complete manner his innate possibilities.

The question arises: What is the basis of the influence of the social heredity, of the forces, in the character of the person born in a social group? Certain aspects of this we must deal with later, in order to keep to a unified presentation of the subject. Other aspects are pertinently to be discussed now.

The link that binds man to man is called the social instinct, though perhaps it would be better to call it the group of social instincts. The link is one of feeling, primarily, though it has associated with it, in an indissoluble way, purpose and action. The existence of the social instinct is undisputed; its explanation is varied and ranges from the mystical to the evolutionary. For the mystical (which crops out in Bergson, Butler and even in Galton), the unity of life is its basis, and there is a sort of recognition of parts formerly united but now separate individuals. This does not explain hate, racial and individual. The evolutionary aspect has received its best handling in recent years in Trotter's "The Herd," where the social instincts are traced in their relation to human history. One writer after another has placed as basic in social instinct, sympathy, imitation, suggestibility and the recognition of "likeness." These are merely names for a spreading of emotion from one member of a group to another, for a something that makes members of the group teachable and makes them wish to teach; that is back of the wish to conform and help and has two sets of guiding forces, reward and its derivative praise; punishment and its derivative blame. Perhaps the term "derivative" is not correct, and perhaps praise and blame are primary and reward and punishment secondary.

So eminent a philosopher as the elder Mill declared the distribution of praise and blame is the greatest problem of society." This view of the place of praise and blame in the organization of character and in directing the efforts and activity of men is hardly exaggerated. From birth to death the pleasure of reward and praise and the pain of punishment and blame are immensely powerful human motives. It is true that now and then individuals seek punishment and blame, but this is always to win the favor of others or of the most important observer of men's actions,—God, The child is trained through the effect of reward and punishment, praise and blame; and these are used to set up, on the one hand, habits of conduct, and on the other an inner mentor and guide called Conscience. It may be true that conscience is innate in its potentialities, but whether that is so or not, it is the teaching and training of the times or of some group that gives to conscience its peculiar trend in any individual case. And before a child has any inward mentor it depends for its knowledge of right and wrong upon the efforts of its parents, their use of praise-reward and blame-punishment; it reacts to these measures in accordance with the strength and vigor of its social instincts and in accordance with its fear of punishment and desire for reward. The feelings of duty and the prickings of conscience serve to consolidate a structure already formed.

Here we must discuss a matter of fundamental importance in character analysis. Men are not born equal in any respect. This inequality extends to every power, possibility and peculiarity and has its widest range in the mental and character life. A tall man is perhaps a foot taller than a very short man; a giant is perhaps twice as tall as a dwarf. A very fleet runner can "do" a hundred yards in ten seconds, and there are few except the crippled or aged who cannot run the distance in twenty seconds. Only in the fables has the hero the strength of a dozen men. But where dexterity or knowledge enters things become different, and one man can do what the most of men cannot even prepare to do. Where abstract thought or talent or genius is involved the greatest human variability is seen. There we have Pascals who are mathematicians at five and discoverers at sixteen; there we have Mozarts, composers at three; there we have our inspired boy preachers already consecrated to their great ideal of work; and we have also our Jesse Pomeroys, fiendish murderers before adolescence. I believe with Carlyle that it is the heroes, the geniuses of the race, to whom we owe its achievements; and the hero and the genius are the men and women of "greatest variability" in powers. The first weapon, the starting of fire, the song that became "a folk song" were created by the prehistoric geniuses and became the social heritage of the group or race. And "common man" did little to develop religions or even superstitions; he merely accepted the belief of a leader.

This digression is to emphasize that children and the men and women they grow to be are widely variable in their native social feeling, in their response to praise, blame, reward and punishmept. One child eagerly responds to all, is moved by praise, loves reward, fears punishment and hates blame. Another child responds mainly to reward, is but little moved by praise, fears punishment and laughs at blame. Still another only fears punishment, while there is a type of deeply antisocial nature which goes his own way, seeking his own egoistic purposes, uninfluenced by the opinion of others, accepting reward cynically and fighting against punishment. More than that, each child shows peculiarities in the types of praise, reward, blame and punishment that move him. Some children need corporal punishment [14] and others who are made rebels by it are melted into conformity by ostracism.

The distribution of praise and blame constitutes the distribution of public opinion. Wherever public opinion is free to exercise its power it is a weapon of extraordinary potency before which almost nothing can stand. One might define a free nation as one where public opinion has no limits, [15] where no one is prevented from the expression of belief about the action of others, and no one is exempted from the pressure of opinion. Conversely an autocracy is one where there is but little room for the public use of praise and but little power to blame, especially in regard to the rulers. But in all societies, whether free or otherwise, people are constantly praising, constantly blaming one another, whether over the teacups or the wine glasses, in the sewing circle or the smoking rooms, in the midst of families, in the press, in the great halls of the states and nations. These are "the mallets" by which society beats or attempts to beat individuals into the accepted shape.

Men and women and children all strive to be praised, if not by their own group, by some other group or by some generation. It is, therefore, a high achievement to introduce a new ideal of character and personality to

---

[14] It is a wishy-washy ideal of teaching that regards pain as equivalent to cruelty. On the contrary, it may be real cruelty to spare pain,—cruelty to the future of the child. Pain is a great teacher, whether inflicted by the knife one has been told not to play with, or by the parent when the injunction not to play with the knife has been disregarded.

[15] In fact, Oliver Wendell Holmes has defined as the great object of human society the free growth and expression of human thought. How far we are from that ideal!

the group. Men—whose opinion as to desirability and praiseworthiness has been the prepotent opinion—love best of all beauty in woman. Therefore, the ideal of beauty as an achievement is a leading factor in the character formation of most girls and young women. The first question girls ask about one another is, "Is she pretty?" and in their criticism of one another the personal appearance is the first and most, important subject discussed. A personal beauty ideal has little value to the character; in fact, it tends to exaggerate vanity and triviality and selfishness; it leads away from the higher aspects of reality. If you ask the majority of women which would they rather be, very beautiful or very intelligent, most will say without question (in their frank moments) that they would rather be very beautiful. Those who are attempting to introduce the ideal of intelligence as a goal to women need of course to balance it with other ideals, but if successful they will revolutionize the attitude of women toward life and change the trend of their character.

Such ideals as beauty and wealth, however, do not acquire their imperativeness unless at the same time they gratify some deep-seated group of desires or instincts. Wealth gives too many things to catalogue here, but fundamentally it gives power, and so beauty which may lead to wealth is always a source of power, although this power carries with it danger to the owner. Mankind has been praising unselfishness for thousands of years, and all men hate to be called selfish, but selfishness still rules in the lives of most of the people of the world. Chastity and continence receive the praise of the religious of the world, as well as of the ascetic-minded of all types, yet the majority of men, in theory accepting this ideal, reject it in practice. Selfishness leads to self-gratification and pleasure; chastity imposes a burden on desire, and praise and blame are in this instance not powerful enough to control mankind's acts, though powerful enough to influence them. Wherever social pressure and education influence men and women to conduct which is contrary to the gratification of fundamental desires, it causes an uneasiness, an unhappiness and discomfort upon which Graham Wallas [16] has laid great stress as the balked desire. The history of man is made up of the struggle of normal instincts, emotions and purposes against the mistaken inhibitions and prohibitions, against mistaken praise and blame, reward and punishment. Moral and ethical ideals develop institutions, and these often press too heavily upon the life and activities of those who accept them as authoritative.

We have spoken as if praise and blame invariably had the same results. On the contrary, though in general they tend to bring about uniformity and conformity, people vary remarkably from one another in their reaction and the same person is not uniform in his reactions. The reaction to praise is on the whole an increased happiness and vigor, but of course it may, when undeserved, demoralize the character and lead to a foolish vanity and to inefficiency. To those whose conscience is highly

---

[16] See his book "The Great Society" for a fine discussion of this important matter.

developed, undeserved praise is painful in that it leads to a feeling that one is deceiving others. Speaking broadly, this is a rare reaction. Most people accept praise as their due, just as they attribute success to their merits. [17] The reaction to blame may be anger, if the blame is felt to be undeserved, and there are people of irritable ego who respond in this way to all blame or even the hint of adverse criticism. The reaction may be humiliation and lowered self-valuation, greatly deenergizing the character and lowering efficiency. There, again, though this reaction occurs in some degree to all, others are so constituted that all criticism or blame is extremely painful and needs to be tempered with praise and encouragement. Where blame is felt to be deserved, and where the character is one of striving after betterment, where the ego is neither irritable nor tender, blame is an aid to growth and efficiency. Many a man flares up under blame who "cools" down when he sees the justice of the criticism, and changes accordingly.

Therefore, in estimating the character of any individual, one must ask into the nature of his environment, the traits and teachings of the group from which he comes and among whom he has lived. To understand any one this inquiry must be detailed and reach back into his early life. Yet not too much stress must be laid upon certain influences in regard to certain qualities. For example, the average child is not influenced greatly by immorality until near puberty, but dishonesty and bad manners strike at him from early childhood. The large group, the small group, family life, gang life influence character, but not necessarily in a direct way. They may act to develop counter- prejudices, for there is no one so bitter against alcoholism as the man whose father was a drunkard and who himself revolts against it. And there is no one so radical as he whose youth was cramped by too much conservatism.

One might easily classify people according to their reaction to reward, praise, punishment and blame. This would lead us too far afield. But at least it is safe to say that in using these factors in directing conduct and character the individual must be studied in a detailed way. The average child, the average man and woman is found only in statistics. Everywhere, to deal successfully, one must deal with the individual.

There is a praise-reacting type to whom praise acts as a tonic of incomparable worth, especially when he who administers the praise is respected. And there are employers, teachers and parents who ignore this fact entirely, who use praise too little or not at all and who rely on adverse criticism. The hunger for appreciation is a deep, intense need, and many of the problems of life would melt before the proper use of praise.

---

[17] A very striking example of this was noticeable during the Great War. American business men in general, producers, distributors, wholesalers, retailers and speculators all got "rich,"—some in extraordinary measure. Did many of them attribute this to the fact that there was a "sellers' market" caused by the conditions over which the individual business man had no control? On the contrary, the overwhelming majority quite complacently attributed the success (which later proved ephemeral) to their own ability.

"Fine words butter no parsnips" means that reward of other kinds is needed to give substance to praise. Praise only without reward losses its value. "I get lots of 'Thank you's' and 'You are a good fellow'," complained a porter to me once, "but I cannot bring up my family on them." In their hearts, no matter what they say, the majority of people place highly him who is just in compensation and reward and they want substantial goods. Many a young scientist of my acquaintance has found that election to learned societies and praise and respect palled on him as compared to a living salary. Money can be exchanged for vacations, education, books, good times and the opportunity of helping others, but praise has no cash exchange value.

Blame and punishment are intensely individual matters. Where they are used to correct and to better the character, where they are the tools of the friends and teacher and not the weapons of the enemy, great care must be used. Character building is an aim, not a technique, and the end has justified the means. Society has just about come to the conclusion that merely punishing the criminal does not reform him, and merely to punish the child has but part of the effect desired. In character training punishment and blame must bring PAIN, but that pain must be felt to be deserved (at least in the older child and adult) and not arouse lasting anger or humiliation. It must teach the error of the ways and prepare the recipient for instruction as to the right away. Often enough the pain of punishment and blame widens the breach between the teacher and pupil merely because the former has inflicted pain without recompense.

One might put it thus: The pleasure of praise and reward must energize, the pain of blame and punishment. must teach, else teacher and society have misused these social tools.

"Very well," I hear some readers say, "is conscience to be dismissed so shortly? Have not men dared to do right in the face of a world that blamed and punished; have they not stood without praise or reward or the fellowship of others for the actions their conscience dictated?"

Yes, indeed. What, then, is conscience? For the common thought of the world it is an inward mentor placed by God within the bosom of man to guide him, to goad him, even, into choosing right and avoiding wrong. Where the conception of conscience is not quite so literal and direct it is held to be an immanent something of innate origin. Whatever it may be, it surely does not guide us very accurately or well, for there are opposing consciences on every side of every question, and opponents find themselves equally spurred by conscience to action and are equally convinced of righteousness. In the long run it would be difficult to decide which did more harm in the world, a conscientious persecutor or bigot, an Alvarez or James the First, or a dissolute, conscienceless sensualist like Charles the Second. Certainly consciences differ as widely as digestions.

Conscience, so it seems to me, arises in early childhood with the appearance of fixed purposes. It is entirely guided at first by teaching and by praise and blame, for the infant gives no evidence of conscience. But the infant (or young child) soon wants to please, wants the favour and smiles of its parents. Why does it wish to please? Is there a something irreducible in the desire? I do not know and cannot pretend to answer.

This, however, may be definitely stated. Conscience arises or grows in the struggle between opposing desires and purposes in the course of which one purpose becomes recognized as the proper guide to conduct. Let us take a simple case from the moral struggles of the child.

A three-year-old, wandering into the kitchen, with mother in the back yard hanging out the clothes, makes the startling discovery that there is a pan of tarts, apple tarts, on the kitchen table, easily within reach, especially if Master Three-Year-Old pulls up a chair. Tarts! The child becomes excited, his mouth waters, and those tarts become the symbol and substance of pleasure,—and within his reach. But in the back of his mind, urging him to stop and consider, is the memory of mother's injunction, "You must always ask for tarts or candy or any goodies before you take them." And there is the pain of punishment and scolding and the vision of father, looking stern and not playing with one. These are distant, faint memories, weak forces,—but they influence conduct so that the little one takes a tart and eats it hurriedly before mother returns and then runs into the dining room or bedroom. Thus, instead of merely obeying an impulse to take the tart, as an uninstructed child would, he has now become a little thief and has had his first real moral struggle.

But it is a grim law that sensual pleasures do not last beyond the period of gratification. If this were not so there could be no morality in the world, and conscience would never reach any importance. Whether we gratify sex appetite or gastric hunger, the pleasure goes at once. True, there may be a short afterglow of good feeling, but rarely is it strongly affective, and very often it is replaced by a positive repulsion for the appetite. On the other hand, to be out of conformity with your group is a permanent pain, and the fear of being found out is an anxiety often too great to be endured. And so our child, with the tart gone, wishes he had not taken it, perhaps not clearly or verbally; he is regretful, let us say. Out of this regret, out of this fear of being found out, out of the pain of nonconformity, arises the conscience feeling which says, "Thou shalt not" or "Thou shalt," according to social teaching.

It may be objected that "Conscience often arrays itself against society, against social teaching, against perhaps all men." It is not my place to trace the growth in mind of the idea of the Absolute Good, or absolute right and wrong, with which a man must align himself. I believe it is the strength of the ego feeling which gives to some the vigor and unyieldingness of their conscience. "I am right," says such a person, "and the rest of the world is wrong. God is with me, my conscience and future times will agree," thus appealing to the distant tribunal as James pointed out. All the insane hospitals have their sufferers for conscience's sake, paranoid personalities whose egos have expanded to infallibility and whose consciences are correspondingly developed.

Conscience thus represents the power of the permanent purposes and ideals of the individuals, and it wars on the less permanent desires and impulses, because there is in memory the uneasiness and anxiety that resulted from indulgence and the pain of the feeling of inferiority that results when one is hiding a secret weakness or undergoing reproof or punishment. This group of permanent purposes, ideals and aspirations corresponds closely to the censor of the Freudian concept and here is an example where a new name successfully disguises an age-old thought.

In other words, conscience is social in its origin, developing differently in different people according to their teaching, intelligence, will, ego-feeling, instincts, etc. From the standpoint of character analysis there are many types of people in regard to conscience development.

In respect to the reactions to praise and blame the following types are conspicuous:

1. A "weak" group in whom these act as apparently the sole motives.

2. A group energized by love of praise.

3. A group energized mainly by fear of blame.

4. A type that scorns anything but material reward.

5. Another, that "takes advantage" of reward; likes praise but is merely made conceited by it, hates blame but is merely made angry by it, fears punishment and finds its main goad to good conduct in this fear.

6. Then there are those in whom all these motives operate in greater or lesser degree,—the so-called normal person. In reality he has his special inclinations and dreads.

7. The majority of people are influenced mainly by the group with which they have cast their positions, the blame of others being relatively unimportant or arousing anger. For there is this great difference between our reactions to praise and blame: that while the praise of almost any one and for almost any quality is welcome, the blame of only a few is taken "well," and for the rest there is anger, contempt or defiance. The influence of blame varies with the respect, love and especially acknowledged superiority of the blamer. The "boss" has a right to blame and so has father or mother while we are children, but we resent bitterly the blame of a fellow employee; "he has no right to blame," and we rebel against the blame of our parents when we grow up. In fact, the war of the old and new generations starts with the criticism of the elder folk and the resentment of the younger folk.

It will be seen that reaction to praise and blame, etc., will depend upon the irritability of ego feeling, the love of superiority and the dislike for inferiority. This basic situation we must defer discussing, but what is of importance is that the primitive disciplinary weapons we have discussed never lose their cardinal value and remain throughout life and in all societies the prime modes of thought and conduct.

In similar fashion the conscience types might be depicted. From the over-conscientious who rigidly hold themselves to an ideal, who watch every departure from perfection with agony and self-reproach, and who may either reach the highest level or "break down" and become inefficient to the almost conscienceless group, doing only what seems more profitable, are many intermediate types merging one with the other.

There are people whose conscience is localized, as the self-sacrificing father who is a pirate in business, or as the policeman who holds rigidly to conscience in courage and loyalty to his fellows, but who finds no internal reproach when he takes a bribe or perjures himself about a criminal. What we call a code is really a localized conscience, and there are many men whose consciences do not permit seduction of the virgin but who are quite easy in mind about an intrigue with a married woman. So, too, you may be as wily as you please in business but find cheating at cards base and unthinkable. Conscience in the abstract may be a divine entity, but in the realities of everyday life it is a medley of motives, purposes and teachings, varying from the grotesque and mischief-working to the sublime and splendid.

CHAPTER III
MEMORY AND HABIT

There are two qualities of nervous tissues (possibly of all living tissue) that are basic in all nervous and mental processes. They are dependent upon the modificability of nerve cells and fibers by stimuli, e. g., a light flashing through the pupil and passing along the optical tracts to the occipital cortex produces changes which constitute the basis of visual memory. Experience modifies nervous tissue in definite manner, and SOMETHING remembers. Who remembers? Who is conscious? Believe what you please about that, call it ego, soul, call it consciousness dipped out of a cosmic consciousness; and I have no quarrel with you.

Memory has its mechanics, in the association of ideas, which preoccupied the early English psychologists and philosophers; it is the basis of thought and also of action, and it is a prime mystery. We know its pathology, we think that memories for speech have loci in the brain, the so-called motor memories in Broca's area. [18] We know that a hemorrhage in these areas or in the fibers passing from them, or a tumor pressing on them may destroy or temporarily abolish these memories, so that a man may KNOW what he wishes to say, understand speech and be unable to say it, though he may write it (motor aphasia). In sensory aphasia the defect is a loss of the capacity to understand spoken speech, though the patient may be able to say what he himself wishes. (It is fair to say that the definite location of these capacities in definite areas has been challenged by Marie, Moutier and others, but this denial does not deny the organic brain location of speech memories; it merely affirms that they are scattered rather than concentrated in one area.)

In its widest phases memory alters with the state of the brain. In childhood impressibility is high, but until the age or four or five the duration of impression is low, and likewise the power of voluntary recall. In youth (eighteen-twenty) all these capacities are perhaps at their highest. As time goes on impressibility seems first of all to be lost, so that it becomes harder and harder to learn new things, to remember new faces, new names.

The typical difficulty of middle age is to remember names, because these have no real relationship or logical value and must be arbitrarily remembered. The typical senile defect is the dropping out of the recent memories, though the past may be preserved in its entirety. With any disease of the brain, temporary or permanent, amnesia or memory loss may and usually is present (e. g., general paresis, tumor, cerebral arteriosclerosis, etc.). As the result of Carbon monoxide poisoning, as after

---

[18] Foot of the left or right third frontal convolutions, auditory speech in the supramarginal, etc.

accidental or attempted suicidal gas inhalation, the memory, especially for the most recent events, is impaired and the patient cannot remember the events as they occur; he passes from moment to moment unconnected to the recent past, though his remote past is clear. Since memory is the basis of certainty, of the feeling of reality, these unfortunates are afflicted with an uncertainty, a sense of unreality, that is almost agonizing. As the effects of the poison wear off, which even in favorable cases takes months, the impressibility returns but never reaches normality again.

Unquestionably there is an inherent congenital difference in memory capacity. There are people who are prodigies of memory as there are those who are prodigies of physical strength,—and without training. The IMPRESSIBILITY for memories can in no way be increased except through the stimulation of interest and a certain heightening of attention through emotion. For the man or woman concerned with memory the first point of importance is to find some value in the fact or thing to be learned. Before a subject is broached to students the teacher should make clear its practical and theoretic value to the students. Too often that is the last thing done and it is only when the course is finished that its practical meaning is stressed or even indicated. In fact, throughout, teaching the value of the subject should constantly be emphasized, if possible, by illustrations from life. There are only a few who love knowledge for its own sake, but there are many who become eager for learning when it is made practical.

The number of associations given to a fact determines to a large extent its permanence in memory and the power of recalling it. In my own teaching I always instruct my students in the technique of memorizing, as follows:

1. Listen attentively, making only as many notes as necessary to recall the leading facts. The auditory memories are thus given the first place.

2. Go home and read up the subject in your textbooks, again making notes. Thus is added the visual associations.

3. Write out in brief form the substance of the lecture, deriving your knowledge from both the lecture and the book. You thus add another set of associations to your memories of the subject.

4. Teach the subject to or discuss it with a fellow student. By this you vitalize the memories you have, you link them firmly together, you lend to them the ardor of usefulness and of victory. You are forced to realize where the gaps, the lacunae of your knowledge come, and are made to fill them in.

Thus the best way to remember a fact is to find a use for it and to link it to your interests and your purposes. Unrelated it has no value; related it becomes in fact a part of you. After that the mechanics of memory necessitate the making of as many pathways to that fact as possible, and this means deliberately to associate the fact by sound, by speech and by action. The advertised schemes of memory training are simply association schemes, old as the hills, and having value indeed, but too much is claimed for them. A splendid memory is born, not made; but any memory, except where disease has entered, can be improved by training.

It is because lectures on the whole do not supply enough associations or arouse enough interest that the lecture is the poorest method of teaching or learning. Man's mind sticks easily to things, but with difficulty to words about things. To maintain attention for an hour or so, while sitting, is a task, and there develops a tendency either to a hypnoidal state in which the mind follows uncritically, or to a restless uneasiness with wandering mind and fatigue of body. A demonstration, on the other hand, a laboratory experiment with short, personal instruction, a bodily contact with the problem calls into play interest, enthusiasm, curiosity, motor images, the use of the hands, and is THE method of teaching.

There are at present excellent psychological methods of testing out the memory capacity. Every one engaged in any responsible work, or troubled about his memory, should be so tested. While there are other qualities of mind of great importance, memory is basic, and no one can really understand himself who is in doubt about his memory. In such diseases as neurasthenia one of the commonest complaints is the "loss of memory," which greatly troubles the patient. As a matter of fact, what is impaired is interest and attention, and when the patient realizes this he is usually quite relieved. The man who has a poor memory may become very successful if he develops systems of recording, filing, indexing, but his possibilities of knowledge are greatly reduced by his defect. [19]

A second fundamental ability of living tissue, and of particular importance in character, is habit formation. Habit resides in the fact that once living tissue has been traversed by a stimulus and has responded by an act, three things result:

1. The pathway for that stimulus becomes more permeable; becomes, as it were, grooved or like a track laid across the living structure of the nervous system.

2. The responding element is more easily stirred into activity, responds with more vigor and with less effort.

3. Consciousness, at first invoked, recedes more and more, until the habit-action of whatever type tends to become automatic. There is in this last peculiarity a tendency for the habit to establish itself as independent of the personality, and if an injurious or undesired habit, to set up the worst of the conflicts of life,—a conflict between one's intention and an automaton in the shape of a powerfully entrenched habit.

Habits are economical of thought and energy, generally speaking; that is their main recommendation. A dozen examples present themselves

---

[19] It is the growth of the subject matter of knowledge that makes necessary the elaborate systems of indexing, etc., now so important. It is as much as man can do to follow the places where the men work, let alone what they are doing. This growth of knowledge is getting to be an extra-human phenomenon. Of this Graham Wallas has written entertainingly.

at once as illustrative: piano playing, with its intense concentration on each note, with consciousness attending to the action of each muscle, and then practice, habit formation, and the ease and power of execution with the mind free to wander off in the moods suggested by the music, or to busy itself with improvisations, flourishes and the artistic touches. Before true artistry can come, technique must be relegated to habit. So with typewriting, driving an automobile, etc.

More fundamental than these, which are largely skill habits, are the organic habits. One of the triumphs of pediatrics depends upon the realization that the baby's welfare hangs on regular habits of feeding, that he is not to be fed except at stated intervals; as a result processes of digestion are set going in a regular, harmonious manner. In other words, these processes may be said to "get to know" what is expected of them and act accordingly. The mother's time is economized and the strain of nursing is lessened. In adults, regular hours of eating make it possible for the juices of digestion to be secreted as the food is ingested; in other words, an habitual adjustment takes place.

If there were one single health habit that I would have inculcated above all others, it would be the habit of regularly evacuating the bowels. While constipation is not the worst ill in the world, it causes much trouble, annoyance and a considerable degree of ill health, and, in my opinion, a considerable degree of unhappiness. A physician may be pardoned for frank advice: all the matters concerning the bowels, such as coarse foods, plenty of water and exercise, are secondary compared to the habit of going to the stool at the same time each day, whether there be desire or not. A child should be trained in this matter as definitely as he is trained to brush his teeth. In fact, I think that the former habit is more important than the latter. The mood of man is remarkably related to the condition of his gastro-intestinal tract and the involuntary muscle of that tract is indirectly under the control of the will through habit formation.

Sleep [20] the mysterious, the death in life which we all seek each night, is likewise regulated by habit. Arising from the need of relief from consciousness and bodily exertion, the mechanism of sleep is still not well understood. Is there a toxic influence at work? is the body poisoned by itself, as it were, as has been postulated; is there a toxin of fatigue, or is there a "vaso-motor" reaction, a shift of the blood supply causing a cerebral anaemia and thus creating the "sleepy" feeling? The capacity to sleep is a factor of great importance and we shall deal with it later under a separate heading as part of the mechanism of success and failure. At present we shall simply point out that each person builds up a set of habits regarding sleep,—as to hour, kind of place, warmth, companionship, ventilation and even the side of the body he shall lie on, and that a change in these preliminary matters is often attended by insomnia. Moreover, a change from the habitual in the general conduct of life—a new city or town, a strange bed, a disturbance in the moods and emotions—may upset the

---

[20] As good a book as any on the subject of sleep is Boris Sidis's little monograph.

sleep capacity. Those in whom excitement persists, or whose emotions are persistent, become easily burdened with the dreaded insomnia. Sleep is dependent on an exclusion of excitement and exciting influences. If, however, exciting influences become habitual they lose their power over the organism and then the individual can sleep on a battle field, in a boiler factory, or almost anywhere. Conversely, many a New Yorker is lulled to sleep by the roar of the great city who, finds that the quiet of the country keeps him awake.

Sleeplessness often enough is a habit. Something happens to a man that deeply stirs him, as an insult, or a falling out with a friend, or the loss of money,—something which disturbs what we call his poise or peace of mind. He becomes sleepless because, when he goes to bed and the shock-absorbing objects of daily interest are removed, his thoughts revert back to his difficulty; he becomes again humiliated or grieved or thrown into an emotional turmoil that prevents sleep. After the first night of insomnia a new factor enters,—the fear of sleeplessness and the conviction that one will not sleep. After a time the insult has lost its sting, or the difficulty has been adjusted, there is no more emotional distress, but there is the established sleeplessness, based on habitual emotional reaction to sleep. I know one lady whose fear reached the stage where she could not even bear the thought of night and darkness. It is in these cases that a powerful drug used two or three nights in succession breaks up the sleepless habit and reestablishes the power to sleep.

People differ in their capacity to form habits and in their love of habits. The normal habits, thoroughness, neatness and method come easily to some and are never really acquired by others. People of an impetuous, explosive or reckless character, keenly alive to every shade of difference in things, find it hard to be methodical, to carry on routine. The impatient person has similar difficulties. Whereas others take readily to the same methods of doing things day by day; and these are usually non-explosive, well inhibited, patient persons, to whom the way a thing is done is as important as the goal itself.

Here comes a very entertaining problem, the question of the value of habits. Good habits save time and energy, tend to eliminate useless labor and make for peace and quiet. But there is a large body of persons who come to value habits for themselves and, indeed, this is true to a certain extent of all of us. Once an accustomed way of doing things is established it becomes not only a path of least resistance, but a sort of fixed point of view, and, if one may mix metaphors a trifle, a sort of trunk for the ego to twine itself around. There is uneasiness in the thought of breaking up habits, an uneasiness that grows the more as we become older and is deepened into agony if the habit is tinged with our status in life, if it has become a sort of measure of our respectability. Thus a good housekeeper falls into the habits of doing things which were originally a mark of her ability, which she holds as sacred and values above her health and energy. There are people who fiercely resent a new way of doing things; they have woven their most minor habits into their ego feeling and thus make a personal issue of innovations. These are the upholders of the established; they hate change as such; they are efficient but not progressive. In its pathological form this type becomes the "health fiends" who never vary in their diet or in their clothing, who arise at a certain time, take their "plunge" regardless, take their exercise and their breakfasts alike as a health measure without real enjoyment, etc., who grow weary if they stay up half an hour or so beyond their ordinary bedtime; they are the individuals who fall into health cults, become vegetarians, raw food exponents, etc.

Opposed to the group that falls into habits very readily is the group that finds it difficult to acquire habitual ways of working and living. All of us seek change and variety, as well as stability. Some cannot easily form habits because they are quickly bored by the habitual. These restless folk are the failures or the great successes, according to their intelligence and good fortune. There is a low-grade intelligence type, without purpose and energy, and there is a high-grade intelligence type, seeking the ideal, restless under imperfection and restraint, disdaining the commonplace and the habits that go with it. Is their disdain of habit-forming and customs the result of their unconventional ways, or do their unconventional ways result because they cannot easily form habits? It is very probable that the true wanderer and Bohemian finds it difficult, at least in youth, to form habits, and that the pseudo-Bohemian is merely an imitation.

Habit is so intimately a part of all traits and abilities that we would be anticipating several chapters of this book did we go into all the habit types. Social conditions, desire, fatigue, monotony, purpose, intelligence, inhibition, all enter into habit and habit formation. Youth experiments with habit; old age clings to it. Efficiency is the result of good habits but originality is the reward of some who discard habits. A nation forms habits which seem to be part of its nature, until emigration to another land shows the falsity of this belief. So with individuals: a man feels he must eat or drink so much, gratify his sex appetite so often, sleep so many hours, exercise this or that amount, seek his entertainment in this or that fashion,—until something happens to make the habit impossible and he finds that what he thought a deeply rooted mode of living was a superficial routine. Though good habits may lead to success they may also bar the way to the pleasures of experience; that is their danger. A man who finds that he must do this or that in such a way had better beware; he is getting old, no matter what his age. [21] For we grow older as we lose mobility,—in joints, muscles, skin and our ways of doing, feeling and thinking! It is a transitory stage of the final immobility of Death.

---

[21] Says the talkative Autocrat of the Breakfast Table: "There is one mark of age that strikes me more than any of the physical ones; I mean the formation of Habits. An old man who shrinks into himself falls into ways that become as positive and as much beyond the reach of outside influences as if they were governed by clock work."

We have not considered the pathological habits, such as alcoholism, excessive smoking and eating, perverse sex habits. The latter, the perverse sex habits, will be studied when discussing the sex feelings and purposes in their entirety. Alcoholism is not yet a dead issue in this country though those who are sincere in wishing their fellows well hope it soon will be. It stands, however, as a sort of paradigm of bad habit- forming and presents a problem in treatment that is typical of such habits.

Not all persons have a liability to the alcoholic habit. For most people lack of real desire or pleasure prevented alcoholism. The majority of those who drank little or not at all were not in the least tempted by the drug. "Will power" rarely had anything to do with their abstinence and the complacency with which they held themselves up as an example to the drunken had all the flavor of Phariseeism. To some the taste is not pleasing, to others the immediate effects are so terrifying as automatically to shut off excess. Many people become dizzy or nauseated almost at once and even lose the power of locomotion or speech.

In many countries and during many centuries most of those who became alcoholic were such largely through the social setting given to alcohol. Because of the psychological effects of this drug in removing restraint, inhibition and formality, in its various forms it became the symbol of good-fellowship; and because it has an apparent stimulation and heat-producing effect there grew up the notion that it aided hard labor and helped resist hardship. As the symbol of good-fellowship it grew into a tradition of the most binding kind, so that no good time, no coming together was complete without it, and its power is celebrated in picturesque songs and picturesque sayings the world over. Hospitality, tolerance, good humor, kindliness and the pleasant breaking down of the barriers between man and man, and also between man and woman, all these lured generation after generation into the alcoholic habit.

There are relatively normal types of the heavy drinker,—the socially minded and the hard manual worker. But there is a large group of those who find in alcohol a relief from the burden of their moods, who find in its real effect, the release from inhibitions, a reason for drinking beyond the reach of reason. Do you feel that the endless monotony of your existence can no longer be borne,—drink deep and you color your life to suit yourself. Do disappointment and despair gnaw at your love of life so that nothing seems worth while,—some bottled "essence of sunshine" will give new, fresh value to existence. Are you a victim of strange, uncaused fluctuations of mood so that periodically you descend to a bottomless pit of melancholy, —well, then, why suffer, when over the bar a man will furnish you a release from agony? And so men of certain types of temperament, or with unhappy experiences, form the alcoholic habit because it gives them surcease from pain; it deals out to them, temporarily, a new world with happier mood, lessened tension and greater success.

Seeking relief [22] from distressing thoughts or moods is perhaps one

---

[22] This is the main theme of De Quincey's "Confessions of an Opium Eater."

of the main causes of the narcotic habit. The feeling of inferiority, one of the most painful of mental conditions, is responsible for the use not only of alcohol but also of other drugs, such as cocaine, heroin, morphine, etc. One of the most typical cases of this I have known is of a young man of twenty-five, a tall fellow with a very unattractive face who had this feeling of inferiority almost to the point of agony, especially in the presence of young women, but also in any situation where he would be noticed. He was fast becoming a hermit when he discovered that a few drinks completely removed this feeling. From that time on he became a steady drinker, with now and then a short period when he would try to stop drinking, only to resume when he found himself obsessed again by the dreaded inferiority complex.

Similarly a shameful position, such as that of the prostitute or the chronic criminal, is "relieved" by alcohol and drugs, so that the majority of these types of unfortunates are either drunkards or "dopes." Too often have reformers reversed the relationship, believing that alcohol caused prostitution and crime. Of course that relationship exists, but more often, in my experience, the alcohol is used to keep up the "ego" feeling, without which few can bear life.

Curiously enough, one of the sex perversions, masturbation, has in a few cases a similar genesis. I have known patients who, when under the influence of depression, or humiliated in some way or other, found a compensating pleasure in the act. Here we come to a cardinal truth in the understanding of ourselves and our fellows and one we shall pursue in detail later,—that face to face with mental pain, men seek relief or pleasure or both by alcohol, drugs, sensual pleasures of all kinds, and that the secret explanation of all such habits is that they offer compensation for some pain and are turned to at such times. What one man seeks in work, another man seeks in religion, another finds in self-flagellation, and still others seek in alcohol, morphine, sexual excesses, etc.

With the increasing excitement and tension of our times there is a constant search for relief, and here is the origin of much of the smoking. Most men find in the deliberate puff, in the slow inhalation and in the prolonged exhalation with the formation of the white cloud of smoke, a shifting of consciousness from the major businesses of their mind, from a constant tension to a minor business not requiring concentration and thereby breaking up in a pleasurable, rhythmic fashion the sense of effort. When one is alone the fatigue and even the pain of one's thinking is relieved by shifting the attention to the smoking. Keeping one's attention at a high and constant pitch is apt to produce a restless fatigue and this is often offset to the smoker by his habit. Excessive smoking may cause "nervousness" but as a matter of fact it is more often a means by which the excessively nervous try to relieve themselves. Of course it is not good therapeutics under such conditions, but I believe that in moderation smoking does no harm and is an innocent pleasure.

Some of the pathological motor habits, such as the tics, often have a curious background. The most common tics are snuffing, blinking, shaking of the head, facial contortions of one kind or another. These arise usually under exciting conditions or in the excitable, sometimes in the acutely self-conscious. Frequently they represent a motor outlet for this excitement; they are the motor analogues of crying, shouting, laughing, etc. (Indeed, a common habit is the one so frequently heard,—a little laugh when there is no feeling of merriment and no occasion for it.) Motor activity discharges tension and is pleasurable and these tics furnish a momentary pleasure; they relieve a feeling that some of the victims compare to an itch and the habit thus is based on a seeking of relief, even though that relief is obtained in a way that distresses the more settled purposes of the individual.

In the establishment of good habits, those desirable from the point of view of the important issues of life, training is of course essential. But in the training of children, certain things must be kept in mind: the usefulness, the practical value must be presented to the child's mind in a way he can understand, or else various ways of energizing him to help in the formation of the habit must be used—praise and blame, reward and punishment. Further, these habits are not to be held holy; cleanliness and method are desirable acquisitions but not so desirable as a feeling of freedom to play and experiment with life and things. If the child is constantly worried lest he get too dirty, or fears to play in his room because he may disorder it, he is forming the good habits of cleanliness and method but also the worse one of worry.

In the breaking of a bad habit, its root in desire and difficulty must be discovered. Often enough a man does not face the source of his trouble, preferring not to. I am not at all sure that it is best in all cases for a man to know his own weakness; in fact, I feel convinced to the contrary in some cases. But in the majority of difficulties, self-revelation is salutary and makes an intelligent coping with the situation possible. Here is the value of the good friend, the respected pastor, the wise doctor. The human being will always need a confessor and a confidante, and he who is struggling with a habit is in utmost need of such help.

Shall the struggler with a bad habit break it with its thralldom? Shall he say to his chains, "From this time, nevermore!" To some men it is given to win the victory this way, to rise to the heights of a stubborn resolution and to be free. But not to many is this possible. To others there is a long history of repeated effort and repeated failures and then—one day there comes a feeling of power, perhaps through a great love, a great cause, a sermon heard, a chance sentence, or a bitter experience, and then, like a religious conversion, the tracks of the old habit are obliterated, never to be used again.

I have in mind two men, both heavy drinkers but differing in everything else. One was a philosopher who saw the world in that dreadful, clear white light of which Jack London [23] spoke, that light which leaves no cozy, pleasant obscurities, in which Truth, the naked, is horrible to look at, when life seems too unreal, when purposes seem most futile. At such times

---

[23] Jack London's "John Barleycorn."

he would get drunk and be happy for the time being, and afterwards find himself bitterly repentant, though even that was a pleasure compared to the hollow world in which his sober self dwelt. Then one day, when all his friends had given him up as hopeless, as destined for disaster, he read a book. "The Varieties of Religious Experience," by William James, came to him as a clear light comes to a man lost in the darkness; he saw himself as a "sick soul," obsessed with the idea that he saw life relentlessly and clearly. There came to him the conviction that he had been arrogant, a conceited ass, bent on ruin, "a sickly soul," he said. Out of that realization grew resolutions that needed no vowing or pledging, for as simply as a man turns from one road to another he turned from his habit into healthy-minded work.

The other was an essentially healthy-minded man but he loved joviality, freedom and good fellowship. Without ever knowing how he came to it, he found himself a confirmed drinker, holding an inferior place, passed by men of lesser caliber. He struggled fitfully but always slipped when the next "good fellow" slapped him on the back and invited him to have a drink. One day he stepped out of a barroom with a group of his cronies, and though he walked straight there was a reckless, happy feeling in him that pushed him on to his folly. A young lady standing on a street corner waiting for a car caught his eye. Signaling to his companions, he walked up to her, put his arms around her and kissed her. The girl stood as if petrified, then she pushed him off and looked him up and down deliberately with cold scorn in her eyes. Then she took off her glove and slapped him across the face with it, as if disdaining to use her hand. With that she walked away.

The man was a gentleman, and he stood there stricken. The laugh of his companions aroused him. He saw them as if they were himself, with a horror and disgust that made him suddenly run away from them.

"From that moment I never again had the slightest desire for drink. The slap sobered me for good."

While these conversions occur now and then there are certain practical points in the breaking of a habit that need attention in each case.

In the first place it is best in the majority of instances to avoid the particular stimuli and associations that set off the habit. The stimulus is a kind of trigger; pull it and the habit can hardly be checked. Whatever the situation is that acts as the temptation, avoid it. Not for nothing do men pray, "Lead us not into temptation." The will needs no such exercise and rarely stands up well against such strain. This may mean a removal for the time being from the source of temptation, a flying away to gain strength.

Further, a substitution of habit, of purpose, is necessary. Some line of activities must be selected to fill in the vacuum. A hobby is needed, a devotion to some larger purpose, whether it be in work or social activity. "Nature abhors a vacuum"; boredom must be avoided, for that is a pain, awakening desire. The gymnasium, golf, sports of all kinds are substitute pleasures of great value.

Third, harness a friend, a superior or a respected equal to the yoke with you. Pull double harness; let him lend his strength to yours. Throw away pride; confess and receive new energy from his sympathy and wisdom. If you are lucky enough to have such a friend, or some wise counselor, thank God for him. For here is where the true friend finds his highest value.

In the analysis of any character the question of the kind of habits formed demands attention. Since almost all traits become matters of habit, such an inquiry would sooner or later lead to a catalogue of qualities. What is here pertinent is this,—that one might inquire into the kind of habits that are easily formed by the individual and the kind that are not. Habits fall into groups such as these:

1. Relating to care of the body: cleanliness, diet, exercise, bowel function, sleep. Here we learn about personal tidiness or the reverse, foppery, dandyism, gluttony, asceticism, etc.

2. Relating to method, efficiency, neatness in work: some people find it almost impossible to become methodical or neat; others become obsessed by these qualities to the exclusion of mobility.

3. Relating to the pursuit of pleasure: type of pleasure sought, time given to it, hobbies.

4. Relating to special habits: alcohol, tobacco, drugs, sex perversions.

5. Relating to study and advancement: love of books, attendance at lectures.

Especially in the study of children is some such scheme essential, for then one gets a definite idea of their defects and takes definite efforts to make habitual the desired practice, or else one sees the special trend, and, if it is good, fosters it. This, of course, is the long and short of character development.

CHAPTER IV

STIMULATION, INHIBITION, ORGANIZING ENERGY, CHOICE AND CONSCIOUSNESS

There are three fundamental factors in the relation of any organism to the environment and in the relation of the various parts of an organism to each other which we must now consider. To consider a living thing of any kind as something separate from the stimuli the world streams in on it, or to consider it as a real unit, is a mistake that falsifies most of the thinking of the world.

On us, as living things, the universe pours in stimuli of a few kinds. Or rather there are few kinds of stimuli we are specialized to receive and react to; there may be innumerable other kinds to which we cannot react because they do not reach us. The world for us is a collection of things that we see, hear, smell, taste and feel, but there may be vast reaches of things for which we have no avenues of approach,—completely unimaginable things because our images are built upon our senses.

To some of the stimuli the world pours in on us we must react properly or die. Certain "mechanisms" with which we are equipped must respond to these stimuli or the forces of the world destroy us. A lion on the horizon must awaken flight, or concealment, or the modified fight reaction of using weapons; extreme cold or heat must start up impulses and reflexes leading away from their disintegrating effects. Food must, when smelled or seen, lead us to conduct whereby we supply ourselves or we die from hunger. Dangers and needs awaken reactions, both through instinctive responses and through intelligence. The main activities of life are to be classed as "averting" and "acquiring," for if life showers us with the things we would or need to have, it also pelts us with the things we fear, hate or despise. It would be interesting to know which activities are the most numerous; presumably the lucky or successful man is busy acquiring while the unlucky or unsuccessful finds himself busiest averting. The averting activities are directed largely against the disagreeable, disgusting, dangerous and the undesired; the acquiring activities are directed toward the pleasant, the necessary, the desired. The problems of life are to know what is really good or bad for us and how to acquire the one and avert the other. While there are certain things that "naturally" [24] are deemed good or

---

[24] I place in quotations NATURALLY because it is difficult to know what is "natural" and what is cultural. In the widest sense everything is natural; in the narrowest very few things are natural. Cooked food, clothing, houses, marriages, education, etc., are not found in a state of nature, any more than clocks and plays by Ibsen are. Our judgment as to what is good and bad is mainly instinctive leaning directed or smothered by education.

bad, there are more that are so regarded through training and education. Morality and Taste are alike concerned with bringing about attitudes that will determine the "right" response to the stimuli of the world.

The stimuli that thus pour in upon the individual, and to which he must react, must find an organism ready to respond in some way or other. A sleeping man naturally does not adjust himself to danger, nor does a paralyzed man fly. The most attractive female in the world causes no response in the very young male child and perhaps stirs only reminiscences in the aged. Food, which causes the saliva to flow in the mouth of the hungry, may disgust the full. Throughout life there are factors in the internal life of the organism instantly changing one's reaction to things of physical, mental and moral significance. He talks loudest of restraint and control who has no desire; and in satiation even the sinner sees the beauty of asceticism. There must be a coincidence of stimulus, readiness and opportunity for the full, successful response to take place. [25]

The simplest response to any stimulus from the outer world is the reflex act. Theoretically a reflex act is dependent upon the interaction of a sensory surface, a sensory nerve cell, a motor nerve cell and a muscle, i. e., a receptive apparatus and a motor apparatus in such close union that the will and intelligence play no part. Thus if one puts his finger on a hot stove he withdraws it immediately, and such responses are present even in the decapitated frog and human for a short time. So if light streams in on the wide-open pupil of the eye, it contracts, grows smaller, without any effort of the will, and in fact entirely without the consciousness of the individual. Swallowing is a series of reflexes in a row, so that food in the back part of the mouth sets a reflex going that carries it beyond the epiglottis; another reflex carries it to the esophagus and then one reflex after the other transports the food the rest of the way. Except for the first effort of swallowing, the rest is entirely involuntary and even unconscious. Those readers who are interested would do well to read the work of Pavlow on the conditioned reflex, in which the great Russian physiologist builds up all action on a basis of a modification of the primitive reflex which he calls the "conditioned reflex." [26]

The simple reflex, immediate response to a stimulus, has only a

---

[25] A slang epigram puts it better: The time, the place, and the girl.

[26] Pavlow is one of the scientists who regard all mental life as built up out of reflexes. The immediate reflex is only one variety; thought, emotion, etc., are merely reflexes placed end to end. Pavlow divides action into two trends, one due to an unconditioned reflex, of innate structure, and the other a modified or conditioned reflex which arises because some stimulus has become associated with the reflex act. Thus saliva dripping from a dog's mouth at the smell of food is an unconditioned reflex; if a bell is heard at the same time the food is smelled then in the course of time the saliva flows at the sound of the bell alone,—a conditioned reflex. A very complex system has been built up of this kind of facts, which I have criticized elsewhere.

41

limited field in human life or adult life. Sherrington points out in his notable book, "The Integrative Action of the Nervous System," that there is a play of the entire organism on each responding element, and there is also a competition throughout each pathway to action. Let us examine this a little closer.

A man is hungry, let us say; i. e., there arise from his gastro-intestinal tract and from the tissues stimuli which arouse motor mechanisms to action and the man seeks food. The need of the body arouses desire in the form of an organic sensation and this arouses mechanisms whose function is to satisfy that desire. Let us assume that he finds something that looks good and he is about to seize it when an odor, called disagreeable, assails his nostrils from the food, which stops him. Then there arises a competition for action between the desire for food and the visual stimulus, associated memories, etc., on the one hand, and the odor, the awakened fear, memories, disgust, etc., on the other hand. This struggle for action, for use of the mechanisms of action, is the struggling of choosing, one of the fundamental phenomena of life. In order for a choice to become manifest, what is known as inhibition must come into play; an impulse to action must be checked in order that an opposing action can be effective. The movement of rejection uses muscles that oppose the movement of acquirement; e. g., one uses the triceps and the other the biceps, muscles situated in opposite sides of the upper arm and having antagonistic action. In order for triceps to act, biceps must be inhibited from action, and in that inhibition is a fundamental function of the organism. In every function of the body there are opposing groups of forces; for every dilator there is a contractor, for every accelerator of action there is inhibition. Nature drives by two reins, and one is a checkrein.

This function of inhibition, then, delays, retards or prevents an action and is in one sense a higher function than the response to stimulation. Its main seat is the cerebrum, the "highest" nervous tissue, whereas reflex and instinctive actions usually are in the vegetative nervous system, the spinal cord, the bulbar regions and the mid-brain, all of which are lower centers. Choice, which is intimately associated with inhibition, is par excellence a cerebral function and in general is associated with intense consciousness. The act of choosing brings to the circumstances the whole past history of the individual; it marshals his resources of judgment, intelligence, will, purposes and desires. In choice lies the fate of the personality, for it is basically related to habit formation. Further, in the dynamics of life a right, proper choice, an appropriate choice, opens wide the door of opportunity, whereas an unfortunate choice may commit one to the mercies of wrecking forces. Education should aim to teach proper choosing and then proper action.

The capacity for perceiving and responding to stimuli, for inhibiting or delaying action and for choosing, are of cardinal importance in our study. But there is another phase of life and character without which everything else lacks unity and is unintelligible. From the beginning of life to the end there is choice. Who and what chooses? From infancy one sees the war of purposes and desires and the gradual rise of one purpose or set of purposes into dominance,—in short, the growth of unity, the growth of personality. The common man calls this unity his soul, the philosopher speaks of the ego and implies some such thing as this organizing energy of character.

But a naturalistic view of character must reject such a metaphysical entity, for one sees the organizing energy increase and diminish with the rest of character through health, age, environment, etc. Further, there is at work in all living things a similar something that organizes the action of the humblest bit of protoplasm. This organizing energy of character will be, for us, that something inherent in all life which tends to individualize each living thing. It is as if all life were originally of one piece and then, spreading itself throughout the world, it tended to differentiate and develop (according to the Spencerian formula) into genera, species, groups and individuals. This organizing energy works up the experiences of the individual so that new formulae for action develop, so that what is experienced becomes the basis of future reaction.

It must be remembered that the world we live in has its great habits. Night follows day in a cycle that never fails, the seasons are repeated each year, and there is a periodicity in the lives of plants and animals that is manifested in growth, nutrition, mating and resting. Things happen again and again, though in slightly altered form, and our desires, satisfied now, soon repeat their urge. The great organic needs and sensations repeat themselves and with the periodic world of outer experience must be dealt with according to a more or less settled policy. It is the organizing energy that works out the policy, that learns, inhibits, chooses and acts,—and it is the essential character-developing principle. For like our bodily organs which are whipped into line by the nervous system, our impulses, instincts, and reflexes [27] have their own policy of action and therefore need, for the good of the entire organism, discipline and coordination. It may sound as if the body were made up of warring entities and states and that there gradually arose a centralized good, and though the analogy may lead to error, it offers a convenient method of thinking.

Moreover, the organizing energy seems often to be at work when consciousness itself is at rest, as in sleep. Often enough a man debates and debates on lines of conduct and wakes up with his problem solved. Or he works hard to learn and goes to bed discouraged, because the matter is a jumble, and wakes up in the morning with an orderly and useful arrangement of the facts. A writer seeks to find the proper opening,—and gives up in a frenzy of despair. He is perhaps walking or driving when

---

[27] Roux, the great French biologist, has shown that each tissue and each cell competes with the other tissues and the other cells. The organism, though it reaches a practical working unity as viewed by consciousness, is nevertheless no entity; it is a collection, an aggregate of living cells which are organized on a cooperation basis just as men are, but maintain individuality and competition nevertheless.

suddenly he lifts his head as one does who is listening to a longed-for voice, and in himself he finds the phrases that he longs for. Something within has set itself, so it seems, the task of bringing the right associations into consciousness. What we call quickness of mind, energy of mind, is largely this function.

It is this which adapts us to different situations, different groups, by calling into play organized modes of talking or acting. We pass from a group of ladies in whose presence we have been friendly but decorous, perhaps unconventionally formal, to a group of business intimates, men of long acquaintance. Without even being conscious of it we lounge around, feet on the table, carelessly dropping cigarette ash to the floor, using language chosen for force rather than elegance; we discuss sports, women, business and a whole group of different emotions, habits and purposes come to the surface, though we were not at all conscious of having repressed them while in the presence of the ladies. A faux pas is where the organizer has "slipped" on his job; lack of tact implies in part a rigid organizing energy, neither plastic nor versatile enough.

We are now ready to face certain developments of these three main factors, viz., the response to stimuli; choice and inhibition, and the organizing energy. Largely we might classify people according to the type of vigor of their reactions to stimuli, the quality and vigor of choice and of inhibition, and the quality and vigor of the organizing energy. We note that there are people who have, as it were, exquisitely sensitive feelers for the stimuli of one kind or another and who react vigorously, perhaps excessively; that there are others of a duller, less reactive nature, largely because they are stimuli-proof. Others are under-inhibited, follow desire or outer stimulus without heed, without a brake; others are over-inhibited, too cautious, too full of doubt, unable to choose the reaction that seems appropriate. The organizing energy of some is low; they never seem to unify their experiences into a code of life and living; they are like a string of beads loosely strung together with disharmonious emotions, desires, purposes. In others this energy is high, they chew the cud of every experience and (to change the metaphor) they weld life's happenings, their memories, their emotions and purposes into a more unified ego, a real I, harmonious, self-enlightened; clearly conscious of aim and end and striving bravely towards it. Or there is over-unification and fanaticism, with narrow aim and little sympathy for other aims. Sketched in this very broad way we see masses of people, rather than individuals, and we are not finely adjusted to our subject.

Psychologists rarely concern themselves to any extent with these matters; they deal mainly with their outgrowths,—emotions, instinct, intelligence and will. We are at once beset with difficulties which are resolved mainly by ignoring them. In such a book as this we are not concerned with the fundamental nature of these divisions of the mental life, we must omit such questions as the relation of instinct to racial habit, or the evolution of instinct from habit, if that is really its origin. Again I must repeat that we shall deal with these as organic, as arising in the sensitized individual as a result of environmental forces, as manifestations of a life which is as yet—and perhaps always will be—mysterious to us. We shall best consider these manifestations of mental activity as an interplay of the reactions of stimulation, inhibition, choice, organizing energy, and not as separate and totally different matters. We shall see that probably emotion is one aspect of reaction to the world, while instinct is merely another aspect; that intelligence is a cerebral shift of instinct, and that will is no unity but the energy of instincts and purposes.

Before we go farther we must squarely face a problem of human thought. Man, since he started reflecting about himself, has been puzzled about his consciousness. How can a person be aware of himself, and what identifies and links together each phase of consciousness? There is an enormous range of thought on this subject: from those who identified consciousness as the only reality and considered what the average person holds as realities—things and people—as only phases of consciousness, to those who, like Huxley, regard consciousness as an "epi-pbenomenon," a sort of overture to brain activity and having nothing whatever to do with action, nothing to do with choice and plan, so that, as Lloyd Morgan points out, "An unconscious Shakespeare writes plays acted by an unconscious troupe of actors to an unconscious audience." The first extreme view, that of Berkeley and the idealists, nullifies all other realities save that of the individual thinker and reduces one to the absurdities of Solipsism where a man writes books to convince persons conjured up by himself and having no existence outside of himself; the other view nullifies that which seems to each of us the very essence of himself.

I shall take a very simple view of consciousness, [28] simply because I shall deliberately dodge the great difficulties. Consciousness is the result of the activities of a group of more or less permanently excited areas of the brain—areas having to do with positions of the head, eyes and shoulders; areas having to do with vision, hearing and smell; areas having to do with speech,—these constituting extremely mobile, extremely active parts of the organism. From these consciousness may irradiate to the activities of almost every part of the organism, in different degrees. We are often extremely conscious of the activities of the hands, in less degree of the legs; we may become wrapped up almost completely in a sensation emanating from the sex organs, and under fear or excitement the heart may pound so that we feel and are conscious of it as ordinarily we can never be. The state of consciousness called interest may shift our feeling of self to any part of our body (as in pain, when a part usually out of consciousness swings into it, or when the hand of a lover grips our own so that the great reality of our life at the moment seems to be the consciousness of the hand) or it may fasten us to an outside object until our world narrows to that object,

---

[28] For discussion of consciousness read Berkeley, Locke, Hume, Spencer, Lotze, Moyan, James, Wundt, Munsterberg and every other philosopher and psychologist. I have not attempted to discuss the matter from the philosopher's point of view for the very obvious reason that I am no philosopher.

nothing else having any conscious value. This latter phenomenon is very striking in children; they become fascinated by something they hear or see and project themselves, as it were, into that object; they become the "soapiness of soap, or the wetness of water" (to use Chesterton's phrase), and when they listen to a story they hold nothing in reserve. Consciousness may busy itself with its past phases, with the preceding thought, emotion, sensation —how, I do not know—or it may occupy itself mainly with the world of things which are hereby declared to have a reality in our theory. In the first instances we have introspection and subjectiveness, and in the second we have extroversion and objectivity.

Since consciousness is most intense when the new or unfamiliar is seen, heard, felt or attempted, we may assume it has a chief function in acquainting the individual with the new and unfamiliar and in the establishment of habitual reactions, We are extraordinarily conscious of a queer, unexplainable thing on the horizon, we bring into the limelight (or IT brings into the limelight) all our possible reactions,—fear, flight, anger, fight, circumvention, curiosity and the movements of investigation; we are thrown into the maelstrom of choice. Choice and consciousness, doubt and consciousness, are directly related; it is only when conduct becomes established as habit, with choosing relegated to the background, that consciousness, in so far as the act is concerned, becomes diminished.

A moderate constant sensation tends to disappear from consciousness, as when we keep our hand in warm water. It then takes a certain increase of the stimulus to keep the sensation from lapsing out of consciousness. This lapsing out of consciousness of the steady stimulus, in its ramifications, is responsible for a good deal of the activity of man, since sensation is a goal of effort. [29] Under emotion we become aware of two sets of things,—the reaction of our body in its sum total of pleasure or the reverse, and second the object that sets up this reaction. Consciousness fastens itself on the body and on the world, and the bodily reaction becomes a guide for future action. Extreme bodily reactions are painful and may result in the abolishing of consciousness.

We assume that consciousness is organic, though we concede that it may be true that it is borrowed from a great pool of consciousness [30] out of

---

[29] The physiologists speak of this phenomenon under the heading of the Weber-Fechner law, after the two physiologists who gave it prominence. James pokes a good deal of fun at the "law," which is expressed mathematically. Perhaps the mathematics should have been eliminated as too "scientific" for our present attainment, but it does remain true that it is not the ACTUAL stimulus increase that is important in sensation or perception, but the RELATIVE stimulus increase. This is behind all of "getting used to things"; it removes the pain from humiliation and also the novelty from joy. It is the reason behind all of the searching for novelty and excitement.

[30] Even if it were true that consciousness is the only reality, nobody really believes it in that nobody acts as if it were true. Conversely, everybody acts as it

which we all come. Consciousness IS organic because a blow on the head may abolish it as may drugs and disease, or a shifting of the blood supply as in emotion or fatigue in the form of sleep, etc. Where does it go to and how does it come back? The savage answered that question by building up the idea of a soul, a thing that might migrate, had an independent existence, took journeys in the form of dreams and lived and flourished after death. Most of these ideas still persist, perhaps as much through the fear of annihilation as anything else, but as to whether or not they are true this book does not concern itself. We have no proof of these matters, but we can prove that we can play on consciousness as we play on a piano, through the body and brain. A blow injures groups of nerve cells and consciousness disappears; when they recover, it returns. Where does any function go when structure is injured? We have practically the same kind of proof for the position of consciousness as a function of the brain and body that we have for gastric juice as a secretion of gastric cells.

However widely we spread the function of consciousness and its domain, we still leave a large field of activities untouched. And so we come to the conception of the subconsciousness. There are two prevailing sets of opinions concerning the subconscious.

The first is quite matter-of-fact. It states that the movements and activities of a large part of the body are outside of the realm of consciousness, such as the activities of the great viscera—heart, lungs, intestines, liver, blood vessels, sex glands—and are largely operated by the vegetative nervous system. [31] There are influences pouring into the brain from these organs, together with influences from muscles, joints, tendons, and these influences, though not consciously itemized, are the subconsciously received stimuli which give us feelings of vigor, energy, courage, hopefulness, or the reverse, according to the state of the organism. In health the ordinary result of these stimuli is good, though people may have health in that no definite disease is present, and yet there

---

trees, rocks, and people were realities; as if fatigue, sickness, age, etc., affected consciousness. That is why, in this book, we are discarding as irrelevant the "ultimate" truth concerning consciousness. My humble belief is that the ultimate truth in this matter will never concern us because we shall never know it.

[31] This is not the place to describe the vegetative nervous system. (It was formerly called the sympathetic nervous system, but this term is now limited to one part of this system, and the term autonomic to another part, although some writers still use the term sympathetic for the whole, and others [the English] the term autonomic for the whole.) This system is the nervous mechanism of organic life, regulating heart, lungs, blood vessels, intestines, sex organs, acting together with endocrines, etc. A huge amount of work has been done of late years on this system and we know definitely that it stimulates, inhibits and regulates these organs, and also that it records their activities. We are commencing to believe that this system is fully as important, in mental life, as the brain. See Langley, Schaeffer, Higier, etc.

is some deficiency in the energy-arousing viscera which brings a lowered coenesthesia, a lessened vigor and lowered mood. In youth the state of the organs brings a state of well feeling; in old age there is a constant feeling of a low balance of energy and mood, and the person is always on the verge of unpleasant feeling. In the great change periods of life—at puberty and the climacteric (or the menopause)—the sudden change in the activity of the sex organs may produce great alterations [32] in the coenaesthesia and therefore in the energy and mood of the individual.

In addition, these activities, which are so all-important, determine the basic conduct by arousing the basic appetites and desires of the individual. It is the change in the gastro-intestinal tract and in the tissues of the body that starts up the hunger feeling and the impulses which prompt men to seek food; in other words, this type of coenaesthesia has set going all the physical and mental activities relating to food; it is the basic impulse behind agriculture and stock raising, as well as energizing work activities of all kinds. It is the tension in the seminal vessels of the male that wakes up his passion, if it is not the sole source of that passion. Sex desire in the adult male has many elements in it, not pertinent at present, but the coenaesthetic influence of the physical structures is its starting point. In men as well as women there is a cycle of desire, with height due to physical tension and abyss following the discharge or disappearance of tension, that profoundly influences life and conduct. Here the sympathetic nervous system and the internal secretion of the genital glands awaken into sexual activity brain, spinal cord and muscles, so that the individual seeks a mate, plunges into marriage and directs his conduct, conscious of taste and desire, but largely unconscious of the physical condition that is impelling him on. In this sense the subconscious activities dominate in life, because the functions of nutrition and reproduction are largely unconscious in their origin, but there is no organized, plotting subconsciousness at work.

Once a thing is experienced, it is stored in memory. What is the basis and position of a memory when we are not conscious of it, when our conscious minds are busy with other matters? What happens when a desire is repressed, inhibited into inaction; when consciousness revolts against part of its own content? Is a "forgotten" memory ever really lost, or a desire that is squelched and thrust out of "mind" really made inactive? Do our inhibitions really inhibit, or do we build up another self or set of selves that rise to the surface under strange forms, under the guise of disease manifestations?

Sigmund Freud and his followers have made definite answers to the foregoing, answers that are incorporated in a doctrine called Freudianism. Freud is an Austrian Jew, a physician, and one that soon specialized in nervous and mental diseases. Early in his career he did some excellent

---

[32] This is especially true of the menopause in women, and often enough of each menstrual period. That there is a climacteric in men is not so clear, but something corresponding to it occurs, at least in the case of some men.

work in the study of the paralysis of childhood (infantile hemiplegia), but his attention and that of an older colleague, Breuer, were soon drawn (as has occurred to almost every neurologist) to the manifestations of that extraordinary disease, hysteria. Hysteria has played so important a role in human history, and Freud's ideas are permeating so deeply into modern thought that I deem it advisable to devote a chapter to them.

CHAPTER V
HYSTERIA, SUBCONSCIOUSNESS AND FREUDIANISM

Hysteria was known to the ancients and in fact is as old as the written history of mankind. Considered essentially a disease of women, it was given its present name which is derived from "hysteron," the Greek name for the womb. We know to-day that men also are victims of this malady, though it arises under somewhat different circumstances than is the case with the other sex. Men and women, living in the same world and side by side, are placed in greatly different positions in that world, are governed by different traditions and are placed under the influences of differing ambitions, expectations, hopes and fears. Hysteria arises largely out of the emotional and volitional reactions of life, and these reactions differ in the sexes.

It was a group of French neurologists, headed by Charcot—and including very illustrious men, such as Janet and Marie, who paid the first scientific attention to the disease. Under their analyses hysteria was defined as a mental disease in which certain symptoms appeared prominently.

1. Charcot especially paid attention to what are known as the attacks. The hysteric patient (usually a woman, and so we shall speak of the patient as "she") under emotional stress and strain, following a quarrel or a disagreement or perhaps some disagreeable, humiliating situation, shows alarming symptoms. Perhaps she falls (never in a way to injure herself) to the floor and apparently loses consciousness, closes her eyes, rolls her head from side to side, moans, clenches her fists, lifts her body from the floor so that it rests on head and heels (opisthotonic hysteria), shrieks now and then and altogether presents a terrifying spectacle. Or else she twitches all over, weeps, moans, laughs and shouts, and rushes around the room, beating her head on the walls; or she may lie or stand in a very dramatic pose, perhaps indicating passion or fear or anger. The attacks are characterized by a few main peculiarities, which are that the patient usually has had an emotional upset or is in some disagreeable situation, that she does not hurt herself by her falls, that consciousness is never completely abolished and fluctuates so that now she seems almost "awake" and then she seems almost in a complete stupor, and that the expression of emotion in the attack is often very prominent. These symptoms are readily differentiated from what is seen in epilepsy. [33]

---

[33] The French writers of the school of Babinski deny that the above symptom and even the majority of the following have a real existence in hysteria. The English,

50

2. The hysteric paralyses which are featured in all the literatures of the world are curious manifestations and often very stubborn. Following an accident (especially in industry and in war) and after some emotional difficulty there is a paralysis of some part of the body. The arm or some particular part of the arm cannot be moved by the will, is paralyzed; or else the difficulty involves one or both legs. Sometimes speech is gone, or the power of moving the head; occasionally the difficulty is with one side of the face, etc. Usually the paralysis comes on suddenly, but often it comes on gradually. Modern neurology soon discovered that these paralyses were quite unlike those seen when there is "real" injury to the brain, spinal cord or the peripheral nerves. They corresponded to the layman's idea of a part. Thus a paralysis of the arm ends at the shoulder, a paralysis of the feet at the ankle, and in ways not necessary to detail here differ from what occurs when the organic structure of the nervous system is involved. For example, the reflexes in hysteria are unaltered, and stiffness when it occurs is not the stiffness of organic disease. If a neurologist were to have a hysteric paralysis a very interesting problem in diagnosis would be presented.

Further, the paralysis yields in spectacular fashion to various procedures or else disappears spontaneously in remarkable fashion overnight. Paralyses of this type have disappeared under hypnosis, violent electric shocks, "magical" liniments, threats, prayers, the healer's, the fakir's, the doctor's personal influence; under circumstances of danger (a fire, a row, etc.); by pilgrimages to Lourdes, St. Anne de Beaupre, the Temple of Diana, the relic of a saint; by the influence of sudden joy, fear, anger; by the work of the psychoanalyst and by that of the osteopath! Every great religious leader and every savage medicine man beating a tom-tom has had to, prove his pretensions to greatness by healing the sick—so intensely practical is man—and he has proved his divinity by curing the hysterics, so that they threw away their crutches, or jumped blithely out of bed, or used their arms, perhaps for the first time in years. Hysteria has caused more talk of the influence of mind over body than all other manifestations of mental peculiarity put together. Wherever there is anything to be gained by hysteric paralyses, these appear in much greater frequency than under ordinary circumstances. Thus the possibility of recovering damages seems to play a role in bringing about a paralysis that defies treatment until the litigation is settled; similarly the possibility of being removed from the fighting line played a large part in the causation of war hysteric paralysis.

3. A group of sensory phenomena is conspicuous in hysteria, sometimes combined with the paralyses and attacks but often existing alone. A part of the body will become curiously insensitive to stimulation. Thus one may thrust a pin into any part without evoking any pain and APPARENTLY without being felt; one may rub the cornea of the eye, that exquisitely sensitive part, without arousing a reaction; one may push a

---

American and German neurologists and the rest of the French school describe hysteria substantially as I am here describing it.

throat stick against the uvula as it hangs from the palate without arousing the normal and very lively reflex of "gagging." These insensitive areas, known as stigmata, played a very important role in the epidemic of witchcraft hunting of the sixteenth and seventeenth centuries, when the witch was so diagnosed if she felt no pain when a needle was thrust into her. Mankind has often enough worshiped the insane and mentally aberrant and has as often been diabolically cruel to them.

What has been stated of the paralyses is true of the insensitive areas; they correspond to an idea of a part and not to an anatomical unit. Thus a loss of sensation will reach up to the wrist (glove type) all around, front and back, or to the elbow or the shoulder, etc. No organically caused anaesthetic area ever does this, and so the neurologist is able, usually, to separate the two conditions. And the anaesthesias yield as do the hysteric paralyses to a variety of agents, from prayer and persuasion to a bitter tonic or a blow. I confess to a weird feeling in the presence of a hysteric whose arm can be thrust through and through with a needle without apparently suffering any pain, and it seems to me that this may be the explanation of the fortitude of those martyrs who have astonished and sometimes converted their persecutors by their sublime resistance to torture.

There has been described as part of hysteria the hysteric temperament. The characteristics of this temperament are the emotional instability, the strong desire for sympathy, the effort to obtain one's desire through weakness, through the appeal to the sympathy of others, an irritable egoism never satisfied and without firm purpose. It is true that the majority of peace-time hysterics show this peculiar temperament, but it is also true that the war-time hysterics often enough were of "normal" character, without prior evidence of weakness.

As I before mentioned, Freud became greatly interested in this group of patients and especially in the female patients, since in ordinary neurological practice the male hysteric is not common. Out of his experience and effort he built up a system of beliefs and treatment, the evolution of which is interesting, but which is not here important.

At the present time the Freudian doctrine hangs on the following beliefs:

1. That from the beginning to the end of life everything in the mental activities of man has a cause and a meaning, and that these causes and meanings may be traced back to infancy. No slip of the tongue is accidental; it has purpose and this purpose can be traced by psychoanalysis. So with hysteric phenomena: the paralyses, the sensory changes, all the queer and startling things represent something of importance and of value to the subconscious.

2. There is in man a subconscious mentality, having wills, purposes, strivings, desires, passions. These trends are the raw, native, uninhibited desires of man; they are our lusts, our crude unsocialized desires, arising out of a metaphysical, undifferentiated yearning called libido. In the Freudian "psychology" the libido is mainly sex desire and takes the form of

homosexual feelings, incest feelings (desire for the father or for the mother—the oedipus complex), desire for the sister or brother. [34] (The human being, according to Freud, goes through three stages in his sex life: first, a sex attachment to himself marked by thumb sucking, masturbation, etc., second, an attachment to the same sex—homosexuality—and, finally, the attachment or desire for the opposite sex.) In the practical application of the Freudian psychology to the patients the sex conflicts (of which we shall speak shortly) are all important; the subconsciousness is largely taken up with sex and with efforts to obtain gratification for these sex desires.

3. But, the theory continues, the conscious personality is the socialized personality, having aims and ends not consistent with desire for mother, homosexual cravings, lust for a married man or woman. So there ensues a battle between desire and inhibition. The inhibiting agent is a something called the censor, who pushes back into the subconsciousness the socially tabooed, the socially abhorrent desires; represses emotions and instincts that are socially out of order. But there is no real victory for the consciousness, for the complex (the name given to a desire or wish with its attendant ideas, emotions and motor manifestations) is still active, subconsciously changing the life of the person, causing him to make slips in his speech, expressing itself in his dreams and his work, and if sufficiently powerful, giving rise to nervous or mental disease of one type or another. Nothing is ever forgotten, according to Freud, and the reason our childhood is not voluntarily remembered is because it is full of forbidden desires and curiosities and the developing censor thrusts it all into the subconsciousness, where it continues to make trouble all the rest of the individual's life. In fact, a cardinal part of Freudianism (which he and his followers are lately modifying) is that it is the results of the "psychic traumata" (psychical injuries) of infancy and childhood that cause the hysteria of the adult; and these psychical traumata are largely (about ninety- nine per cent.) sexual.

4. Freudianism has borrowed the time-honored dictum that every sensation has a natural result in action and has elaborated it into the statement that every affective state, every desire and craving of whatever sort, needs a motor discharge, an avenue of outlet. If the desire or emotion is inhibited, its excitement is transferred with it into the subconscious and that excitement may attach itself to other excitements and break into consciousness as a mental disturbance of one type or another. If you can get at the complex by psychoanalysis, by dragging it to the light, by making it conscious, you discharge the excitement and health is restored. This originally was very important in the Freudian work and was called by the crude term of catharsis.

---

[34] The Freudians would protest against this. Libido is the life energy,—but all the Freudian analyses of actual cases published make libido sex, and usually "perverse." (I put the perverse in quotations because I fear to be called prudish by Freudians.)

5. How can one get at these subterranean cravings and strivings, at the fact that originally one desired one's mother and was jealous of one's father, or vice versa? Here Freud developed an elaborate technique based on the following:

Though the censor sits on the lid of the subconsciousness, that wily self has ways and means of expression. In dreams, in humor, in the slip of the tongue, in forgetfulness, in myths of the race, in the symptoms of the hysteric patient, in the creations of writers and artists, the subconsciousness seeks to symbolize in innocent (or acceptable) form its crude wishes. By taking a dream, for example, and analyzing it by what is known as the free association method, one discovers the real meaning of the terms used, the meaning behind the symbol; and behind the apparent dream-content one sees revealed the wishes and disorganizing desires of the subconscious or the real person. For throughout Freud's work, though not so definitely expressed, there is the idea that the subconscious is by far the most important part of the personality, and that the social purposes, the moral injunctions and feelings are not the real purposes and real desires of the real personality.

In analyzing dreams, the symbols become quite standardized. The horses, dogs, beards, queer situations of the dream (falling, walking without clothes, picking up money, etc.), the demons, ghosts, flying, relate definitely to sex situations, sex organs, sex desires. (The Freudians are apt to deny this theoretically, but practically every dream of the thousands they publish is a sex dream of crude content.) Naturally a "pure" girl is quite shocked when told that because she dreamed she was riding a gray horse in a green meadow that she really has bad (and still is troubled by) incestuous desires for her father, but that is the way to cure her of her neurasthenia or fatigue or obsession of one kind or other.

I have not attempted a detailed account of the technique of free association, nor the Freudian account of humor, etc. There are plenty of books on the market written by Freud himself and his followers. Frankly I advise the average person not to read them. I am opposed to the Freudian account of life and character, though recognizing that he has caused the psychologist to examine life with more realism, to strip away pretense, to be familiar with the crude and to examine conduct with the microscope.

I do not believe there is an ORGANIZED subconsciousness, having a PERSONALITY. Most of the work which proves this has been done on hysterics. Hysterics are usually proficient liars, are very suggestible and quite apt to give the examiner what he looks for, because they seek his friendly interest and eager study. Wherever I have checked up the "subconscious" facts as revealed by the patient as a result of his psychoanalysis or through hypnosis, I have found but little truth. On the other hand, the Freudians practically never check up the statements of their patients; if a woman tells all sorts of tales of her husband's attitude toward her, or of the attitude of her parents, it is taken for granted that she tells the truth. My belief is that had the statements of Freud's patients been carefully investigated he would probably never have evolved his theories.

The Freudians have made no consecutive study of normal childhood, though they lay great stress on this period of life and in fact trace the symptoms of their patients back to "infantile trauma." Most of Freud's ideas on sex development can be traced to, the one four-and-a-half-years-old child he analyzed, who was as representative of normal childhood as the little chess champion of nine years now astounding the world is representative of the chess ability of the average child. Moreover, the basis of the technique is the free association, an association released from inhibitions of all kinds. There isn't any such thing, as Professor Woodworth has pointed out. All associations are conditioned by the physical condition of the patient, by his mood, by the nature of the environment he finds himself in, by the personality of the examiner and his powers of suggesting, his purposes and (very important) by the patient's purposes, which he cannot bid "Disappear!" As for the results of treatment, every neurologist meets patients again and again who have been "psychoanalyzed" without results. Moreover, psychoneurotic patients get well without treatment, as do all other classes of the sick, and the Christian Scientist, the osteopath and the chiropractic also have records of "cures."

This is not the place to discuss in further detail the Freudian ideas (the wish, the symbol, the jargon of transference, etc). The leading follower of Freud, Jung, has already broken away from the parent church, and there is an amusing cry of heresy raised. Soon the eminent Austrian will have the pleasure of seeing a half-dozen schools that have split off from his own,— followers of Bleuler, Jung, Adler and others.

There IS a subconsciousness in that much of the nervous activity of the organism has but little or no relation to consciousness. There are mechanisms laid down by heredity and by the racial structure that accomplish great functions without any but the most indirect effect on consciousness and without any control by the conscious personality. We are spurred on to sex life, to marriage, to the care of our children by instinct; but the instinct is not a personality any more than the automatic heartbeat is. We repress a forbidden desire; if we are successful and really overcome the desire by setting up new desires or in some other way, the inhibited desire is not locked up in a subterranean limbo. There is nothing pathological about inhibition, for inhibition is as normal a part of character as desire, and the social instinct which bids us inhibit is as fundamental as the sex instinct. Most conflicts are on a conscious plane, but most people will not admit to any one else their deeply abhorrent desires. To all of us, or nearly all, come desires and temptations that we would not acknowledge for the world. If a wise examiner succeeds in getting us to admit them, it is very agreeable to find a scapegoat in the form of the subconsciousness. I have often said this to students: if all our thoughts and conscious desires could be exposed, the most of us would almost die of shame. True, we do not clearly understand ourselves and our conflicts and explanation is often necessary, but that is not equivalent to the subconsciousness; it merely means that introspection is not sagacious.

Nor is it true, in my belief, that dreams are important psychical events, nor that the subconsciousness evades a censor in elaborating them. To what end would that be done? What would be the use of it? Suppose that Freud and his school had never been; then dreams would always be useless, for they would have no interpreter. Men have dreamed in the countless ages before Freud was born,—in vain. Think how the poor, misguided subconsciousness has labored for nothing,—and how grateful it should be to Freud! Dreams are results and have the same kind of function that a stomach-ache has.

Things, experiences are forgotten, and whether they are remembered or not depends upon the number of times they are experienced, the attention they are given, the use they are put to and the quality of the brain experiencing them. Disease and old age may lower the recording power of the brain so that experiences and sensations do not stick, and now and then the brain is hypermnesic so that things are remembered with surprising ease.

The conflicts of life are generally conscious conflicts, in my experience. Desires and lusts that one does not know of do no harm; it is the conflict which we cannot settle, the choice we cannot make, the doubt we cannot resolve, that injures. It is not those who find it easy to inhibit a desire or any impulse that are troubled, though they may and do grow narrow. It is those whose unlawful or discordant desires are not easily inhibited who find themselves the theater of a constant struggle that breaks them down. The uneasiness of a desire that arises from the activity of the sex organs is not a manifestation of a subconscious personality, unless we include in our personality our livers, spleen and internal organs of all kinds. Such an uneasiness may not be clearly understood by the individual merely because the uneasiness is diffuse and not localized. But there is no personality, Do will, wish or desire in that uneasiness; it may and does cause to arise in the conscious personality wills and wishes and desires against which there is rebellion and because of which there is conflict.

Upon the issue of the conflicts within the personality hangs the fate of the individual. Race-old lines of conduct are inhibited by custom, tradition, teaching, conformity and the social instinct and its allies. Here is a subject worthy of extended consideration.

Freud has done the thought of our times a great service in emphasizing conflict. From the earliest restriction laid by men on his own conduct, wrestling with desire and temptation has been the greatest of man's struggles. Internal warfare between opposing purposes and desires may proceed to a disruption of the personality, to failure and unhappiness, or else to a solidified personality, efficient, single-minded and successful. Freud's work has directed our attention to the thousand and one aberrant desires that we will hardly acknowledge to ourselves, and he has forced the professional worker in abnormal and normal mental life to disregard his own prejudices, to strip away the camouflage that we put over our motives and our struggles. Together with Jung and Bleuler, he has helped our science of character a great deal through no other method than by arousing it to action against him. In order to fight him, our thought has been forced to arm itself with the weapons that he has used.

CHAPTER VI
EMOTION, INSTINCT, INTELLIGENCE AND WILL

In a preceding chapter we discussed man as an organism reacting against an outside world and spurred on by internal activities and needs. We discussed stimulation, reflexes, inhibition, choice and the organizing activity, memory and habit, consciousness and subconsciousness, all of which are primary activities of the organism. But these are mere theories of function, for the activities we are interested in reside in more definite reactions, of which the foregoing are parts.

We see a dreaded object on the horizon or foresee a calamity,—and we fear. That state of the organism (note I do not say that STATE OF MIND) resulting from the vision is an emotion. We fly at once, we hide, and the action is in obedience to an instinct. But ordinarily we do not fly or hide haphazard; we think of ways and means, if only in a rudimentary fashion; we shape plans, perhaps as we fly; we pick up a stick on the run, hoping to escape but preparing for the reaction of fight if cornered. "What shall I do—what shall I do? finds no conscious answer if the emotion is overwhelming or the instinctive flight a pell-mell affair; but ordinarily memories of other experiences or of teaching come into the mind and some effort is made to meet the situation in an "intelligent" manner.

Here, then, is a response in which three cardinal reactions have occurred and are blended,—the emotion, the instinctive action, and the intelligent action; or to make abstractions, emotion, instinct and intelligence. (Personally, I think half the trouble with our thought is that, we abstract from our experiences a common group of associations and believe that the abstraction has some existence outside our thoughts.) Thus there arise in us, as a result of things experienced, curious feelings and we speak of the feelings as emotions; we make a race-old response to a situation,—an instinctive reaction; our memories, past experiences and present purposes are stirred into activity, and we plan and scheme, and this is an intelligent reaction, but there is in reality no metaphysical entity Emotion, Instinct, Intelligence. I believe that here the philosophers whose mental activities are essentially in the direction of forming abstract ideas have misled us.

What I wish to point out is this: that to any situation all three reactions may take place and modify one another. We are insulted—some one slaps our face—the fierce emotion of anger arises and through us surge waves of feeling manifested on the motor side by tensed muscles, rapid heart, harsh breathing, perhaps a general reddening of face and eyes. Instinctively our fists are clenched, a part of the reaction of fight, and it needs but the slightest increase of anger to send us leaping on the aggressor, to fight him perhaps to the death. But no,—the situation has aroused certain memories and certain inhibitions: the one who struck us has been our friend and we can see that he is acting under a mistaken impression, or else we perceive that he is right, that we have done him a wrong for which his blow is a sort of just reaction. We are checked by these cerebral activities, we choose some other reaction than fight; perhaps we prevent him from further assault, or we turn and walk away, or we start to explain, to mollify and console, or to remonstrate and reprove. In other words, "intelligence" steps in to inhibit, to bring to the surface the possibilities, to choose, and thus overrides the emotional instinctive reaction. It may not succeed in the overriding; we may hesitate, inhibit, etc., for only a second or so, before hot anger overcomes us, and the instinctive response of fight and retaliation takes place.

These examples might be multiplied a thousandfold. Every day of our lives situations come up in which there is a blending or an antagonism between emotional, instinctive and intelligent responses. In fact, very few acts of the organized human being are anything else. For every emotion awakens memories of past emotions and the consequences; every instinct is hampered by other instincts or by the inhibitions aroused by obstacles; and intelligence continually struggles against emotion and blind instinct. Teaching, experience, knowledge, all modify emotional and instinctive responses so that sometimes they are hardly recognizable as such. On the other hand, though intelligence normally occupies the seat of power, it is easily ousted and in reality only steers and directs the vehicle of life, choosing not the goal but the road by which the goal can safely be reached.

In general terms we shall define emotions, instincts and intelligence as follows:

1. For emotions we shall accept a modified James-Lange theory, supplementing it by the developments of science since their day. When a thing is seen or heard (or smelled or tasted or thought), it arouses an emotion; that emotion consists of at least three parts. First, the arousal of memories and experiences that give it a value to the individual, make it a desired object or a dreaded, distasteful object. Second, at the same time, or shortly preceding or succeeding this, a great variety of changes takes place in the organism, changes that we shall call the vaso-visceral-motor changes. This means merely that there is a series of reactions set up in the sympathetic nervous system, in the blood vessels and bodily structures they control and in the glands of internal secretion,—changes which include the blush or the pallor, the rapid heartbeat, the quickened or labored breathing, the changes in the digestive tract which include the vomiting of disgust and the diarrhoea of fear; the changes that passion brings in the male and the female and many other alterations to be discussed again. Third, there is then the feeling of these coenaesthetic changes,—a feeling of pleasantness, unpleasantness mingled with the basic feeling of excitement, and from then on that situation is linked in memory with the feeling that we usually call the emotion but which is only a part of it. Nevertheless, it becomes the part longed for or thereafter avoided; it is the value of the emotion to us, as conscious personalities, although it may be a false, disastrous, dangerous value. Excitement is the generalized mood

change that results in consciousness in consequence of the vaso-visceral-motor changes of emotion; it is therefore based on bodily changes as is the feeling, pleasant or unpleasant, that also occurs. William James said that we laugh and are therefore happy; we weep and are therefore sad; the bodily changes are primary and the feeling secondary. We do not accept this dictum entirely, but we say that the organism reacts in a complicated way and that the feeling—sadness, disgust, anger, joy—springs from the memories and past experiences aroused by a situation as well as from the widespread bodily excitement also so aroused. For the neurologist both the cerebral and the sympathetic- endocrinal components of emotion are important.

For the moment we turn to instinct and instinctive reactions.

2. Man has always wondered that things can be known without teaching. So slow and painful is the process of mastering a technique, whether of handicraftsmanship or of art, so imbued are we with the need of education for the acquirement of knowledge, that we are taken aback by the realization that all around us are creatures carrying on the most elaborate technique, going through the most complicated procedures and apparently possessed of the surest knowledge without the possibility of teaching. The flight of birds, the obstetric and nursing procedures of all animals, and especially the complicated and systematized labors of bees, ants and other insects, have aroused the wonder, admiration and awe of scientists. A chick pecks its way out of its egg and shakes itself,—then immediately starts on the trail of food and usually needs no instruction as to diet. The female insect lays its eggs, the male insect fertilizes them, the progeny go through the states of evolution leading to adult life without teaching and without the possibility of previous experience. Since the parent never sees the progeny, and the progeny assume various shapes and have very varied capacities at these times, there can be no possible teaching of what is remarkably skillful and marvelously adapted conduct.[35]

Herbert Spencer considered the instinct as a series of inevitable reflexes. The carrion fly, when gravid, deposits her eggs in putrid meat in order that the larvae may have appropriate food, although she never sees the larvae or cannot know through experience their needs. "The smell of putrid meat attracts the gravid carrion fly. That is, it sets up motions of the wings which bring the fly to it, and the fly having arrived, the smell, and the contact combined stimulate the functions of oviposition." [36] But as all the critics have pointed out, the theory of compound reflex action leaves out of account that there are any number of stimuli pouring in on the carrion fly at the same time that the meat attracts her. The real mystery lies

---

[35] The nature of instinct has been a subject of discussion for centuries, but it is only within the last fifty years or thereabouts that instinctive actions have really been studied. I refer the reader to the works of Darwin, Romanes, Lloyd Morgan, the Peckhams, Fabre, Hobhouse, and McDougall for details as to the controversies and the facts obtained.

[36] Hobhouse.

in that internal condition which makes the smell of the meat act so inevitably.

In fact, it is this internal condition in the living creature that is the most important single link in instinct. In the non-mating season the sight of the female has no effect on the male. But periodically his internal organs become tense with procreative cells; these change his coenaesthesia; that starts desire, and desire sets going the mechanisms of search, courtship, the sexual act and the care of the female while she is gravid. All instinctive acts have back of them either a tension or a deficit of some kind or other, brought about by the awakening of function of some glandular structure, so that the organism becomes ready to respond to some appropriate outside stimulus and inaccessible to others. During the mating season, with certain animals, the stimulus of food has no effect until there is effected the purposes of the sexual hunger. Changes in the body due to the activity of sex glands or gastric juices or any other organic product have two effects. They increase the stimulation that comes from the thing sought and decrease the stimulation that comes from other things. In physiological language, the threshold for the first is lowered and for the other it is raised.

But this does not explain HOW the changes in glands MAKE the animal seek this or that, except by saying that the animal has hereditary structures all primed to explode in the right way. We may fall back on Bergson's mystical idea that all life is a unity, and that instinct, which makes one living thing know what to do with another—to kill it in a scientific way for the good of the posterity of the killer—is merely the knowledge, unconscious, that life has of life. That pleasant explanation projects us back to a darker problem than ever: how life knows life and why one part of life so obviously seeks to circumvent the purpose of another part of life.

For us it is best to say that instinct arises out of the racial and individual needs; that physically there occur changes in the glands and tissues; that these set up desires which arouse into action simple or elaborate mechanisms which finally satisfy the need of the organs and tissues. [37]

Even in the low forms of life instincts are not perfect at the start, or perfect in details, and almost every member of a species will show individuality in dealing with an obstacle to an instinctive action. In other words, though there is instinct and this furnishes the basis for action in the lowest forms of life, there is also the capacity for learning by experience,— and this is Intelligence. "The basis of instinct is heredity and we can impute an action to pure instinct only if it is hereditary. The other class of actions are those devised by the individual animal for himself on the basis

---

[37] Kempf in his book on the vegetative nervous system goes into great detail the way the visceral needs force the animal or human to satisfy them. Life is a sort of war between the vegetative and the central nervous system. There is just enough truth in this point of view to make it very entertaining.

of his own experience and these are called generally intelligent. Of intelligence operating within the sphere of instinct there is ample evidence. There are modifications of instinctive action directly traceable to experience which cannot be explained by the interaction of purely hereditary tendencies and there are cases in which the whole structure of the instinct is profoundly modified by the experience of the individual." Hobhouse, whom I quote, goes on to give many examples of instinctive action modified by experience and intelligence in the insect and lower animal world.

What I wish especially to point out is that man has many instinctive bases for conduct, but instincts as such are not often seen in pure form in man. They are constantly modified by other instincts and through them runs the influence of intelligence. The function of intelligence is to control instincts, to choose ways and means for the fulfillment of instincts that are blocked, etc. Moreover, the effects of teachings, ethics, social organization and tradition, operating through the social instincts, are to repress, inhibit and whip into conformity every mode of instinctive conduct. The main instincts are those relating to nutrition and reproduction, the care of the young, to averting danger or destroying it, to play and organized activity, to acquiring, perhaps to teaching and learning and to the social relations generally. But manners creep in to regulate our methods of eating and the things we shall eat; and we may not eat at all unless we agree to get the things to eat a certain way. We may not cohabit except under tremendous restriction, and marriage with its aims and purposes is sexual in origin but modified largely and almost beyond recognition by social consideration, taste, esthetic matters, taboos and economic conditions. We may not treat our enemy as instinct bids us do,—for only in war may one kill and here one kills without any personal purpose or anger, almost without instinct. We may be compelled through social exigencies to treat our enemy politely, eat with him, sleep with him and help him out of difficulties and thus completely thwart one instinctive set of reactions. Play becomes regulated by rules and customs, becomes motivated by the desire for superiority, or the desire for gain, and may even leave the physical field entirely and become purely mental. And so on. It does no special practical good to discuss instincts as if they operated in man as such. They become purposes. Therefore we shall defer the consideration of instincts and purposes in detail until later chapters of this book.

Since instincts are too rigid to meet the needs of the social and traditional life of man, they become intellectualized and socialized into purposes and ambitions, sometimes almost beyond recognition. Nevertheless, the driving force of instinct is behind every purpose, every ambition, even though the individual himself has not the slightest idea of the force that is at work. This does not mean that instinct acts as a sort of cellar- plotter, roving around in a subconsciousness, or at least no such semi-diabolical personality need be postulated, any more than it need be postulated for the automatic mechanism that regulates heartbeat or digestion. The organic tensions and depressions that constitute instinct are not conscious or subconscious; they affect our conscious personalities so that we desire something, we fit that desire in with the rest of our desires, we seek the means of gratifying that desire first in accordance with means that Nature has given us and second in accordance with social teaching and our intelligence. If the desire brings us sharply in contact with obstacles imposed either by circumstances or more precious desire, we inhibit that desire,—and thus the instinct. Because organic tensions and depressions are periodic and are dependent upon the activities of glands and tissues not within our control, the desires may never be completely squelched and may arise as often as some outer stimulus brings them into activity, to plague and disorder the life of the conscious personality.

3. With this preliminary consideration of instinct, we pass on to certain of the phases of intelligence. How to define intelligence is a difficulty best met by ignoring definition. But this much is true: that the prime function of intelligence is to store up the past and present experiences so that they can be used in the future, and that it adds to the rigid mechanism of instinct a plastic force which by inhibiting and exciting activity according to need steers the organism through intricate channels.

Instinct, guided by a plan, conveniently called Nature's plan, is not itself a planner. The discharge of one mechanism discharges another and so on through a series until an end is reached,—an end apparently not foreseen by the organism but acting for the good of the race to which the organism belongs. Intelligence, often enough not conscious of the plans of Nature, [38] indeed, decidedly ignorant of these plans, works for some good established by itself out of stimuli set up by the instincts. It plans, looks backward and forward, reaches the height of reflecting on itself, gets to recognize the existence of instinct and sets itself the task of controlling instinct. Often enough it fails, instinct breaks through, takes possession of the means of achievement, accomplishes its purpose—but the failure of intelligence to control and the misguided control it attempts and assumes are merely part of the general imperfections of the organism. A perfect

---

[38] We are at this stage in a very dark place in human thought. We say that instincts seek the good of the race, or have some racial purpose, as the sexual instinct has procreation as its end. But the lover wooing his sweetheart has no procreation plan in his mind; he is urged on by a desire to win this particular girl, a desire which is in part sexual, in part admiration of her beauty, grace, and charm; again it is the pride of possession and achievement; and further is the result of the social and romantic ideals taught in books, theaters, etc. He may not have the slightest desire for a child; as individual he plans one thing,—but we who watch him see in his approach the racial urge for procreation and even disregard his purposes as unimportant. Who and what is the Race, where does it reside, how can it have purposes? Call it Nature, and we are no better off. We must fall back on an ancient personalization of forces, and our minds rest easier when we think of a Planner operating in all of us and perhaps smiling as He witnesses our strivings.

intelligence would be clearly able to understand its instincts, to give each of them satisfaction by a perfect compromise, would pick the methods for accomplishment without error, and storing up the past experiences without loss, would meet the future according to a plan.

As we study the nervous systems of animals, we find that with the apparent growth of intelligence there is a development of that part of the brain called the cerebrum. In so far as certain other parts of the brain are concerned—medulla, pons, mid-brain, basal ganglia cerebellum—we who are human are not essentially superior to the dog, the cow, the elephant or the monkey. But when the neopallium, or the cerebrum, is considered, the enormous superiority of man (and the superiority of the higher over the lower animals) becomes striking. Anatomically the cerebrum is a complex elaboration of cells and fibers that have these main purposes: First, to record in perfect and detailed fashion the EXPERIENCES of the organism, so that here are memory centers for visual and auditory experiences, for skin, joint and bone experiences of all kinds, speech memories, action memories, and undoubtedly for the recording in some way not understood of the pleasure-pain feelings. Second, it has a hold, a grip on the motor mechanism of the body, on the muscles that produce action, so that the intelligence can nicely adapt movement to the circumstances, to purpose, and can inhibit the movements that arise reflexly. Thus in certain diseases, where the part of the brain involved in movement is injured, voluntary movement disappears but reflex action is increased. Third, the neopallium, or cerebrum, is characterized by what are known as association tracts, i.e., connections of intricate kinds which link together areas of the brain having different functions and thus allow for combinations of activity of all kinds. The brain thus acts to increase the memories of the past, and, as we all know, man is probably the only animal to whom the past is a controlling force, sometimes even an overpowering force. It acts to control the conduct of the individual, to delay or to inhibit it, and it acts to increase in an astonishing manner the number of reactions possible. One stimulus arousing cerebral excitement may set going mechanisms of the brain through associated tracts that will produce conduct of one kind or another for years to come.

We spoke in a previous chapter of choice as an integral function of the organism. While choice, when two competing stimuli awake competing mechanisms, may be non-cerebral in its nature, largely speaking it is a function of the cerebrum, of the intelligence. To choose is a constant work of the intelligence, just as to doubt is an unavailing effort to find a choice. Choice blocked is doubt, one of the unhappiest of mental states. I shall not pretend to solve the mystery of WHO chooses,—WHAT chooses; perhaps there is a constant immortal ego; perhaps there is built up a series of permanently excited areas which give rise to ego feeling and predominate in choice; perhaps competing mechanisms, as they struggle (in Sherrington's sense) for motor pathways, give origin to the feeling of choice. At any rate, because we choose is the reason that the concept of will has arisen in the minds of both philosopher and the man in the street, and much of our feeling of worth, individuality and power—mental factors of huge importance in character—arises from the power to choose. Choice is influenced by—or it is a net result of—the praise and blame of others, conscience, memory, knowledge of the past, plans for the future. It is the fulcrum point of conduct!

That animals have intelligence in the sense in which I have used the term is without doubt. No one who reads the work of Morgan, the Peckhams, Fabre, Hobhouse and other recent investigators of the instincts can doubt it. Whether animals think in anything like the form our thought takes is another matter. We are so largely verbal in thought that speech and the capacity to speak seem intimately related to thought. For the mechanics of thought, for the laws of the association of ideas, the reader is referred to the psychologists. That minds differ according to whether they habitually follow one type of associations or another is an old story. The most annoying individual in the world is the one whose associations are unguided by a controlling purpose, who rambles along misdirected by sound associations or by accidental resemblances in structure of words, or by remote meanings,—who starts off to tell you that she (the garrulous old lady) went to the store to get some eggs, that she has a friend in the country whose boy is in the army (aren't the Germans dreadful, she's glad she's born in this country), city life is very hard, it isn't so healthy as the country, thank God her health is good, etc., etc.," and she never arrives at the grocery store to buy the eggs. The organizing of the associations through a goal idea is part of that organizing energy of the mind and character previously spoken of. The mind tends automatically to follow the stimuli that reach it, but the organizing energy has as one of its functions the preventing of this, and controlled thinking follows associations that are, as it were, laid down by the goal. In fatigue, in illness, in certain of the mental diseases, the failure of the organizing energy brings about failure "to concentrate" and the tyranny of casual associations annoys and angers. The stock complaint of the neurasthenic that everything distracts his attention is a reversion back to the unorganized conditions of childhood, with this essential difference: that the neurasthenic rebels against his difficulty in thinking, whereas the child has no rebellion against that which is his normal state. Minds differ primarily and hugely in their power of organizing experience, in so studying and recording the past that it becomes a guide for the, future. Basic in this is the power of resisting the irrelevant association, of checking those automatic mental activities that tend to be stirred up by each sound, each sight, smell, taste and touch. The man whose task has no appeal for him has to fight to keep his mind on it, and there are other people, the so-called absent-minded, who are so over-concentrated, so wedded to a goal in thought, that lesser matters are neither remembered nor noticed. In its excess overconcentration is a handicap, since it robs one of that alertness for new impressions, new sources of thought so necessary for growth. The fine mind is that which can pursue successfully a goal in thought but which picks en route to that goal, out of the irrelevant associations, something that enriches its conclusions.

Not often enough is mechanical skill, hand-mindedness, considered as one of the prime phases of intelligence. Intelligence, en route to the conquest of the world, made use of that marvelous instrument, the human hand, which in its opposable thumb and little finger sharply separates man from the rest of creation. Studying causes and effects, experimenting to produce effect, the hand became the principal instrument in investigation, and the prime verifier of belief. "Seeing is believing" is not nearly so accurate as "Handling is believing," for there is in touch, and especially in touch of the hands and in the arm movements, a Reality component of the first magnitude. But not only in touching and investigating, but in pushing and pulling and striking, IN CAUSING CHANGE, does the hand become the symbol and source of power and efficiency. Undoubtedly this phase of the hands' activities remained predominant for untold centuries, during which man made but slow progress in his career toward the leadership of the world. Then came the phase of tool-making and using and with that a rush of events that built the cities, bridged the waters, opened up the Little and the Big as sources of knowledge and energy for man and gave him the power which he has used,—but poorly. It is the skill of human hands upon which the mind of man depends; though we fly through the air and speed under water, some one has made the tools that made the machine we use. Therefore, the mechanical skill of man, the capacity to shape resisting material to purpose, the power of the detailed applications of the principles of movement and force are high, special functions of the intelligence. That people differ enormously in this skill, that it is not necessarily associated with other phases of intelligence are commonplaces. The dealer in abstract ideas of great value to the race may be unable to drive a nail straight, while the man who can build the most intricate mechanism out of crude iron, wood and metal may be unable to express any but the commonplaces of existence. Intelligence, acting through skill, has evolved machinery and the industrial evolution; acting to discover constant principles operating in experience, it has established science. Seeking to explain and control the world of unknown forces, it has evolved theory and practice. A very essential division of people is on the one hand those whose effort is to explain things, and who are called theorists, and those who seek to control things, the practical persons. There is a constant duel between these two types of personalities, and since the practical usually control the power of the world, the theorists and explainers have had rather a hard time of it, though they are slowly coming into their own.

Another difference between minds is this: that intelligence deals with the relations between things (this being a prime function of speech), and intelligence only becomes intellect when it is able to see the world from the standpoint of abstract ideas, such as truth, beauty, love, honor, goodness, evil, justice, race, individual, etc. The wider one can generalize correctly, the higher the intellect. The practical man rarely seeks wide generalizations because the truth of these and their value can only be demonstrated through the course of long periods of time, during which no good to the individual himself is seen. Besides which, the practical man knows that the wide generalization may be an error. Practical aims are usually immediate aims, whereas the aims of intellect are essentially remote and may project beyond the life of the thinker himself.

We speak of people as original or as the reverse, with the understanding that originality is the basis of the world's progress. To be original in thought is to add new relationships to those already accepted, or to substitute new ones for the old. The original person is not easily credulous; he applies to traditional teaching and procedure the acid test of results. Thus the astronomers who rejected the theological idea that the earth was the center of the universe observed that eclipses could not be explained on such a basis, and Harvey, as he dissected bullocks' hearts and tied tourniquets around his arms, could not believe that Galen's teaching on circulation fitted what he saw of the veins and valves of his arm. The original observer refuses to slide over stubborn facts; authority has less influence with him than has an apple dropping downward. In another way the original thinker is constantly taking apart his experiences and readjusting the pieces into new combinations of beauty, usefulness and truth. This he does as artist, inventor and scientist. Most originality lies in the rejection of old ideas and methods as not consonant with results and experience; in the taking apart and the isolation of the components of experience (analysis) and in their reassemblage into new combinations (synthesis). The organizing activity of the original mind is high, and curiosity and interest are usually well maintained. Unless there is with these traits the quality called good judgment (i.e., good choice), the original is merely one of those "pests" who launch half-baked reforms and projects upon a weary world.

We have spoken of intelligence as controlling and directing instinct and desire, as inhibiting emotion, as exhibiting itself in handicraftsmanship, as the builder up of abstractions and the principles of power and knowledge; we have omitted its relationship to speech. Without speech and its derivatives, man would still be a naked savage and not so well off in his struggle for existence as most of the larger animals. It is possible that we can think without words, but surely very little thinking is possible under such circumstances. One might conduct a business without definite records, but it would be a very small one. Speech is a means not only of designating things but of the manifest relations between things. It "short-cuts" thought so that we may store up a thousand experiences in one word. But its stupendous value and effects lie in this, that in words not only do we store up ourselves (could we be self-conscious without words?) and things, but we are able to interchange ourselves and our things with any one else in the world who understands our speech and writings. And we may truly converse with the dead and be profoundly changed by them. If the germ plasm is the organ of biological heredity, speech and its derivatives are the organs of social heredity!

The power of expressing thought in words, of compressing

experiences into spoken and written symbols, of being eloquent or convincing either by tongue or pen, is thus a high function of intelligence. The able speaker and writer has always been powerful, and he has always found a high social value in promulgating the ideas of those too busy or unfitted for this task, and he has been the chief agent in the unification of groups.

The danger that lies in words as the symbols of thought lies in the fact pointed out by Francis Bacon [39] (and in our day by Wundt and Jung) that words have been coined by the mass of people and have come to mean very definitely the relations between things as conceived by the ignorant majority, so that when the philosopher or scientist seeks to use them, he finds himself hampered by the false beliefs inherent in the word and by the lack of precision in the current use of words. Moreover, words are also a means of stirring up emotions, hate, love, passion, and become weapons in a struggle for power and therefore obscure intelligence.

Words, themselves, arise in our social relations, for the solitary human would never speak, and the thought we think of as peculiarly our own is intensely social. Indeed, as Cooley pointed out, our thought is usually in a dialogue form with an auditor who listens and whose applause we desire and whose arguments we meet. In children, who think aloud, this trend is obvious, for they say, "you, I, no, yes, I mustn't, you mustn't," and terms of dialogue and social intercourse appear constantly. Thought and words offer us the basis of definite internal conflict: one part of us says to the other, "You must not do that," and the other answers, "What shall I do?" Desire may run along smoothly without distinct, internal verbal thought until it runs into inhibition which becomes at once distinctly verbal in its, "No! You musn't!" But desire obstructed also becomes verbal and we hear within us, "I will!"

We live secure in the belief that our thoughts are our own and cannot be "read" by others. Yet in our intercourse we seek to read the thoughts of others—the real thoughts—recognizing that just as we do not express ourselves either accurately or honestly, so may the other be limited or disingenuous. Whenever there occurs a feeling of inferiority, the face is averted so the thoughts may not be read, and it is very common for people mentally diseased to believe that their thoughts are being read and published. Indeed, the connection between thoughts and the personality may be severed and the patient mistakes as an outside voice his own thoughts.

A large part of ancient and modern belief and superstition hinges on the feeling of power in thought and therefore in words. Thought CAUSES things as any other power does. Think something hard, use the appropriate word, and presto,—what you desire is done. "Faith moves mountains," and the kindred beliefs of the magic in words have plunged the world into abysses of superstition. Thought is powerful, words are powerful, if

---

[39] This is Bacon's "Idols of the Market Place."

combined with the appropriate action, and in their indirect effects. All our triumphs are thought and word products; so, too, are our defeats.

It is not profitable for us at this stage to study the types of intelligence in greater detail. In the larger aspects of intelligence we must regard it as intimately blended with emotions, mood, instincts, and in its control of them is a measurement of character. We may ask what is the range of memory, what is the capacity for choosing, how good is the planning ability, how active is the organizing ability, what is the type of associations that predominate and how active is the stream of thought? What is the skill of the individual? How well does he use words and to what end does he use them? Intelligence deals with the variables of life, leaving to instinct the basic reactions, but it is in these variables that intelligence meets situations that of themselves would end disastrously for the individual.

Not a line, so far, on Will. What of the will, basic force in character and center of a controversy that will never end? Has man a free will? does his choice of action and thought come from a power within himself? Is there a uniting will, operating in our actions, a something of an integral indivisible kind, which is non-material yet which controls matter?

Taking the free-will idea at its face value leads us nowhere in our study of character. If character in its totality is organic, so is will, and it therefore resides in the tissues of our organism and is subject to its laws. In some mental diseases the central disturbance is in the will, as Kraepelin postulates in the disease known as Dementia Praecox. The power of choice and the power of acting according to choice disappear gradually, leaving the individual inert and apathetic. The will may alter its directions in disease (or rather be altered) so that BECAUSE of a tumor mass in the brain, or a clot of blood, or the extirpation of his testicles, he chooses and acts on different principles than ever before in his life. Or you get a man drunk, introduce into his organism the soluble narcotic alcohol, and you change his will in the sense that he chooses to be foolish or immoral or brutal, and acts accordingly. When from Philip drunk we appeal to Philip sober, we acknowledge that the two Philips are different and will different things. And the will of the child is not the will of the adult, nor is that the will of the old man. If will is organic it cannot be free, but is conditioned by health, glandular activity, tissue chemistry, age, social setting, education, intelligence.

Moreover, behind each choice and each act are motives set up by the whole past of the individual, set up by heredity and training, by the will of our ancestors and our contemporaries. Logically and psychologically, we cannot agree that a free agent has any conditions; and if it has any conditions, it cannot in any phase be free. To set up an argument for free will one has to appeal to the consciousness or have a deep religious motive. But even the ecclesiastical psychologists and even so strong a believer in free will as Munsterberg take the stand that we may have two points of view, one—as religiously minded—that there is a free will, and the other— as scientists—that will is determined in its operations by causes that reach back in an endless chain. The power to choose and the power to act may be heightened by advice and admonitions. In this sense we may properly tell a man to use his will, and we may seek to introduce into him motives that will fortify his resolution, remove or increase his inhibitions, make clearer his choice. But that will is an entity, existing by itself and pulling at levers of conduct without itself being organic, need not be entertained by any serious-minded student of his kind.

Is there a unit, will? A will power? I can see no good evidence for this belief except the generalizing trend of human thought and the fallacy that raises abstractions into realities. Napoleon had a strong will in regard to his battles and a weak one regarding women. Pitt was a determined statesman but could not resist the lure of drink. Socrates found no difficulty in dying for his beliefs, but asked not to be tempted by a beautiful youth. Francis Bacon took all knowledge to be his province, and his will was equal to the task, but he found the desire for riches too great for him. In reality, man is a mosaic of wills; and the will of each instinct, each desire, each purpose, is the intensity of that instinct, desire or purpose. In each of us there is a clash of wills, as the trends in our character oppose one another. The united self harmonizes its purposes and wills into as nearly one as possible; the disunited self is standing unsteadily astride two or more horses. We all know that it is easy for us to accomplish certain things and difficult to make up our minds to do others. Like and dislike, facility or difficulty are part of each purpose and enter into each will as parts.

Such a view does not commit one to fatalism, at least in conduct. Desiring to accomplish something or desiring to avoid doing something, both of which are usually considered as part of willing, we must seek to find motives and influences that will help us. We must realize that each choice, each act, changes the world for us and every one else and seek to harmonize our choice and acts with the purposes we regard as our best. If we seek to influence others, then this view of the will is the only hopeful one, for if will is a free entity how can it possibly be influenced by another agent? The very essence of freedom is to be noninfluenced. Seeking to galvanize the will of another, there is need to search for the influences that will increase the energy of his better purposes, to "appeal to his better self," meaning that the spurs to his good conduct are applied with greater force, but that first the nature of the particular things that spur him on must be discovered. Praise? Blame? Reward? Punishment? Education? Authority? Logic? Religion? Emotional appeal? Substitution of new motives and associations?

The will is therefore no unit, but a sum total of things operating within the sphere of purpose. Purpose we have defined as arising from instinct and desire and intellectualized and socialized by intelligence, education, training, tradition, etc. Will is therefore best studied under the head of purpose and is an outgrowth of instinct. Each instinct, in its energy, its fierceness, its permanence, has its will. He who cannot desire deeply, in whom some powerful instinct does not surge, cannot will deeply.

If we look at character from the standpoint of emotion, instinct, purpose and intelligence, we find that emotion is an internal discharge of energy, which being FELT by the individual becomes an aim or aversion of his life; that instinctive action is the passing over of a stimulus directly into hereditary conduct along race-old motor pathways for purposes that often enough the individual does not recognize and may even rebel against; that instinct is without reflection, but that purpose, which is an outgrowth of instinct guided and controlled by intelligence, is reflective and self-conscious. Purpose seeks the good of the individual as understood by him and is often against the welfare of the race, whereas instinct seeks the good of the race, often against the welfare of the individual. Intelligence is the path of the stimulus or need cerebrally directed, lengthened out, inhibited, elaborated and checked. Often enough faulty, it is the chief instrument by which man has become the leading figure on the world stage.

CHAPTER VII
EXCITEMENT, MONOTONY AND INTEREST

No matter what happens in the outside world, be it something we see, hear or feel, in any sense-field there is an internal reverberation in our bodies,—excitement. Excitement is the undifferentiated result of stimuli, whether these come from without or from within. For a change in the glands of the body heaps up changes within us, which when felt, become excitement. Thus at the mating period of animals, at the puberty of man, there is a quite evident excitement demonstrated in the conduct of the animal and the adolescent. He who remembers his own adolescence, or who watches the boy or girl of that age, sees the excitement in the readiness to laugh, cry, fight or love that is so striking.

Undoubtedly the mother-stuff of all emotion is the feeling of excitement. Before any emotion reaches its characteristic expression there is the preparatory tension of excitement. Joy, sorrow, anger, fear, wonder, surprise, etc., have in them as a basis the same consciousness of an internal activity, of a world within us beginning to seethe. Heart, lungs, blood stream, the great viscera and the internal glands, cerebrum and sympathetic nervous system, all participate in this activity, and the outward visage of excitement is always the wide-open eye, the slightly parted lips, the flaring nostrils and the slightly tensed muscles of the whole body. Shouts, cries, the waving of arms and legs, taking the specific direction of some emotion, make of excitement a fierce discharger of energy, a fact of great importance in the understanding of social and pathological phenomena. On the other hand, excitement may be so intensely internal that it shifts the blood supply too vigorously from the head and the result is a swoon. This is more especially true of the excitement that accompanies sorrow and fear than joy or anger, but even in these emotions it occurs.

There are some very important phases of excitement that have not been given sufficient weight in most of the discussions.

1. In the very young, excitement is diffuse and spreads throughout the organism. An infant starts with a jump at a sudden sound and shivers at a bright light. A young child is unrestrained and general in his expression of excitement, no matter what emotional direction that excitement takes. Bring about any tension of expectation in a child—have him wait for your head to appear around the corner as you play peek-a-boo, or delay opening the box of candy, or pretend you are one thing or another—and the excitement of the child is manifested in what is known as eagerness. Attention in children is accompanied by excitement and is wearying as a natural result, since excitement, means a physical discharge of energy. A child laughs all over and weeps with his entire body; his anger

involves every muscle of his body and his fear is an explosion. The young organism cannot inhibit excitement.

As life goes on, the capacity for localizing or limiting excitement increases. We become better organized, and the disrupting force of a stimulus becomes less. Attention becomes less painful, less tense, i.e., there is less general muscular and emotional reaction. Expectation is less a physical matter—perhaps because we have been so often disappointed—and is more cerebral and the emotions are more reflective and introspective in their expression and less a physical outburst. Indeed, the process often enough goes too far, and we long for the excitement of anticipation and realization. We do not start at a noise, and though a great crowd will "stir our blood" (excitement popularly phrased and accurately), we still limit that excitement so that though we cheer or shout there is a core of us that is quiet.

This is the case in health. In sickness, especially in that condition known as neurasthenia, where the main symptoms cluster around an abnormal liability to fatigue, and also in many other conditions, there is an increase in the diffusion of excitement so that one starts all over at a noise, instead of merely turning to see what it is, so that expectation and attention become painful and fatiguing. Crowds, though usually pleasurable, become too exciting, and there is a sort of confusion resulting because attention and comprehension are interfered with. The neurasthenic finds himself a prey to stimuli, his reaction is too great and he fatigues too readily. He finds sleep difficult because the little noises and discomforts make difficult the relaxation that is so important. The neurasthenic's voluntary attention is lowered because of the excitement he feels when his involuntary attention is aroused.

In the condition called anhedonia, which we shall hear of from time to time, there is a blocking or dropping out of the sense of desire and satisfaction even if through habit one eats, drinks, has sexual relationship, keeps up his work and carries out his plans. This lack of desire for the joys of life is attended by a restlessness, a seeking of excitement for a time, until there arises a curious over-reaction to excitement. The anhedonic patient finds that noises are very troublesome, that he becomes unpleasantly excited over music, that company is distressing because he becomes confused and excited, and crowds, busy scenes and streets are intolerable. Many a hermit, I fancy, who found the sensual and ambitious pleasure of life intolerable, who sought to fly from crowds to the deserts, was anhedonic but he called it renunciation. (Whether one really ever renounces when desire is still strong is a nice question. I confess to some scepticism on this point.)

2. Seeking excitement is one of the great pleasure-trends of life. In moderation, tension, expectation and the diffuse bodily reactions are agreeable; there is a feeling of vigor, the attention is drawn from the self and there is a feeling of being alive that is pleasurable. The tension must not be too long sustained, nor the bodily reaction too intense; relaxation

73

and lowered attention must relieve the excitement from time to time; but with these kept in mind, it is true that Man is a seeker of excitement.

This is a factor neglected in the study of great social phenomena. The growth of cities is not only a result of the economic forces of the time; it is made permanent by the fact that the cities are exciting. The multiplicity and variety of the stimuli of a city—social, sexual, its stir and bustle—make it difficult for those once habituated ever to tolerate the quiet of the country. Excitement follows the great law of stimulation; the same internal effect, the same feeling, requires a greater and greater stimulus, as well as new stimuli. So, the cities grow larger, increase their modes of excitement, and the dweller in the city, unless fortified by a steady purpose, becomes a seeker of excitement.

Not only is excitement pleasurable when reached through the intrinsically agreeable but it can be obtained from small doses of the intrinsically disagreeable. This is the explanation of the pleasure obtained from the gruesome, from the risk of life or limb, or from watching others risk life or limb. Aside from the sense of power obtained by traveling fast, it is the risk, THE SLIGHT FEAR, producing excitement, that makes the speed maniac a menace to the highways. And I think that part of the pleasure obtained from bitter foods is that the disagreeable element is just sufficient to excite the gastro-intestinal tract. The fascination of the horrible lies in the excitement produced, an excitement that turns to horror and disgust if the disagreeable is presented too closely. Thus we can read with pleasurable excitement of things that in their reality would shock us into profoundest pain. The more jaded one is, the more used to excitement, the more he seeks what are, ordinarily, disagreeable methods of excitement. Thus pain in slight degree is exciting, and in the sexual sphere pain is often sought as a means of heightening the pleasure, especially by women and by the roue. I suspect also that the haircloth shirt and the sackcloth and ashes of the anhedonic hermit were painful methods of seeking excitement.

Sometimes pain is used in small amounts to relieve excitement. Thus the man who bites his finger nails to the quick gets a degree of satisfaction from the habit. Indeed, all manner of habitual and absurd movements, from scratching to pacing up and down, are efforts to relieve the tension of excitement. One of my patients under any excitement likes to put his hands in very hot water, and the pain, by its localization, takes away from the diffuse and unpleasant excitement. The diffuse uncontrolled excitement of itching is often relieved by painful biting and scratching. Here is an effort to localize a feeling and thus avoid diffuse discomfort, a sort of homeopathic treatment.

3. As a corollary to the need of excitement and its pleasure is the reaction to monotony. Monotony is one of the most dreaded factors in the life of man. The internal resources of most of us are but small; we can furnish excitement and interest from our own store for but a short time, and there then ensues an intense yearning for something or somebody that will take up our attention and give a direction to our thought and action.

Under monotony the thought turns inward, there is daydreaming and introspection, [40] which are pleasurable only at certain times for most of us and which grow less pleasurable as we grow older. Watch the faces of people thinking as they travel alone in cars,—and rarely does one see a happy face. The lines of the face droop and sighs are frequent. Monotony and melancholy are not far apart; monotony and a restless seeking for excitement are almost synonymous. Of course, what constitutes monotony will differ in the viewpoint of each person, for some are so constituted and habituated (for habit is a great factor) that it takes but few stimuli to arouse a well-sustained interest, and others need or think they need many things, a constantly changing set of circumstances for pleasure.

Restlessness, eager searching for change, intense dissatisfaction are the natural fruit of monotony. Here is an important item in the problems of our times. Side by side with growth of the cities and their excitement is the growing monotony of most labor. The factory, with its specialized production, reduces the worker to a cog in the machinery. In some factories, in the name of efficiency, the windows are whitewashed so that the outside world is shut out and talking is prohibited; the worker passes his day performing his unvaried task from morning to night. Under such circumstances there arises either a burning sense of wrong, of injustice, of slavery and a thwarting of the individual dignity, or else a yearning for the end of the day, for dancing, drinking, gambling, for anything that offers excitement. Or perhaps both reactions are combined. Our industrial world is poorly organized economically, as witness the poor distribution of wealth and the periodic crises, but it is abominably organized from the standpoint of the happiness of the worker. Of this, more in another place.

Monotony brings fatigue, because there is a shutting out of the excitement that acts as an antidote to fatigue-feeling. A man who works without fatigue six days a week is tired all day Sunday and longs for Monday. The modern housewife, [41] with her four walls and the unending, uninteresting tasks, is worn out, and her fatigue reaction is the greater the more her previous life has been exciting and varied. Fatigue often enough is present not because of the work done but because the STIMULUS TO WORK HAS DISAPPEARED. Monotony is an enemy of character. Variety, in its normal aspect, is not only the spice of life; it is a great need. Stabilization of purpose and work are necessary, but a standardization that stamps out the excitement of variety is a deadly blow to human happiness.

Under monotony certain types of personalities develop an intense inner life, which may be pathological, or it may be exceedingly fruitful of productive thought.

Some build up a delusional thought and feeling. For delusion merely means uncorrected thought and belief, and we can only correct by contact and collision. The whole outer world may vanish or become hostile and

---

[40] Stanley Hall, in his book "Adolescence," lays great stress on monotony and its effects. See also Graham Wallas' "The Great Society."

[41] See my book "The Nervous Housewife!"

true mental disease develop. Perhaps it is more nearly correct to say that minds predisposed to mental disease find in monotony a circumstance favoring disease.

On the other hand, a vigorous mind shut out from outer stimuli [42] finds in this circumstance the time to develop leisurely, finds a freedom from distraction that leads to clear views of life and a proper expression. A periodic retirement from the busy, too-busy world is necessary for the thinker that he may digest his material, that he may strip away unessential beliefs, that he may find what it is he really needs, strives for and ought to have.

4. Here we come to another corollary of the need for excitement, the need of relaxation. At any rate, satisfaction and pleasure need periods of hunger in order to be felt. In the story of Buddha he is represented as being shielded from all sorrow and pain, living a life filled with pleasure and excitement, yet he sought out pain. So excitement, if too long continued—or rather if a situation that produces excitement of a pleasurable kind be too long endured—will result in boredom. "Things get to be the same," whether it be the excitement of love, the city, sports or what not. This is a basic law of all pleasures. In order that life may have zest, that excitement may be easily and pleasurably evoked and by normal means, we need relaxation, periods free from excitement, or we must pass on to a costly chase for excitement that brings breakdown of the character.

5. If the seeking of excitement, as such, is one of the prime pleasures of life, organized excitement in the form of interest is the directing and guiding principle of activity. At the outset of life interest is in the main involuntary and is aroused by the sights, sounds and happenings of the outer world. As time goes on, as the organism develops, as memories of past experiences become active, as peculiarities of personality develop, and as instincts reach activity, interest commences to take definite direction, to become canalized, so to speak. In fact, the development of interest is from the diffuse involuntary form of early childhood to a specialization, a condensation into definite voluntary channels. This development goes on unevenly, and is a very variable feature in the lives of all of us. Great ability expresses itself in a sustained interest; a narrow character is one with overdeformed, too narrow interest; failure is often the retention of the childish character of diffuse, involuntary interest. And the capacity to sustain interest depends not only on the special strength of the various abilities of the individual, but remarkably on his energy and health. Sustained "voluntary" interest is far more fatiguing than involuntary interest, and where fatigue is already present it becomes difficult and perhaps impossible. Thus after much work, whether physical or mental, during and after illness—especially in influenza, in neurasthenic states generally, or where there is an inner conflict—interest in its adult form is at a low ebb.

---

[42] Perhaps this is why real genius does not flourish in our crowded, over-busy days, despite the great amount of talent.

There are two main directions which interest may take, because there are two worlds in which we live. There is the inner world of our feelings, our thoughts, our desires and our struggles, [43] —and there is the outer world, with its people, its things, its hostilities, its friendships, its problems and facts, its attractions and repulsions. Man divides his interest between the two worlds, for in both of them are the values of existence. The chief source of voluntary interest lies in desire and value, and though these are frequently in coalescence, so that the thing we desire is the thing we value, more often they are not in coalescence and then we have the divided self that James so eloquently describes. So there are types of men to whom the outer world, whether it is in its "other people," or its things, or its facts, or its attractions and repulsions, is the chief source of interest and these are the objective types, exteriorized folks, whose values lie in the goods they can accumulate, or the people they can help, or the external power they exercise, or the knowledge they possess of the phenomena of the world, or the things they can do with their hands. These are on the whole healthy-minded, finding in their pursuits and interest a real value, rarely stopping from their work to ask, "Why do I work? To what end? Are things real?" Contrasted with them are those whose gaze is turned inward, who move through life carrying on the activities of the average existence but absorbed in their thoughts, their emotions, their desires, their conflicts,—perhaps on their sensations and coenaesthetic streams. Though there is no sharp line of division between the two types, and all of us are blends in varying degrees, these latter are the subjective introspective folk, interiorized, living in the microcosmos, and much more apt than the objective minded to be "sick souls" obsessed with "whys and wherefores." They are endlessly putting to themselves unanswerable questions, are apt to be the mentally unbalanced, or, but now and then, they furnish the race with one whose answers to the meaning of life and the direction of efforts guide the steps of millions.

There is a good and a bad side to the two types of interest. The objective minded conquer the world in dealing with what they call reality. They bridge the water and dig up the earth; they invent, they plow, they sell and buy, they produce and distribute wealth, and they deal with the education that teaches how to do all these things. They find in the outer world an unalterable sense of reality, and they tend rather naively to accept themselves, their interests and efforts as normal. In their highest forms they are the scientist, reducing to law this tangle of outer realities, or the artist, who though he is a hybrid with deep subjective and objective interest, nevertheless remodels the outer world to his concept of beauty. These objective-minded folk, the bulk of the brawn and in lesser degree of the brain of the world, are apt to be "materialists," to value mainly quantity and to be self-complacent. Of course, since no man is purely objective, there come to them as to all moments of brooding over the eggs of their

---

[43] Herbert Spencer's description of these two worlds is the best in literature. "Principles of Psychology."

inner life, when they wonder whether they have reached out for the right things and whether the goods they seek or have are worth while. Such introspective interest comes on them when they are alone and the outer world does not reach in, or when they have witnessed death and misfortune, or when sickness and fatigue have reduced them to a feeling of weakness. For it is true that the objective minded are more often robust, hearty, with more natural lust, passion and desire than your introspectionists, more virile and less sensitive to fine impressions.

The introspectionists, culling, chewing the cud of their experiences and sensations, find in their own reactions the realities. In fact, interested in consciousness, they are sometimes bold enough to deny the realities of anything else. Where the others build bridges, they build up the ideas of eternal good and bad, of beauty, of the transitory and the permanent, of now and eternity. They deal with abstract ideas, and they luxuriate in emotions. They build up beliefs where thought is the only reality and is omnipotent. They are the founders of religious, cults, fads and fancies. They inculcate the permanent ideals, because they are the only ones who interest themselves in something beside the show of the universe.

But too often they are the sick folk. Without the hardihood and the energy to conquer the outer world, they fall back on a world requiring less energy to study, less energy to conquer. Sometimes they develop a sense of unreality which vitiates all their efforts to succeed; or they become hypochondriacs, feeling every flutter of the heart and every vague ache and pain. The Hamlet doubting type is an introspectionist and oscillates in his mind from yea to nay on every question. Such as this type develop ideas of compensation and power and become cranks and fake prophets. Or else, and this we shall see again, they become imbued with a sense of inferiority, feel futile as against the red-blooded and shrink from others through pain.

Everywhere one sees these phases of interest in antagonism and cooperation. The "healthy-minded" acknowledge the leadership of a past introspectionist but despise the contemporary one as futile and light-headed. The introverted (to use a Freudian term) call the others Philistines, and mock them for their lack of spiritual insight, yet in everything they do they depend for aid and sustenance upon them. Introspection gives no exact measurements of value, but it gives value and without it, there can be no wisdom. But always it needs the correction of the outer world to keep it healthy.

While we have dealt here with the extremes of extrospection and introspection, it is safe to say that in the vast majority of people there is a definite and unassailable interest in both of these directions. Interest in others is not altruism and interest in the self is not self-interest or egoism. But, on the whole, they who are not interested in others never become philanthropists; they who are not interested in things never become savants; and they who do not dig deep into themselves are not philosophers. There are, therefore, certain practical aspects to the study of interest which are essential parts of the knowledge of character.

1. Is the interest of the one studied controlled by some purpose or purposes, or is it diffuse, involuntary, not well directed?

2. Is it narrow, so that it excludes the greater part of the world, or is it easily evoked by a multiplicity of things? In the breadth of interest is contained the breadth of character, but not necessarily its intensity or efficiency. There are people of narrow but intense successful interest, and others of broad, intense successful interest, but one meets, too frequently, people quickly interested in anything, but not for long or in a practical fashion. There is a certain high type of failure that has this difficulty.

3. Is its main trend outward, and if so, is there some special feature or features of the world that excite interest?

4. Is its main trend inward, and is he interested in emotions, thoughts, sensations,—In his mind or his body, in ideas or in feelings? For it is obvious that the man interested in his ideas is quite a different person than he who is keenly aware of his emotions, and that the hypochondriac belongs in a class by himself.

5. If there are special interests, how do these harmonize with ability and with well-defined plan and purpose. It is not sufficient to be keenly interested, though that is necessary. One of the greatest disharmonies of life is when a man is interested when he is not proficient, though usually proficiency develops interest because it gives superiority and achievement.

Interest is heightened by the success of others, for we are naturally competitive creatures, or by admiration for those successful in any line of activity. The desire to emulate or excel or to get power is a mighty factor in the maintenance of interest. "See how nicely Georgie does it," is a formula for both children and adults, and if omitted, interest would not be easily aroused or maintained. In other words, the competitive feeling and desire in its largest sense are necessary for the concentrated excitement of interest. So any scheme of social organization that proposes to do away with competition and desire for superiority labors under the psychological handicap of removing the basis of much of the interest in work and study and must find some substitute for the lacking incentives before it can seriously ask for the adherence of those with a realistic view of human nature. One might, it is true, establish traditions of work, bring about a livelier social conscience as to service, but these are not sufficient to arouse real interest in the vast majority of the race. Here and there one finds a man in whom interest is aroused by the unsolved problem, by the reward of fame and the pleasure of achievement, but such persons are rare. The average man (and woman), in my experience, loses interest in anything that does not directly benefit him or in which his personal competitive feeling is not aroused. Interest becomes vague and ill-defined the farther the matter concerned is from the direct personal good of the individual, and proportionately it becomes difficult to sustain it.

That is why in our day "dollars and cents" appeals to interest are made; away with abstracts, away with sentiment; the publicity man working for a good cause now uses the methods of the man selling shoes or automobiles: he attempts to show that one's interest and cooperation are demanded and necessary because one's direct personal welfare is involved. Whether or not ethically justifiable, it is a recognition of the fact that interest is aroused and sustained, for the majority, by some direct personal involvement.

Thus in education, a fact to be learned, or a subject to be studied, should be first sketched or placed in some use value to the student. Knowledge for knowledge's sake is appealing only to the rare scholar, he who palpitates with interest over the relationship of things to one another, he who seeks to discover values. Now and then one finds such a person, one thrown into sustained excitement by learning, but the great majority of students, whether in medicine, law or mathematics, are "practical," meaning that their interests are relatively narrow and the good they seek an immediate one to be reaped by themselves. Recognizing this fact in the abstract, the most of teaching is conducted on the plane of the real scholar, and the average student is left to find values for himself. From first to last in teaching I would emphasize usevalue; true, I would seek to broaden the conception of usevalue, so that a student would see that usefulness is a social value, but no matter how abstract and remote the subject, its relationship to usefulness would be preliminary and continuously emphasized in order to sustain interest.

Interest, like any other form of excitement, needs new stimuli and periods of relaxation. People under the driving force of necessity continue at their work for longer periods of time and more constantly than is psychologically possible for the maintaining of interest. So it disappears, and then fatigue sets in at once,—a fatigue that is increased by the effort to work and the regret and rebellion at the change. The memory seems to suffer and a fear is aroused that "I am losing my memory"; the threat to success brings anguish and often the health becomes definitely impaired. Overconcentrated, too long maintenance of interest brings apathy,—an apathy that cannot be dispelled except by change and rest. Here there is wide individual variation from those who need frequent change and relaxation periods to those who can maintain interest in a task almost indefinitely.

A hobby, or a secondary object of interest, is therefore a real necessity to the man or woman battling for a purpose, whose interest must be sustained. It acts to relax, to shift the excitement and to allow something of the feeling of novelty as one reapproaches the task.

As a matter of fact, excitement and interest are not easily separated from their derivatives and elaborations. Desire, purpose, ambition, imply a force; interest implies a direction for that force. Interest may be as casual as curiosity aroused by the novel and strange, or as deep-seated and specialized as a talent. The born teacher is he who knows how to arouse and maintain and direct interest; the born achiever is the man whose interest, quickly aroused, is easily maintained and directs effort. To find the activity that is natively interesting and yet suited to one's ability is the aim in vocational guidance.

There are some curious pathological aspects to interest —"conflict" aspects of the subject. A man finds himself palpitatingly interested in what is horrible to him, as a bird is fascinated by a snake. Sex abnormalities have a marvelous interest to everybody, although many will not admit it. Stories of crime and bloodshed are read by everybody with great avidity,— and people will go miles to the site of grim tragedy. Court rooms are packed whenever a horrible murder is aired or a nauseating divorce scandal is tried. A chaste woman will read, on the sly and with inner rebellion, as many pornographic tales as she can get hold of, and the "carefully" brought up, i. e., those whose interest has been carefully directed, suddenly become interested in the forbidden; they seek to peek through windows when they should be looking straight ahead.

As a matter of fact, interest is as much inhibited as conduct. "You mustn't ask about that" is the commonest answer a child gets. "That's a naughty question to ask" runs it a close second. Can one inhibit interest, which is the excitement caused by the unknown? The answer is that we can, because a large part of education is to do this very thing. "Can we inhibit any interest without injuring all interests?" is a question often put. My answer would be that it is socially necessary that interest in certain directions be inhibited, whether it hurts the individual or not. But the interest in a forbidden direction can be shifted to a permitted direction, and this should be done. In my opinion, sex interest can be so handled and a blunt thwarting of this interest should be avoided. Some explanation leading the child to larger, less personal aspects of sex should be given.

The interest of the child is often thwarted through sheer laziness. "Don't bother me" is the reply of a parent shirking a sacred duty. Interest is the beginning of knowledge, and where it is discouraged knowledge is discouraged. Any inquiry can be met on the child's plane of intelligence and comprehension, and the parent must arrange for the gratification of this fundamental desire. How? By a question hour each day, perhaps a children's hour, a home university period where the vital interest of the child will be satisfied.

To return to the morbid interests: do they arise from secret morbid desires? The Freudian answer to that would be yes. And so would many another answer. It is the answer in many cases, especially where the desire is not so much morbid as forbidden. The virgin, the continent who are intensely interested in sex are not morbid, even though they have been forbidden to think of a natural craving and appetite. But when the interest is for the horrible it is often the case that the excitement aroused by the subject is pleasurable, because it is a mild excitement and does not quite reach disgust. Confronted with the real perversity, the disgust aroused would quite effectually conquer interest.

And here is a fundamental law of interest: it must lead to a profitable, pleasurable result or else it tends to disappear. If this is too bold a statement, let me qualify it by stating that a profitable, pleasurable result must be foreseen or foreseeable. Either in some affective state, or in some tangible good, interest seeks fulfillment. Disappointment is the foe of interest, and too prolonged a "vestibule of satisfaction" (to use Hocking's phrase) destroys or impairs interest.

CHAPTER VIII

THE SENTIMENTS OF LOVE, FRIENDSHIP, HATE, PITY AND DUTY. COMPENSATION AND ESCAPE

I shall ignore the complexities that arise when we seek to organize our reactions into various groups by making a simple classification of feeling, for the purposes of this book. There is a primary result of any stimulation, whether from within ourselves or without, which we have called excitement. This excitement may have a pleasurable or an unpleasurable quality, and we cannot understand just what is back of pleasure and pain in this sense. Such an explanation, that pleasure is a sign of good for the organism and pain a sign of bad, is an error in that often an experience that produces pleasure is a detriment and an injury. If pleasure were an infallible sign of good, no books on character, morals or hygiene would need to be written.

This primary excitement, when associated with outer events or things, becomes differentiated into many forms. Curiosity (or interest) is the focusing of that excitement on particular objects or ends, in order that the essential value or meaning of that object or individual become known. Curiosity and interest develop into the seeking of experience and the general intellectual pursuits. We have already discussed this phase of excitement.

An object of interest may then evoke further feeling. It may be one's baby, or one's father or a kinsman or a female of the same species. A type of feeling FAVORABLE to the object is aroused, called "tender feeling," which is associated with deep-lying instincts and has endless modifications and variations. Perhaps its great example is the tender feeling of the mother for the baby, a feeling so strong that it leads to conduct of self-sacrifice; conduct that makes nothing of privation, suffering, even death, if these will help the object of the tender feeling, the child. Tender feeling of this type, which we call love, is a theme one cannot discuss dryly, for it sweeps one into reveries; it suggests softly glowing eyes, not far from tears, tenderly curved lips, just barely smiling, and the soft humming of the mother to the babe in her arms. It is the soft feeling which is the unifying feeling, and when it reaches a group they become gentle in tone and manners and feel as one. The dream of the reformer has always been the extension of this tender feeling from the baby, from the child and the helpless, to all men, thus abolishing strife, conquering hate, unifying man. This type of love is also paternal, though it is doubtful whether as such it ever reaches the intensity it does in the mother. By a sort of association it spreads to all children, to all little things, to all helpless things, except where there exists a counter feeling already well established.

Though typical in the mother, child relationship, tender feeling or love, exists in many other relationships. The human family, with its close association, its inculcated unity of interests, in its highest form is based on the tender feeling. The noble ideal of the brotherhood of man comes from an extension of the feeling found in brothers. The brotherly feeling is emphasized, though the sisterly feeling is fully as strong, merely because the male member of genus homo has been the articulate member, he has written and talked as if he, and not his sister, were the important human personage. So fraternal feeling is tender feeling, existing between members of the same family, or the love that we conceive ought to be present. Is such love instinctive, as is the maternal love? If it is, that instinct is very much weaker, and hostile feeling, indifference, rivalry, may easily replace it. We rarely conceive of a mortal world where so intense a love as that of the mother will be the common feeling; all we dare hope for is a world in which there will be a fine fraternal feeling.

Fraternal feeling is born of association together, any task undertaken en masse, any living together under one roof. Even when men sit down to eat at the same table, it tends to appear. So college life, the barracks, secret orders, awaken it, but here, as always, while it links together the associated, it shuts out as non-fraternal those not associated.

What we call friendly feeling is a less vehement, more intellectualized form of tender feeling. It demands a certain equality and a certain similarity in tastes, though some friendships are noted for the dissimilarity of the friends. Friendship lives on reciprocal benefits, tangible or intangible, though sentimentalists may take exception to this. Primary in it is the good opinion of the friends and interest in one another; we cannot be friends with those who think we are foolish or mean or bad. We ALLOW a friend to say that we have acted wrongly because we think he has our interest at heart, because he has shown that he has this interest at heart, though his saying so sometimes strains the friendship for a while. Friendship ideally expects no material benefits, but it lives on the spiritual benefit of sympathy and expressed interest and the flattery of a taste in common. It is a unification of individuals that has been glorified as the perfect relationship, since it has no classifiable instinct behind it and is in a sense democracy at its noblest. Friendship is easiest formed in youth, because men are least selfish, least specialized at that time. As time goes on, alas, our own interests and purposes narrow down in order that we may succeed; there is less time and energy for friendship.

Sex love is only in part made up of tender feeling. Passion, admiration of beauty, desire of possession, the love of conquest, take away from the "other" feeling that is the basis of tenderness or true love. We desire so much for ourselves in sex love that we have not so much capacity for tender feeling as we usually think we have. The protests of eternal devotion and unending self-sacrifice are sincere enough but they have this proviso in the background: "You must give yourself to me." If the lovers can also be friends, if they have a real harmony of tastes, desires and ambitions, if they can recede their ego feeling, know how to compromise, then this added to sex feeling makes the most genuinely satisfying of all human relations, or at least the most reciprocal. But the two human beings who fall in love are rarely enough alike, and their relationship is rarely one of equality; traditional duties and rights are not equal; they will seek different things, and their relationship is too close and intimate to be an easy one to maintain. Sex love and marriage are different matters, for though they may be the same, too often they are not. Rarely does sex love maintain itself without marriage and marriage colors over sex love with parental feelings, financial interests, home and its emotions, etc. In sex gratification [44] there is the danger of all sensuous pleasure: that a periodic appetite gratified often leaves behind it an ennui, a distaste,—sometimes reaching dislike—of the entire act and associations.

Is all tender feeling, all love, sexual in its essential nature? The Freudians say yes to this, or what amounts to yes. All mother love arises from the sex sphere, and it cannot be denied that in the passionate desire to fondle, to kiss and even to bite there is something very like the excitement of sex. But there is something very different in the wish for self-sacrifice, the pity for the helpless state, the love of the littleness. Women, when they love men, often add maternal feeling to it, but mainly they love their strength, size and vigor; and there tenderness and passion differ. Certainly there seems little of the sexual in the love of a father for his baby, [45] though the Freudians do not hesitate in their use of the term homosexual. Apparently all children have incestuous desire for their parents, if we are to trust Freud. Without entering into detailed reasoning, I disavow any truly sexual element in tender feeling. It is part of the reception we give to objects having a favorable relation to ourselves. Indeed, we give it to our houses, our dogs, our cattle; our pipes are hallowed by friendly association, and so with our books, our clothes and our homes. We extend it in deep, full measure to the very rocks and rills of our native land or to some place where we spent happy or tender days. Tender feeling, love, is inclusive of much of the sex emotion, and the characteristic mistake of the Freudians of identifying somewhat similar things has here been made.

Love, then, is this tender feeling made purposive and intelligent. It is a sentiment, in Shand's phrase, and seeks the good of its object. It may be narrow, it may be broad, it may be intense or feeble, but in its organized

---

[44] Stanley Hall says that after sex gratification there is "taedium vitae," weariness of life. In unsanctioned sex gratification this is extreme and takes on either bitter self-reproach or else a hate of the partner. But this is due to the inner conflict rather than the sex act.

[45] It's a very difficult world to live in, if we are to trust the Freudians. If your boy child loves his mother, that's heterosexual; if he loves his father, that's homosexual; and the love of a girl child for her parents simply reverses the above formula. If your wife says of the baby boy, "How I love him! He looks just like my father," be careful; that's a daughter-father complex of a dangerous kind and means the most unhallowed things, and may cause her to have a nervous breakdown some day!

sense it plans, fights and cherishes. It has organized with it the primary emotions,—fear if the object is in danger, or anger is evoked according to the circumstances; joy if the object of love is enhanced or prospers; sorrow if it is lost or injured under circumstances that make the lover helpless. Love is not only the tenderest feeling, but it is also the most heroic and desperate fighter in behalf of the loved one. Here we are face to face with the contradictions that we always meet when we personify a quality or make an abstraction. Love may do the most hateful things; love may stunt, the character of the lover and the beloved. In other words, love, tender feeling, must be conjoined with intelligence, good judgment, determination and fairness before it is useful. It would be a nice question to determine just how much harm misguided love has done.

What is pity? Though objects of love always elicit pity, when helpless or injured, objects of pity are not necessarily objects of love. In fact, we may pity through contempt. Objective pity is a type of tender feeling in which there is little or no self-feeling. We do not extend the ego to the piteous object. We desire to help, even though the object of pity is an enemy or disgusting. One of the commonest struggles of life is that between self-interest and pity,—and the selfish resent any situation that arouses their pity, because they dislike to give. Pity tends to disappear from the life of the soldier and is, indeed, a trait he does not need; in the lives of the strong and successful, pity is apt to be a hindering quality. In a world in which competition is keen, the cooperative gentle qualities hinder success. The weak seek the pity of others; they need it; and the pity-seeker is a very distinct type. The strong and proud hate to be pitied, and when wounded they hide, shun their friends and keep the semblance of strength with a brave face. Pity directed toward oneself as the object is self-pity,—a quality found in children and in a certain amiable, weak, egoistic type, whose eyes are always full of tears as they talk of themselves. Of course, at times, we are all prone to this vice of character, but there are some chronically afflicted.

Certain so-called sentimentalists are those who die, tribute their pity in an erratic fashion. These are the vegetarians who are sad because it is wrong to kill for food; yet they wear without compunction the leather of cattle who have neither committed suicide nor died of old age. And the anti-vivisectionists view without any stir of pity the children of the slums and the sick of all kinds. Pity raises man to the divine but, like all the gentle qualities, it needs guidance by reason and common sense before it is of any value.

Just as there are objects and individuals recognized or believed to be as somehow favorable and who evoke tender feeling, so there are objects and individuals regarded as unfavorable, perhaps dangerous, who arouse aversion and hatred. The feeling thus produced is the other great sentiment of life, which on the whole organizes character and conduct on a great plane. Hatred, a decidedly primitive reaction, still is powerful in the world and is back of dissension of all kinds, from lawsuits to war. When one hates he is attached to the hated object in a fashion just the reverse of the attachment of love; joy, anger, fear and sorrow arise under exactly the opposite circumstances, and the aim and end of hate is to block, thwart and destroy the hated one. The earlier history of man lays emphasis on the activities of hate,—war, feats of arms, individual feuds. Hate, unlike love, needs no moral code or teaching to bring it into activity; it springs into being and constantly needs repression. Unlikeness alone often brings it to life; to be too different from others is recognized as a legitimate reason for hatred. The most important cause is conflict of interest and wounding of self-feeling and pride. Revengeful feeling, fostered by tradition and "patriotism," caused many wars and in its lesser spheres of operation is back of murders, assaults, insults and the lesser categories of injuries of all kinds.

The prime emotion of hatred is anger; in its less intense aspect of aversion it is disgust. The aim and end of anger is destruction of the offending object; the aim and end of aversion is removal, ejection. Hate may be and often is a noble sentiment, though the trend of modern thought, as it minimizes personal responsibility, is to eliminate hate against persons and intellectualize hate so that it is reserved for the battle against ideas. Whether you can really summon all your effort against any one, against his plans, opinions and actions, unless you have built up the steady sentiment of hatred for him, is a nice psychological question. Hate is most intense in little people, in persons absolutely convinced that their interests, opinions and plans are sacred, sure of their superiority and righteousness. Once let insight into yourself, your weakness and your real motives creep into your mind and your hate against opponents and obstructors must lessen. Those who realize most the fallibility of men and women, to whom Pilate's question "What is truth?" has added to it a more sceptical question, "What is right," find it hard to hate. Therefore, such persons, the broad-minded and the most deeply wise, are not the best fighters for a cause, since their efforts are lessened by sympathy for the opponent. Here is the marvel of Abraham Lincoln; rich with insight, he could hate slavery and secession and yet not hate the southern people. In that division of himself lies his greatness and his suffering.

The disappearance of personal hate from the world can only come when men realize the essential unity of mankind. For part of the psychological origin of hate lies in unlikeness. Great unlikeness in color and facial line seems to act as a challenge to the feeling of superiority. Wherever a "different" group challenges another's superiority, or enters into active competition for the goods of life, there hate enters in its most virulent form. The disappearance of the "unlike" feeling is very slow and is hindered by the existence of small "particular" groups. Little nationalities, [46] small sects, even exclusive clubs and circles are means of generating difference and thus hate.

We shall not enter into the origin of hate through the danger to

---

[46] The more nationalities, each with its claim to a great destiny, the more wars! There is the essential danger and folly of tribal patriotism.

purpose, through rivalry among those not separated by unlikeness. Hate seems to be a chronic anger, or at least that emotion kept at a more or less constant level by perception of danger and the threat at personal dignity and worth. Obstructed love or passion and the feeling of "wrong," i. e., injury done that was not merited, that the personal conscience does not justify, furnish the most virulent types of hatred. "Love thine enemies" is still an impossible injunction for most men.

We cannot hope to trace the feeling of revenge in its effects on human conduct. Though at present religion and law both prohibit revengeful acts, the desire "to get even" flames high in almost every human breast under all kinds of injury or insult. This form of hate may express itself crudely in the vendetta of the Sicilian, the feud of the Tennessee mountaineer, or the assault and battery of an aggrieved husband; it is behind the present-day conflict in Ireland, and it threatened Europe for forty years after the Franco-Prussian War, —and no man knows how profoundly it will influence future world affairs because of the Great War. Often it disguises itself as justice, the principle of the thing, in those who will not admit revenge as a motive; and the eclipsed and beaten take revenge in slander, innuendo and double-edged praise. To some revenge is a devil to be fought out of their hearts; to others it is a god that guides every act. We may define nobility of character as the withdrawal from revenge as a motive and the substitution for it of justice.

Some hatred expresses itself openly and fearlessly and as such gains some respect, even from its own object. Other hatred plots and schemes, the intelligence lends itself to the plans completely and the whole personality suffers in consequence. Some hatred, weak and without self-confidence, or seeking the effect of surprise, is hypocritical, dissimulates, affects friendly feeling, rubs its hands over insults and awaits the opportune moment. This type is associated in all minds with a feeling of disgust, for at bottom we rather admire the "good" hater.

We have spoken of these three specialized and directed outgrowths of excitement, interest, love and hatred as if they were primarily directed to the outside world, though in a previous chapter we discussed the introspective interest. What shall we call the love and hatred a man has for himself? Is the self-regarding sentiment any different than the sentiment of love for others? Is that hate and disgust we feel for ourselves, or for some action or thought, different from the hate and disgust we have for others?

Judged by Shand's dicta that anger and fear are aroused if the object of love is threatened, joy is aroused as it prospers, and sorrow if it is deeply injured or lost, self-love remarkably resembles other-love. The pride we take in our own achievements is unalloyed by jealousy, and there is always a trace of jealousy in the pride we take in the achievements of others, but there is no difference in the pride itself. There is no essential difference in the "good" we seek for ourselves and in the good we seek for others, for what we seek will depend on our idea of "good." Thus the ambitious mother seeks for her daughter a rich husband and the idealist seeks for his son a career of devotion to the ideal. And the sensualist devoted to the good of his belly and his pocket loves his child and shows it by feeding and enriching him.

There seems to be lacking, however, the glow of tender feeling in self-love. The projection of the self-interest to others has a passion, a melting in it that self-love never seems to possess, though it may be constant and ever-operating. Self-regard, self-admiration or conceit may be very high and deeply felt, but though more common than real admiration for others, it seldom reaches the awe and reverence that the projected emotion reaches.

In mental disease, of the type known as Maniac Depressive insanity, there is a curious oscillation of self-love and self-admiration. This disease is cyclic, in that two opposing groups of symptoms tend to appear and displace each other. In the manic, or excited state, there is greatly heightened activity with correspondingly heightened feeling of power. Self-love and admiration reach absurd levels: one is the most beautiful, the richest and wisest of persons, infallible, irresistible, aye, perhaps God or Christ. Sometimes the feeling of grandeur, the euphoria, is less fantastic and the patient imagines himself a great inventor, a statesman of power and wisdom, a writer of renown, etc. Suddenly, or perhaps gradually, the change comes; self-feeling drops into an abyss. "I am the most miserable of persons, the vilest sinner, hated and rightly by God and man, cause of suffering and misery. I am no good, no use, a horrible odor issues from me, I am loathsome to look at, etc., etc." Desperate suicidal attempts are made, and all the desires that tend to preserve the individual disappear, including appetite for food and drink, the power to sleep. It is the most startling of transitions; one can hardly realize that the dejected, silent person, sitting in a corner, hiding his face and hardly breathing, is the same individual who lately tore around the wards, happy, dancing, singing and boasting of his greatness of power. Indeed, is he the same individual? No wonder the ancients regarded such insanity as a possession by an evil spirit. We of a later day who deal with this disease on the whole are inclined to the belief that some internal factor of a physical kind is responsible, some neuronic shift, or some strange, visceral endocrinal disorder.

While self-hate in this pathological aspect is relatively uncommon, in every person there are self-critical, self-condemning activities which sometimes for short periods of time reach self-hatred and disgust. McDougall makes a good deal of the self-abasing instinct which makes us lower ourselves gladly and willingly. This seems to me to be an aspect of the emotion of admiration and wonder, for we do not wish ordinarily to kneel at the feet of the insignificant, debased; or it is an aspect of fear and the effort to obtain conciliation and pity. But the establishment of ideals for ourselves to which we are not faithful brings with it a disgust and loathing for self that is extremely painful and leads to a desire for penance of any kind In order that we may punish ourselves and feel that we have made amends. The capacity for self-hate and self-disgust depends largely upon the development of these ideals and principles of conscience, of expectation of the self. Frequently there is an overrigidity, a ceaseless self-examination that now and then produces miracles of character and achievement but more often brings the breakdown of health. This is the seeker of perfection in himself, who will not compromise with his instincts and his human flesh. There seekers of perfection are among the noblest of the race, admired in the abstract but condemned by their friends as "too good," "impractical," as possessors of the "New England conscience." One of the effects of a Puritanical bringing-up is a belief that pleasure is unworthy, especially in the sex field and even in marriage. Now and then one meets a patient caught between perfectly proper desire and an obsession that such pleasure is debasing; and a feeling of self-disgust and self-hatred results that is the more tragic since it is useless.

There are those in whom self-love and self-esteem is at a lower pressure than with the average man, just as there are those in whom it is at a much higher pressure. Such people, when fatigued or when subject to the hostile or even non-friendly opinion of others, become so-called self-conscious, i. e., are afflicted with fear and a feeling of inferiority. This may deepen into self-contempt and self-hatred. Part of what is called confidence in oneself is self-esteem, and under fatigue, illness, after punishment of a physical or mental nature, it is apt to disappear. Very distressing is this in those who have been accustomed to courage and self-confidence, perhaps whose occupation makes these qualities necessary. Soldiers, after gassing or cerebral concussion, men completely without introspection, fearless and gay with assurance, become apprehensive, self-analytical and without the least faith in themselves, so that they approach their work in fear. So with men who work in high places or where there is risk, such as steeplejacks, bridge builders, iron workers, engineers; let an accident happen to them, or let there occur an exhausting disease with its aftermath of neurasthenia, and the self-esteem and self-confidence disappear so that in many cases they have to give up their job.

Because self-disgust and hatred are so painful, compensatory "mechanisms" have been set up. There is in many people a tendency to project outward the blame for those acts or thoughts which they dislike. In the pathological field we get those delusions of influence that are so common. Thus a patient will attribute his obscene thoughts and words to a hypnotic effect of some person or group of persons and saves his own face by the delusion. In lesser pathological measure, men have fiercely preached against the snares and wiles of women, refusing to recognize that the turmoil of unwelcome desire into which they were thrown was internal in the greater part of its origin and that the woman often knew little or not at all of the effect she helped produce. One of the outstanding features in the history of the race has been this transfer of blame from the desire of men to the agent which aroused them. Of course, women have played on the desires of men, but even where this was true the blame for VULNERABILITY has seldom been fully accepted. Whenever any one has been "weak" or "foolish" or "sinful," his mind at once seeks avenues of escape from the blame, from the painful feeling of inferiority and self-reproach. The avenue of escape selected may be to blame others as tempting or not warning and not teaching, may become entirely delusional, or it may take the religious form of confession, expiation and repentance. There are some so hardy in their self-esteem that they never suffer, never seek any escape from self-reproach, largely because they never feel it; and others, though they seek escape, are continually dragged by conscience to self-imposed torture. Most of us seek explanations for our unwelcome conduct on a plane most favorable to our self-esteem, and there arises an elaborate system of self-disguise, expiation, repentance and confession that is in a large part the real inner life of most of us. To explain failure especially are the avenues of escape utilized. Wounded in his self-esteem, rare is the one who frankly acknowledges inferiority. "Pull," "favoritism," "luck," explain the success of others as do the reverse circumstances explain our failures to ourselves. Sickness explains it, and so the defeated search in themselves for the explanation which will in part compensate them. Escape from inferiority follows many avenues, —by actual development of superiority, by denying real superiority to others, or by explaining the inferiority on some acceptable basis.

Here (as elsewhere in character) there is evident an organic and a social basis for feeling. We have not emphasized sufficiently a peculiarity of all human feeling, all emotions, all sentiments. They have their value to the individual in organizing his conduct, his standard of value. They are of enormous importance socially. A great law of feeling of whatever kind, of whatever elaboration, is this; it tends to spread from individual to individual and excites whole groups to the same feeling; tender feeling is contagious, and so is hate. We are somehow so made that we reverberate at a friendly smile in one way and to the snarl and stern look of hate in another way. Ordinarily love awakens love and hate awakens hate, though it may bring fear or contempt. It is true that we may feel so superior or cherish some secret hate that will make another's love odious to us, and also we may admire and worship one who hates us. These are exceptional cases and are examples of exceptional sentimental stability. It is of course understood that by love is not meant sex passion. Here the curious effect of coldness is sometimes to fan the flame of passion. Desire obstructed often gains in violence, and the desire to conquer and to possess the proud, that we all feel, adds to the fire of lust.

Self-esteem, self-confidence, hateful to others if in excess or if obtrusive, is an essential of the leader. His feeling is extraordinarily contagious, and the morale of the group is in his keeping. He must not show fear, or self-distrust or self-lowering in any way. He must be deliberate, but forceful, vigorous, masterful. If he has doubts, he must keep them to himself or exhibit them only to one who loves him, who is not a mere follower. It is a law of life that the herd follows the unwounded, confident, egoistic leader and tears to pieces or deserts the one who is wearying.

The basic sentiments of interest, love and hate, projected outward or inward, organize personality. Men's characters and their destinies rest in the things they find interesting, the persons they love and hate, their self-confidence and self-esteem, their self-contempt and hatred. And it is true that often we hate and love the same person or circumstance; we are divided, secretly, in our tenderest feelings, in our fiercest hate, more often, alas, in the former. For occasionally admiration and respect will mitigate hate and render impotent our aim, but more commonly we are jealous of or envy son, brother, sister, husband, wife, father, mother and friend. We love our work but hate its tyranny, and even the ideal that we cherish, when we examine it too closely, seems overconventionalized, not enough our own, and it stifles and martyrs too many unpleasant desires. We rebel against our own affections, against the love that chains us perhaps to weakness and forces us, weary, to the wheel.

How deeply the feeling of "right" enters into the sentiments and their labors needs only a little reflection to understand. Here we come to the effect of the sentiment of duty, for as such it may be discussed. The establishment of conscience as our inner guide to conduct, and even to thought and emotions, has been studied briefly. On a basis of innate capacity, conscience arises from the teaching and traditions of the group (or groups). The individual who has a susceptibility or a readiness to believe and a desire to be in conformity accepts or evolves for himself principles of conduct, based on obligation, expectation of reward and fear of punishment, these entering in various proportions, according to the type of person. In children, or the very young child, expectation of reward and fear of punishment are more important than obligation, and this remains true of many people throughout life. Gradually right, what we call duty, becomes established as a guiding principle; but it must struggle with impulse and the desire for immediate pleasure throughout life. In fact, one of the dangers of the development of the feeling of duty lies in the view often held by those guided by principle and duty that pleasure is in itself somehow wrong and needs justification. Whereas, in my opinion, pleasure is right and needs no justification and is wrong only when it offends the fundamental moralities and purposes of Society.

The feeling of "right" depends to a certain extent on the kind of teaching in early childhood, but more on the nature of the individual. It is based on his social feeling, his desire to be in harmony with a group or a God that essentially stands above any group. For the idea of God introduces an element having more authority than the group whom He leads. Here also is a factor of importance: choice is difficult for the great majority. Placed in a situation where more than one response is possible, an unhappy state of bewilderment results unless there are formulae for action. The leader is the chooser for the group; religion is an established system of choices even in its "Thou shalt not" injunctions, and to be at one with God implies that one is following an infallible leader, and doubt and uncertainty disappear. Trotter [47] points out clearly the role the feeling of certitude plays in developing codes. As life becomes more complex, as

---

[47] "The Herd and its Instincts in Peace and War."

more choices appear, the need of an established method of choosing becomes greater. The careful, cautious, conscientious types develop a system of principles for choice of action; they discard the uncertainty of pleasure as a guide for the certainty of a code laid down and fixed. Duty is the north star of conduct!

In passing, an interesting development of our times is worth noticing. The tendency is to discard established codes, to weaken dogma and to throw more responsibility on the individual conscience. That is the meaning of the Protestant reformation, and it is the meaning of the growth of Unitarianism within the Protestant church; it is also the meaning of the reform movement in Judaism. The Catholic church has felt it in the breaking away of state after state from its authority, which virtually means that the states have thrown their citizens back on their own consciences and the state laws. In fact, reliance on law is in part an effort to escape the necessity of choosing. The pressure of external authority has its burden, but in giving up its certainty man also gives up tranquillity. Much of modern neurasthenia is characterized by a feeling of uncertainty, unreality, doubt: what is right, what is real? True, as religion in the dogmatic sense relinquishes its power, ethics grow in value and men seek some other formula which will compensate for the dogma. It is no accident that as the old religions lose their complete control new ones appear, with all-embracing formula, like Christian Science, New Thought, etc. Though these start with elastic general principles, sooner or later the directions for conduct become minute and then fixed. The tragedy of a great founder of religion like Buddha or Christ is that though he gives out a great pure principle, his followers must have, demand and evolve a dogmatic religion with fixed ceremonials. Man, on the whole, does not want to choose; he wants to have the feeling that he ought to do this or that according to a code laid down by authority. This will make a real democracy always impossible.

However the sentiment of duty arises, it becomes the central feeling in all inner conflicts, and it wrestles with inclination and the pleasant choice. Duty is the great inhibitor, but also it says "Thou shalt!" Ideally, duty involves self-sacrifice, and practically man dislikes self-sacrifice save where love is very strong. Duty chains a man to his task where he is inclined for a holiday. Duty may demand a man's life, and that sacrifice seems easier for men to make than the giving up of power and pelf. (In the late war it was no great trouble to pass laws conscripting life; it was impossible to pass laws conscripting wealth. It was easier for a man to allow his son to go to war than to give up his wealth en masse.)

The power of the feeling of duty and right over men is very variable. There are a few to whom the feeling of "ought" is all powerful; they cannot struggle against it, even though they wish to. All of their goings, comings and doings are governed thereby, and even though they find the rest of the world dropping from them, they resist the herd. For the mass of men duty governs a few relationships—to family and country—and even here self-interest is camouflaged by the term "duty" in the phrase "a man owes a duty to himself." This is the end of real duty. The average man or woman makes a duty of nonessentials, of ceremonials, but is greatly moved by the cry of duty if it comes from authority or from those he respects. He fiercely resents it if told he is not doing his duty, but is quick to tell others they are not doing theirs.

There is also a group in whom the sense of duty is almost completely lacking, or rather fails to govern action. Ordinarily these are spoken of as lacking moral fiber, but in reality the organizing energy of character and the inhibition of the impulse to seek pleasure and present desire is feeble. Sometimes there is lack of affection toward others, little of the real glow of tender feeling, either towards children [48] or parents or any one. Though these are often emotional, they are not, in the good meaning of the term, sentimental.

Is the sentiment of duty waning? The alarmists say it is and point to the increase of divorce, falling off in church attendance, and the unrest among the laboring classes as evidence that there is a decadence. Pleasure is sought, excitement is the goal, and sober, solid duty is "forgotten." They point out a resemblance to the decadent days of Rome, in the rise of luxury and luxurious tastes, and indicate that duty and the love of luxury cannot coexist. Woman has forgotten her duty to bear children and to maintain the home and man has forgotten his duty to God.

Superficially these critics are right. There is a demand for a more satisfying life, involving less self sacrifice on the part of those who have in the past made the bulk of the sacrifices. Woman, demanding equality, refuses to be regarded as merely a child bearer and is become a seeker of luxury. The working man, looking at the world he has built, now able to read, write and vote, asks why the duty is all on his side. In other words, a demand for justice, which is merely reciprocal, universal duty, has weakened something of the sense of duty. In fact, that is the first effect of the feeling of injustice, of unjust inequality. Dealing with the emancipated, the old conception of duty as loyalty under all conditions has not worked, and we need new ideals of duty on the part of governments and governing groups before we can get the proper ideals of duty in the governed.

Some of those ideals are commencing to be heard. International duty for governments is talked of and some are bold to say that national feeling prevents a real feeling of duty to the world, to man. These claim that duty must have its origin in the extension of tender feeling, in fraternity, to all men. In a lesser way business is commencing to substitute for its former motto, "Handelschaft ist keine Bruderschaft" (business is no brotherhood), the ideal of service, as the duty of business. Everywhere we are commencing to hear of "social duty," of obligation to the lesser and unfortunate, of the responsibility of the leaders to the led, of the well to the

---

[48] It is again to be emphasized that the most vital instincts may be lacking. Even the maternal feeling may be absent, not only in the human mother but in the animal mother. So we need not be surprised if there are those with no sense of right or duty.

sick, of the law-abiding to the criminal. Strange notion, this last, but one at bottom sound and practical.

In the end, the true sense of duty is in a sense of individual responsibility. Our age feels this as no other age has felt it. Other ages have placed responsibility on the Church, on God and on the State. Difficult and onerous as is the burden, we are commencing to place duty on the individual, and in that respect we are not in the least a decadent generation.

CHAPTER IX
ENERGY RELEASE AND THE EMOTIONS

One of the problems in all work is to place things in their right order, in the order of origin and importance. This difficulty is almost insoluble when one studies the character of man. As we see him in operation, the synthesis is so complete that we can hardly discern the component parts. Inheritance, social pressure, excitement, interest, love, hate, self-interest, duty and obligation, —these are not unitary in the least and there is constantly a false dissection to be made, an artefact, in order that clearness in presentation may be obtained.

We see men as discharging energy in work and play, in the activities that help or hurt themselves and the race. They obtain that energy from the world without, from the sunshine, the air, the plants and the animals; it is built up in their bodies, it is discharged either because some inner tension builds up a desire or because some outer stimulus, environmental or social, directs it. Though we have no way of measuring one man's energy against another, we say, perhaps erroneously, "He is very energetic," or "He is not"; "He is tireless," or "He breaks down easily." As students of character, we must take this question of the energies of men into account as integral in our study.

Granting that the human being takes in energy as food and drink and builds it up into dischargeable tissues, we are not further concerned with the details of its physiology. How does the feeling of energy arise, what increases the energy discharge and what blocks, inhibits or lowers it? For from day to day, from hour to hour, we are conscious either of a desire to be active, a feeling of capacity or the reverse. We depend on that feeling of capacity to guide us, and though it is organic, it has its mysterious disappearances and marvelous reenforcements.

It arises, so we assume, from the visceral-neuronic activities, subconsciously, in the sense we have used that word. It therefore fluctuates with health, with fatigue, with the years. We marvel at the energy of childhood and youth, and the deepest sadness we have is the depletion of energy-feeling in old age. We love energy in ourselves and we yield admiration, willing or unwilling, to its display in others. The Hero, the leader, is always energetic. In our times, in America, we demand "pep," action and energy-display as an essential in our play and in our work, and we worship quite too frankly where all men have always worshiped.

What besides the organic activity, besides health and well-being, excites the feeling of energy and what depresses it?

1. This feeling is excited by the society of others, by the herd-feeling, and depressed by long-continued solitude or loneliness. The stimuli that come from other people's faces, voices, contacts—their emotions, feelings and manifestations of energy—are those we are best adapted to react to,

95

those most valuable in stirring us up. Scenery, the grandeur of the outer world, finally depress the most of us, and we can bear these things best in company. Who has not, on a long railroad journey, watched with weariness and flickering interest valley and hill and meadow swing by and then sat up with energy and definite attention as a human being passed along on some rural road? Lacking these stimuli there is monotony and monotony always has with it as one of its painful features a subjective sense of lowered energy, of fatigue. This is the problem of the housewife and the solitary worker everywhere,—there is failure of the sense of energy due to a failure to receive new stimuli in their most potent form, our fellows.

2. The disappearance or injury of desire and purpose. Let there be a sudden blocking of a purpose or an aim, so that it seems impossible of fulfillment, and energy-feeling drops; movement, thought, even feeling seem painful. The will flags, and the whole world becomes unreal. This is part of the anhedonia we spoke of.

In reality, we have the disappearance of hope as basic in this adynamia. Hope and courage are in part organic, in part are due to the belief that a desired goal can be reached. Whether that goal is health, when one is sick, or riches, or fame, or love and possession, if it is a well-centralized goal toward which our main energies are bent, and then seems suddenly impossible to reach, there is a corresponding paralysis of energy.

Here is where a great difference is seen between individuals and between one time of life and another. There are some to whom hope is a shining beacon light never absent; whatever happens, hope remains, like the beautiful fable of Pandora's box. There are others to whom any obstruction, any discouraging feature, blots out hope, and who constantly need the energy of others; their persuasions and exhortations, for a renewal of energy. Here, as elsewhere in life, some are givers and others takers of energy. In the presence of the hopeless it is hard to maintain one's own feeling of energy and that is why the average man shuns them. He guards as priceless his own enthusiasm.

Curiously enough, when energy tends to disappear in the face of disaster to one's plans, a tonic is often enough the reflection, "it might have been worse" or "there are others worse off." [49] Though one rebels against the encouraging effect of the last statement, it does console, it does renew hope. For hope and energy and desire are competitive, as is every other measure of value. So long as one is not the worst off, then there is something left, there is a hopeful element in the situation. Similarly a certain rough treatment helps, as when Job is told practically, "After all, who is Man that he should ask for the fulfillment of his hopes?" A sense of littleness with the rest of the race acts to bring resignation, and after that has been established, hope can reappear. For resignation is rarely a prolonged state of mind; it is a doorway through which we reenter into the vista-chambers of Hope.

---

[49] A humorous use of this fact is in the popular "Cheer up, the worst is yet to come!" This acts as a rough tonic.

And one clearly sees the benefit of a belief, a faith in God. "Gott in sein Mizpah ist gerecht," cries the orthodox Jew when his hope is shattered,—"God's decree is just." This is Hope Eternal; "my purposes are blocked, but were they God's purposes? No. He would not then block them. I must seek God's purposes." Faith is really a transcendent Hope, renewing the feeling of energy.

3. The belief that one has the good opinion of others is a powerful stimulus to energy and feeling. We have already considered the effect of praise and blame. Some are so constituted that they need the approval of others at all times; they are at the mercy of any one who gives them a cold look or a harsh word. Others cling to the need of their own self-approval; they are aristocrats, firm and secure in their self-estimate. Let their self-esteem crumble, and these proud and haughty ones are humble, weak, inefficient. We fiercely resent criticism because in it is a threat to our source of energy, our very feeling of being alive.

One has shrewdly to examine his fellow men from this angle: "Does he work up his own steam; are his boilers of energy heated by his own enthusiasm and his own self-approval? Or does he borrow; can he work only if others add their fire to his; does his light go out if his neighbors turn away or are too busy to help him?" One type of man may be as admirable as another in his gifts, but the types need different treatment.

Self-valuation is to a large extent our opinion of the valuation of others of ourselves. [50] We believe people like us, think we are fine and able, or beautiful, and we react with energy to difficulties. We may be wrong; they may call us a conceited ass and laugh at us behind our backs, but so long as we do not find it out, it doesn't matter. There is, however, no blow quite so severe as the sudden realization that we have mistaken the opinion of others, we have been "fooled." To be fooled is to be lowered in one's own self-esteem, and we like sincerity and hate insincerity largely because our self-esteem stands on some solid basis in the one case and on none whatever in the other. Most of us would rather have people say bad things of us to our face than run the risk of the ridicule and the foolish feeling that comes with insincerity. There are some who are always suspicions that people are insincere in praise or friendly words; they hate being fooled, they know of no criterion of sincerity and such people are in an adynamic state most of the time. The difference between the trusting and the suspicious is that one responds with energy and belief to the manifestations of friendliness in everybody, and the other has no such inner response to guide his energy and his actions. Trust in others is a releaser of energy; distrust paralyzes it.

4. Doubt and inability to choose may be contrasted with certitude and clear choice in their effect on energy release. Of course, one of the signs of lowered energy is doubt, as a sign of high energy is certainty. Nevertheless, a situation of critical importance, in which choice is difficult

---

[50] To paraphrase Doctor Holmes the biggest factor in John's self-valuation is HIS idea of Jane's idea of John.

or digagreeable, inhibits energy feeling [51] and discharge perhaps as much as any other mental factor. Especially is this true when the inhibition concerns a moral situation—"Ought I to do this or that"—and where the fear of being wrong or doing wrong operates so that the individual does nothing and develops an obsession of doubt. This "to be or not to be" attitude is typical of many intelligent people, yes, even intellectual people. They we so many angles to a situation, they project so far into the future in their thoughts, that a weary discouragement comes. To such as these, the counsel of "action right or wrong but action anyway!" is good, but the difficulty is to make them overcome their doubts. Their cerebral oscillation makes them weary but they cannot seem to stop it; their pendulum of choice never stops at action.

If one wishes to destroy the energy of any one, the best way to do it is to sow the seeds of doubt. "Your ideal is a fine one, my friend, but—isn't it a little sophomoric?" "A nice piece of work, but—who wants it?" On the other hand, to one obsessed by doubt it may happen that a whole-hearted endorsement, a resolution of the doubt, brings with it first relief and then a swing of energy into the channels of action.

5. Competition is a great factor in energy release. Every one has seen a horse ambling along, apparently without sufficient energy to go more than four miles an hour. Suddenly he cocks up his ears as the sounds of the hoof beats of a rapidly traveling horse are heard. He shakes his head and to the amazement or amusement of his driver sets off in rivalry at a two-minute clip. Intensely cooperative and gregarious as man is, he is as intensely competitive, spurred on by his observations of the other fellow. Introduce a definite system of rivalry into a school or an office, and you release energies never manifested before. There are some to whom this is the main releaser of energy; struggle, competition and victory over another is their stimulus. They can play no game unless there is competition, and the solitary pleasures and satisfactions, like reading, exploring, a row on the river or a walk in the woods, cannot arouse them. Others dislike rivalry or competition; they are too sympathetic to wish victory over another and also they dread to lose. They prefer team play and cooperation. The world will always seem different to these two types. This may be said now that for most of us, who are somewhat of a blend in this matter, rivalry is pleasant and stimulating when there is a show of success, but we prefer cooperation when we foresee failure.

This brings up the interesting phase of precedent in energy release. Early success, unless it brings too high a self-valuation, which is its great danger, is remarkably valuable in releasing energy, and failure establishes a precedent that may bring doubt, fear and the attendant inhibition of energy. Of course, failure may bring with it caution and a recasting of plans and thus constitute the most valuable of experiences. But if it is too great, or if there is lacking a certain fortitude, it may act as a paralyzer of energy

---

[51] See William James' "Varieties of Religious Experiences," for beautiful examples. The Russian writers are often narrators of this struggle.

thenceforth. In the prize ring this is often noted; the spirit of a man goes with a defeat and he never again has self-confidence; thereafter his energy is constantly inhibited.

Emotions have long been studied in their effects on energy. In fact, every animal that bristles and snarls as it faces a foe is, unconsciously, attempting to paralyze with fear its opponent, to render it helpless through the inhibition of action. So with the lurking tiger; it waits in silence for the prey and seeks the fascination of surprise as a factor in victory. On the other hand, the emotion of fear may be a releaser of energy for the prospective victim; it may release the energies of flight and add to the power of the animal. In this, there is a unique and neglected phase of emotion, i.e., if you shake your fist at your enemy and he runs away or knocks you down, then your manifestation of anger has been unsuccessful for you but his reaction has been successful for him. If he becomes so paralyzed with fear that you can work your will with him, then your anger is successful while his fear is not. Most of the psychologists have neglected this phase of emotion. Thus it is hard to understand the use fainting from terror has to the victim. The answer is it is useful to him who has caused the victim to faint.

6. For the individual, the emotion of fear has as its function a preparation for a danger that is foreseen to be too powerful to be met with effective resistance. Fear says, "It's no use to fight, fly or hide." Therefore, normally there is a heightening of energy feeling and action in these two directions. There are plenty of recorded incidents where fear has enabled men to run distances utterly impossible to them otherwise. In the fear states of mental disease, the resistance a frail woman will offer to her attendants is such that the utmost strength of several people is required to restrain her. Under these circumstances fear acts as an energizer, causing physical reactions not ordinarily within the will of the person. "Fear lends wings," is the time-honored way of expressing this. The trapped animal makes "frantic" efforts to escape.

Fear is extraordinarily contagious, perhaps because as herd members the cry of fear sets us all racing for safety. This is the grimmest danger from fires in public places or the presence of a coward in a military unit. Panic occurs with its blind unreasoning flight, and the result is disastrous. I emphasize again that emotions are poorly adapted to the welfare of the individual. Business panics are in large measure the result of the contagiousness of fear; timidity spreads like wildfire, distrust and suspicion are aroused and stagnation results without a "real" basis. In President Wilson's phrase, the panic is "purely psychological."

Intellectualized, fear becomes one of the driving forces of life, as Hobbes [52] pointed out. Fear of punishment undoubtedly deters from crime, though it is not in itself sufficient, and the kind of punishment becomes important. Fear of hunger has brought prudence, caution, agriculture into the world. Life insurance has its root in fear for others,

---

[52] Hobbes made fear the most important motive in the conduct of man.

who are really part of one's self; the fear of the rainy day is back of most of the thrift, though the acquisitive feeling and duty may also operate powerfully. Fear of venereal disease impels many a man to continence who otherwise would follow his desire. And fear of the bad opinion of others is the most powerful deterrent force in the world. "What will people say" is, at bottom, fear that they will say bad things, and though it keeps men from the "bad" conduct, it inhibits the finer nobler actions as well. There is a great deal of unconventional untrammeled belief in the world that never finds expression because of fear.

How deeply the fear of death modifies the life of people it is impossible to state. To every one there comes the awful reflection that he, that warmly pulsating being, in love with the world and with living, "center of the universe," HE himself must die, must be cold and still and have no will, no power, no feeling; be buried in the ground. Most of the essential melancholy of the world is due to this realization, and most of the feeling of pessimism and futility thus has its origin. Mortal man—a worm of the earth—a brief flower doomed to perish—and all of it finds final expression in Gray's marvelous words:

"The boast of heraldry, the pomp of pow'r,
   And all that beauty, all that wealth e'er gave,
  Await alike the inevitable hour.
   The paths of glory lead but to the grave."

"Why strive, thou poor creature, for wealth and power; sink thyself in the, Godhead!" "Turn, turn from vain pursuits; fame, the bubble, is bound to break as thou art." This is one type of reaction against this fear,—for men react to the fear of death variously. If man is mortal, God is not, and there is a life everlasting. The life everlasting—whether a reality or not—is conjured up and believed in by an effort to compensate for the fear of death.

I have a son who, when he was three, manifested great emotion if death were to enter in a story. "Will anything happen?" he would ask, meaning, "Will death enter?" And if so, he would beg not to have that story told. But when he was four, he heard some one say that there were people who took old automobiles apart, fixed up the parts and these were then placed in other automobiles.

"That's what God does to us," he cried triumphantly. "When we die, He takes us apart and puts us into babies, and we live again." Thereafter he would discuss death as fearlessly as he spoke of dinner, and all his fears vanished. Here was a typical rationalization of fear, one that has helped to shape religion, philosophies, ways of living. And the widespread belief in immortality is a compensation and a rationalization of the fear of death.

If some men rationalize in this fashion, others take directly opposite means. "Eat, drink and be merry, for to-morrow we die." The popularity of Omar Khayyam rests upon the aptness of his statement of this side of the case of Man vs. Death, and many a man who never heard of him has recklessly plunged into dissipation on the theory, "a short life and a merry one." This is more truly a pessimism than is the ascetic philosophy.

"Well, then, I must die," says another. "Oh, that I might achieve before death comes!" So men, appalled by the brief tenure of life and the haphazard way death strikes, work hard, spurred on by the wish to leave a great work behind them. This work becomes a Self, left behind, and here the fear of death is compensated for by a little longer life in the form of achievement.

Many a father and mother, looking at their children, feel this as part of their compensation for parenthood. "I shall die and leave some one behind me," means, "I shall die and yet I shall, in another form, live." Part of the incentive to parenthood, in a time which knows how to prevent parenthood and which shirks it as disagreeable, is the fear of death, of personal annihilation. For there is in death a blow to one's pride, an indignity in this annihilation,—Nothingness.

There is a still larger reaction to the fear of death. I have stated that the feeling of likeness is part of the feeling of brotherhood and in death is one of the three great likenesses of man. We are born of the labor of our mothers, our days are full of strife and trouble and we die. Men's minds have lingered on these facts. "Man that is born of a woman, is of few days, and full of trouble." Job did not add to this that he dies, but elsewhere it appears as the bond for mankind. Reacting to this, the reflective minds of the race have felt that here was the unity of man, here the basis of a brotherhood. True, the Fatherhood of God was given as a logical reason, but always in every appeal there is the note, "Do we not all die? Why hate one another then?"

So to the fear of death, as with every other fear, man has reacted basely and nobly. Man is the only animal that foresees death and he is the only one to elaborate ethics and religion. There is more than an accidental connection between these two facts.

Fear in its foreseeing character is termed worry. As a phase of character, the liability to worry is of such importance that book after book has dealt with the subject,—emphasizing the dangers, the futility and cowardice of it. It is surely idle to tell people not to worry who live continually on the brink of economic disaster, or who are facing real danger. But there are types who find in every possibility of injury a formidable threat, who are thrown into anguish when they contemplate any evil, remote or unlikely as it may be. The present and future are not faced with courage or equanimity; they present themselves as a never-ending series of threats; threat to health, to fortune, to family, reputation, everything. Horace Fletcher called this type of forethought "fear thought." Men and women, brave enough when face to face with actualities, are cowards when confronting remote possibilities. The housewife especially is one of these worriers, and her mind has an affinity for the terrible. I have described her elsewhere, [53] but she has her prototype among men.

Fear of this type is an injury to the body and character both and is one of the causes and effects of the widespread neurasthenia of our day.

---

[53] "The Nervous Housewife."

For fear injures sleep, and this brings on fatigue and fatigue breeds more fear, —a vicious circle indeed. Fear disturbs digestion and the energy of the organism is thereby lowered. The greatest damage by worry is done in the hypochondriac, the worrier about health. Here, in addition to the effects of fear, introspection and a minute attention to every pain and ache demoralize the character, for the sufferer cannot pay attention to anything else. He becomes selfish, ego-centric and without the wholesome interest in life as an adventure. I doubt if there is enough good in too minute a popular education on disease and health preservation. Morbid attention to health often results, an evil worse than sickness.

Sometimes, instead of the indiscriminate fear of worry, there are localized fears, called phobias, which creep or spring into a man's thoughts and render him miserable. Thus there is fear of high places, of low places, of darkness, of open places, of closed places,—fear of dirt, fear of poison and of almost everything else. A bright young man was locked, at the age of fourteen, in a closed dark shanty; when released he rushed home in the greatest terror. Since then he has been afflicted with a fear of leaving home. He dares venture only about fifty feet and then is impelled to run back. If anybody hinders his return he attacks them; if the door is locked he breaks through a window. He is in a veritable panic, and yet presents no other fears; is a reader and thinker, clever at his work (he is a painter), but his fear remains inaccessible and uncontrollable. Often one experience of this kind builds up an obsessive fear; the associations left by the experience give the fear an open pathway to consciousness, without any inhibiting power. As in this case, the whole life of the individual becomes changed.

Throughout history the man without fear has been idolized. The hero is courageous, that he must be; the coward is despised, whatever good may be in him. Consequently, there is in most men a fear of showing fear; and pride, self-respect, often urge men on when they really fear. This pride is greater in some races than others—in the Indian and the Anglo-Saxon—but the Oriental does not think it wrong to be afraid. In the Great War this fear of showing fear played a great role in producing shell shock, in that men shrank from actual cowardice but easily developed neuroses which carried them from the fighting line.

There is this to add to this little sketch of fear: it turns easily to anger for both are responses to a threat. I remember in my boyhood being mortally afraid of a larger boy who one day chased me, caught me and started to "beat me up." Before I knew it, the fear had gone and I was fighting him with such fierceness and fury that in amazement he ran away. So a rat, cornered, becomes fierce and blood-thirsty and there is always the danger, in the use of fear as a weapon, that it become changed quite readily into the fighting spirit.

7. Anger is a primitive reaction and is the backbone of the fighting spirit. It tends to displace fear, though it may be combined with it, in one of the most unhappy —because helpless—mental states. Anger in its commonest form is a violent energizer and in the stiffened muscles, the set jaw, bared teeth, and the forward-thrust head and arms one sees the

animal prepared to fight. Anger is aroused at any obstruction, any threat or injury, from physical violences to the so-called "slight." In fact, it is the intent of the opponent as understood that makes up the stimulus to anger in the human being. We forgive a blow if it is accidental, but even a touch, if in malice or in contempt, arouses a fierce reaction.

We call becoming angry too readily "losing the temper," and there is a type known as the irascible in whom anger is the readiest emotion. The bluff English squire, the man in authority, is this type, and his anger lasts. In its lesser form anger becomes irritability, a reaction common to the neurotic and the weak. When anger is not frank, but manifests itself by a lowered brow and sidelong look, we speak of sullenness or surliness. The sullen or surly person, chronically ill-tempered and hostile, is regarded as unsocial and dangerous, whereas the most lovable persons are quick to anger and quick to repent.

As a man's anger, so is he. There are some whose anger is always a reaction against interference with their comfort, their dignity, their property and their will; it never by any chance is aroused by the wrongs of others. Usually, however, these folk camouflage their motive. "It's the principle of the thing I object to," is its commonest social disguise, which sometimes successfully hides the real motive from the egoist himself. Wherever wills and purposes meet in conflict, there anger, or its offshoot, contempt, is present, and the more egoistic one is, the more egoistic the sources of anger.

The explosiveness of the anger will depend on the power of inhibition and the power of the intelligence, as well as on the strength of the opponent. There are enough whose temper is uncontrolled in the presence of the weak who manage to be quite calm in the presence of the strong. I believe there is much less difference amongst races in this respect than we suspect, and there is more in tradition and training. There was a time when it was perfectly proper for a gentleman to lose his temper, but now that it is held "bad form," most gentlemen manage to control it.

If it is common for men to become angry at ego-injury, there are in this world, as its leaven of reform, noble spirits who become angry at the wrongs of others. The world owes its progress to those whose anger, sustained and intellectualized, becomes the power behind reform; to those like Abraham Lincoln, who vowed to destroy slavery because he saw a slave sold down the river; to the Pinels, outraged by the treatment of the insane; to the sturdy "Indignant Citizen," who writes to newspapers about what "is none of his business," but who is too angry to keep still, and whose anger makes public opinion. Whether anger is useful or not depends upon its cause and the methods it employs. Righteous anger, whether against one's own wrongs or the wrongs of others, is the hall-mark of the brave and noble spirit; mean, egoistic anger is a great world danger, born of prejudice and egoism. A violent-tempered child may be such because he is outraged by wrong; if so, teach him control but do not tell him in modern wishy-washy fashion that "one must never get angry." Control it, intellectualize it, do not permit it to destroy effectiveness, as it is prone to do; but it cannot be eliminated without endangering personality.

Fear and anger have this in common: whenever the controlling energy of the mind goes, as in illness, fatigue or early mental disease, they become more prominent and uncontrolled. This cannot be overemphasized. When a man (or woman) finds himself continually getting apprehensive and irritable, then it is the time to ask, "What's the matter with me," and to get expert opinion on the subject.

These two emotions are in more need of rationalizing and intelligent control than the other emotions, for they are more explosive. Certainly of anger it is truly said that "He who is master of himself is greater than he who taketh a city." The angry man is disliked, he arouses unpleasant feelings, he is unpopular and a nuisance and a danger in the view of his fellows. The underlying idea underneath courtesy and social regulations is to avoid anger and humiliation. Controversial subjects are avoided, and one must not brag or display concern because these things cause anger and disgust. Politeness and tact are essential to turn away wrath, to avoid that ego injury that brings anger.

We contrast with the brusque type, careless of whether he arouses anger, the tactful, which conciliates by avoiding prejudice, and which hates force and anger as unpleasant. Against the quick to anger there is the slow type, whose anger may be enduring. We may contrast egoistic anger with the altruistic and oppose the anger which is effective with the anger that disturbs reason and judgment; intellectual anger against brute anger. Rarely do men show anger to their superiors; extreme provocation and desperation are necessary. Men flare up easily against equals but more easily and with mingled contempt against the inferior. Anger, though behind the fighting spirit, need not bluster or storm; usually that is a "worked up" condition intended in a naive way to frighten and intimidate, or through disgust, to win a point. Anger is not necessarily courage, which replaces it the higher up one goes in culture.

8. Disgust, also a primary emotion, is one of the basic reactions of life and civilization. Literally "disagreeable taste," its facial expression, with mouth open and lower lip drawn down, [54] is that preliminary to vomiting. We eject or retract when disgusted; we are not afraid nor are we angry. We say "he—or she, or it—makes me sick," and this is the stock phrase of disgust. Inelegant as it is, it exactly expresses the situation. Disgust easily mingles with fear and anger; it is often dispelled by curiosity and interest, as in the morbid, as in medical science, and it of ten displaces less intense curiosity and interest.

After anything has been accepted as standard in cleanliness, a deviation in a "lower" direction causes disgust. Those who are accustomed to clean tablecloths, clean linen are disgusted by dirty tablecloths, dirty linen. The excreta of the body have been so effectively tabooed, in the

---

[54] See Darwin's "The Expression of Emotions in Man and Animals," —a great book by a great man.

interest perhaps of sanitation, that their sight or smell is disgusting, and they are used as symbols of disgust in everyday language. Indeed, the so-called animal functions have to be decorated and ceremonialized to avoid disgust. We turn with ridicule and repugnance from him who eats without "manners" and one of the functions of manners is to avoid arousing disgust.

Disgust kills desire and passion, and from that fact we may trace a large part of moral progress. Satiety brings a slight disgust; thus after a heavy meal there may be contentment but the sight of food is not at all appealing and often enough rather repelling. In the sex field, a deep repulsion is often felt when lust alone has brought the man and woman together or when the situation is illegal or unhallowed. With satisfaction of desire, the inhibiting forces come to their own, and the violence of repentance and disgust may be extreme. Stanley Hall, Havelock Ellis and other writers lay stress on this; and, indeed, one of the bases of asceticism is this disgust. Further, when we have no desires or passion, the sight of others hugging and kissing, or acting "intimate" in any way, is usually disgusting, an offense against "good taste" based on the "bad taste" it arouses in the observer. In memory we are often disgusted at what we did in the heat of desire, but usually memory itself does not prevent us from repeating the act; desire itself must slacken. Thus the old are often intensely disgusted at the conduct of the young, and it is never wise for a young couple to live with older people. For in the early days of married life the intensity of the intimate feelings needs seclusion in order to avoid disgusting others. It is no accident that Dame Grundy is depicted as an elderly person with a "sour look"; her prudishness has an origin in disgust at that which she has outlived. Sometimes the old are wise—not often enough—and then their humor, love and sympathy keeps them from disgust.

Love counteracts disgust. The young girl who turns in loathing from uncleanliness finds it easy and a pleasure to care for her soiled baby. In fact, tender feeling of any kind overcomes—or tends to overcome—disgust; and pity, the tenderest of all feelings and without passion, impels us to march into the very jaws of disgust. The angry may have no pity,—but they are not less unkind in commission than the disgusted are unkind in omission. Thus a too refined breeding leads people away from effective pity and that sturdiness of conduct which is real philanthropy. Indeed, too much of refinement increases the number of disgusting things in the world; he who must have this or that luxury is not so much pleased with it as disgusted without it. Raising standards in things material cannot increase the happiness or contentment of the world, for it merely makes men impatient and disgusted at lesser standards. We cannot hope to increase happiness through the material improvements of civilization.

Self-disgust and shame are not identical but are so kindred that shame may well be studied here. Shame is lowered self-valuation, brought on by social or self-disapproval. Usually it is acute and, like fear, it tends to make the individual hide or fly. It is based on insight, and there are thus some who are never ashamed, simply because they do not understand disapproval. Shame is essentially a feeling of inferiority, and when we say to a man, "Shame on you," we say, "You have done wrong, humble yourself, be little!" When we say, "I am ashamed of you," we say, "I had pride in you; I enlarged myself through you, and now you make me little." When the community cries shame, it uses a force that redresses wrong by the need of the one addressed to vindicate himself. When a man feels shame he feels small, inferior in his own eyes and in the eyes of others. He feels impelled, if he is generous, to make amends or to do penance, and thus he recovers his self-esteem. Unfortunately, shame arises more frequently and often more violently from a violation of custom and manner than from a violation of ethics or morals. Thus we are more ashamed of the so-called "bad break" than of our failures to be kind. Sometimes our fellow feeling is so strong that we avoid seeing any one who is humiliated or embarrassed, because sympathy spreads his feeling to us. Gentle people are those who dislike to shame any one else, and often one of this type will endure being wronged rather than reprimand or cause humiliation and shame. Let something be said to shame any member of a company and a feeling of shame spreads through the group, except in the case of those who are very hostile.

Disgust, too, is extremely contagious, especially its manifestations. One of the most crude of all manifestations, to spit upon some one, is a symbol taken from disgust, though it has come to mean contempt, which is a mixture of hatred and disgust.

To raise the tastes and not raise the acquisitions is a sure way to bring about chronic disgust, which is really an angry dissatisfaction mixed with disgust. This type of reaction is very common as a factor in neurasthenia. In fact, my motto is "search for the disgust" in all cases of neurasthenia and "search for it in the intimate often secret desires and relationships. Seek for it in the husband-wife relationship, especially from the standpoint of the wife." Women, we say, are more refined in their feelings than men, which is another way of saying they are more easily disgusted and therefore more easily injured. For disgust is an injury, when chronic or too easily elicited, and is then a sign and symbol of weakness.

Thus disgust is a great reenforcer of social taboo and custom, as well as morality. Just as it fails to keep us from eating the wrong kind of foods, so it may fail to keep us from the wrong conduct. Like every emotion it is only in part adapted to our lives, and in those people where it becomes a prominent emotion it is a great mischief worker, subordinating life to finickiness and hindering the growth of generous feeling.

9. We come to two opposite emotions, very readily considered together. One of the linkings of opposites is in the connection of Joy and Sorrow. Whether these are primary emotions or outgrowths of Pleasure and Pain I leave to others. For Shand the fact that Joy tends to prolong a situation in which it occurs raises it into an active emotion.

Joy is perhaps the most energizing of the emotions for it tends to express itself in shouts, smiles and laughter, dancing and leaping. Sorrow ordinarily is quite the reverse and expresses itself by immobility, bowed head and hands that shut out from the view the sights of the world. There is, however, a quiet joy called relief, which is like sailing into a smooth, safe harbor after a tempestuous voyage; and there is an agitated grief, with lamentation, the wringing of hands and self-punishment of a frantic kind. Joy and triumph are closely associated, sorrow and defeat likewise. There are some whose rivalry-competitive feelings are so widespread that they cannot rejoice even at the triumph of a friend, and a little of that nature is in even the noblest of us. There are others who find sorrow in defeat of an enemy, so widespread is their sympathy. This is the generous victor. For the most of us youth is the most joyous period because youth finds in its pleasures a novelty and freshness that tend to disappear with experience. For the same reason the sorrow of youth, though evanescent, is unreasoning and intense.

Joy and sorrow are reactions and they are noble or the reverse, according to the nature of the person. Joy may be noble, sensuous, trivial or mean; many a "jolly" person is such because he has no real sympathy. At the present time not one of us could rejoice over anything could we SEE and sympathize deeply with the misery of Europe and China, to say nothing of that in our own country. Nay, any wrong to others would blast all our pleasure, could we really feel it. Fortunately only a few are so cursed with sympathy. When the capacity for joyous feeling is joined with fortitude or endurance, then we have the really cheerful, who spread their feeling everywhere, whom all men love. Where cheerfulness is due to lack of sympathy and understanding, we speak of a cheerful idiot; and well does that type merit the name. There is a modern cult whose followers sing "La, la, la" at all times and places, who minimize all misfortune, crime, suffering, who find "good in everything,"—the "Pollyana" tribe. My objection to them is based on this,—that mankind must see clearly in order to rid itself of unnecessary suffering. Hiding one's head (and brains) in a desert of optimism merely perpetuates evil, even though one sufferer here and there is deluded into happiness.

Sorrow may enrich the nature or it may embitter and narrow it. Wisdom may spring from it; indeed, who can be wise who has not sorrowed? Says Goethe:
"Wer nie sein Brot in Thranen ass
    Wer nie die kummervollen Nachte
Auf seinem Bette weinend sass
    Er weiss Euch nicht—himmelischen Machte."
The afflicted in their sorrow may turn from self-seeking to God and good deeds. But sorrow may come in a trivial nature from trivial causes; the soul may be plunged into despair because one has been denied a gift or a pleasure. The demonstrativeness of grief or sorrow is not at all in proportion to the emotion felt; it is more often based on the effort to get sympathy and help. For sorrow is "Help, help" in one form or another, even though one refuses to be comforted. All our emotions, because they are socially powerful, become somewhat theatrical; in some completely

theatrical. We are so constituted that emotional display is not indifferent to us; it pleases, repels, annoys, angers, frightens, disgusts or awes us according to the kind of emotion displayed, the displayer and the circumstances.

The psychologists speak of sympathy as this susceptibility to the emotions of others, but there is an antipathy to their emotions, as well. If we feel that our emotions will be "well received," we do not fear to display them, and therein is one of the uses of the friend. If we feel that they will be poorly received, that they will annoy or anger or disgust, we strive to repress them. The expression of emotion, especially of fear and sorrow, has become synonymous with weakness, and a powerful self-feeling operates against their display, especially in adults, men and certain races. It is no accident that the greatest actors are from the Latin and Hebrew races, for there is a certain theatricality in fear and sorrow that those schooled to repression lose. We resent what we call insincerity in emotional expression because we fear being "fooled," and there are many whose experiences in being "fooled" chill sympathy with doubt. We resent insincere sympathy, on the other hand, because we regret showing weakness before those to whom that weakness is regarded as such and who perhaps rejoice at it as ridiculous. We like the emotional expression of children because we can always sympathize, through our tender feeling with them, and their very sincerity pleases as well.

Is there a harm in the repression of emotion? [55] Is emotion a heaped-up tension which, unless it is discharged, causes damage? Shall man inhibit his anger, fear, joy, sorrow, disgust, at least in some measure, or shall he express them in gesture, speech and act? The answer is obvious: he must control them, and in that term control we mean, not inhibition, not expression in its naive sense, but that combination of inhibition, expression and intelligent act we call adjustment. To express fear in the face of danger or anger at an offense might thwart the whole life's purpose, might bring disaster and ruin. The emotions are poor adjustments in their most violent form, their natural form, and invite disaster by clouding the intelligence and obscuring permanent purposes. Therefore, they must be controlled. To establish this control is a primary function of training and intelligence and does no harm unless carried to excess. True, there is a relief in emotional expression, a wiping out of sorrow by tears, an increase of the pleasure of joy in freely laughing, a discharge of anger in the blow or the hot word, even the profane word. There is a time and a place for these things, and to get so "controlled" that one rarely laughs or shows sadness or anger is to atrophy, to dry up. But the emotional expression makes it easy to become an habitual weeper or stormer, makes it easy to become the over-emotional type, whose reaction to life is futile, undignified and a bodily injury. For emotion is in large part a display of energy, and the overemotional rarely escape the depleted neurasthenic state. In fact,

---

[55] Isador N. Coriat's book, "The Repression of Emotions" deals with the subject from psychoanalytic. point of view.

hysteria and neurasthenia are much more common in the races freely expressing emotion than in the stolid, repressed races. Jew, Italian, French and Irish figure much more largely than English, Scotch or Norwegian in the statistics of neurasthenia and hysteria.

10. I have said but little on other emotions,—on admiration, surprise and awe. This group of affective states is of great importance. Surprise may be either agreeable or disagreeable and is our reaction to the unexpected. Its expression, facially and of body, is quite characteristic, with staring eyes and mouth slightly open, raised eyebrows, hands hanging with fingers tensely spread apart, so that a thing held therein is apt to drop. Surprise heightens the feeling of internal tension, and in all excitement it is an element, in that the novel brings excitement and surprise, whereas the accustomed gives little excitement or surprises. In all wit and humor surprise is part of the technique and constitutes part of the pleasure. Surprise usually heightens the succeeding feeling, whether of joy, sorrow, anger, fear, pleasure or pain, or in any form. But sometimes the effect of surprise is so benumbing that an incapacity to feel, to realize, is the most marked result and it is only afterward that the proper emotion or feeling becomes manifest.

The reaction to the unexpected is an important adjustment in character. There are situations beyond the power of any of us quickly to adjust ourselves to and we expect the great catastrophe to surprise and overwhelm. Nevertheless, we judge people by the way they react to the unexpected; the man who rallies quickly from the confusion of surprise is, we say, "cool-headed," keeps his wits about him; and the man who does not so rally or adjust "loses his head,"—"loses his wits." Part of this cool-headedness is not only the rallying from surprise but also the throwing off of fear. A warning has for its purpose, "Don't be surprised!" and training must teach resources against the unexpected. "If you expect everything you are armed against half the trouble of the world." The cautious in character minimize the number of surprises they may get by preparing. The impulsive, who rarely prepare, are always in danger from the unforeseen. Aside from preparation and knowledge, there is in the condition of the organism a big factor in the reaction to the unexpected. Fatigue, neurasthenia, hysteria and certain depressed conditions render a man more liable to react excessively and badly to surprise. The tired soldier has lessened resources in wit and courage when surprised, for fatigue heightens the confusion and numbness of surprise and decreases the scope of intelligent conduct. Choice is made difficult, and the neurasthenic doubt is transformed to impotence by surprise.

Face to face with what is recognized as superior to ourselves in a quality we hold to be good, we fall into that emotional state, a mingling of surprise and pleasure, called admiration. In its original usage, admiration meant wonder, and there is in all admiration something of that feeling which is born in the presence of the superior. The more profound the admiration, the greater is the proportion of wonder in the feeling.

We find it difficult to admire where the competitive feeling is strongly aroused, though there are some who can do so. It is the essence of good sportsmanship, the ideal aimed at, to admire the rival for his good qualities, though sticking fast to one's confidence in oneself. The English and American athletes, perhaps also the athletes of other countries, make this part of their code of conduct and so are impelled to act in a way not entirely sincere. Wherever jealousy or envy are strongly aroused, admiration is impossible, and so it comes about that men find it easy to praise men in other noncompetitive fields or for qualities in which they are not competing. Thus an author may strongly admire an athlete or a novelist may praise the historian; a beautiful woman admires another for her learning, though with some reservation in her praise, and a successful business man admires the self-sacrificing scientist, albeit there is a little complacency in his approval.

He is truly generous-hearted who can admire his competitor. I do not mean lip-admiration, through the fear of being held jealous. Many a man joins in the praise of one who has outstripped him, with envy gnawing at his heart, and waits for the first note of criticism to get out the hammer. "He is very fine—but" is the formula, and either through innuendo, insinuation or direct attack, the "subordinate" statement becomes the most sincere and significant. But there are those who can admire their conqueror, not only through the masochism that lurks in all of us, but because they have lifted their ideal of achievement and character higher than their own possibilities and seek in others the perfection they cannot hope to have in themselves. In other words, where competition is hopeless, in the presence of the greatly superior, a feeling of humility which is really admiration to the point of worship comes over us, and we can glory in the quality we love. To admire is to recede the ego-feeling, is to feel oneself in an ecstasy that becomes mystical, and in that sense the contradiction arises that we feel ourselves larger in a unification with the admired one.

Each age, each country, each group and each family set up the objects and qualities for admiration, in a word, the ideals. Out of these the individual selects his specialties in admiration, according to his nature and training. All the world admires vigor, strength, courage and endurance,— and these in their physical aspects. The hero of all times has had these qualities: he is energetic, capable of feats beyond the power of others, is fearless and bears his ills with equanimity. Beauty, especially in the woman, but also in man, has received an over-great share of homage, but here "tastes differ." We have no difficulty in agreement on what constitutes strength, and we have objective tests for its measurement; but who can agree on beauty? What one race prizes as its fairest is scorned by another race. We laugh at the ideal of beauty of the Hottentot, and the physical peculiarity they praise most either disgusts or amuses us. But what is there about a white skin more lovely than a black one, and why thrill over blue eyes and neglect the brown ones? What is the rationale for the admiration of slimness as against stoutness? Indeed, there are races who would turn with scorn from our slender debutante [56] and worship their more buxom heavy-busted and wide-hipped beauties. The only "rational" beauty in face and figure is that which stands as the outer mask of health, vigor, intelligence and normal procreative function. The standards set up in each age and place usually arise from local pride, from the familiar type. The Mongolian who finds beauty in his slanting-eyed, wide-cheek boned, yellow mate has as valid a sanction as the Anglo-Saxon who worships at the shrine of his wide-eyed, straight-nosed blonde.

When we leave the physical qualities and pass to the mental we again find a lack of agreement as to the admirable. All agree that intelligence is to be admired, but how shall that intelligence be manifested? In practice, the major part of the world admires the intelligence that is financially and socially successful, and the rich and powerful have the greatest share of the world's praise. Power, strength, and superiority command admiration, even from the unwilling, and the philosopher who stands aloof from the world and is without real strength finds himself admiring a crude, bustling fellow ordering men about. True, we admire such acknowledged great intelligences as Plato, Galileo, Newton, Pascal, Darwin, etc., but in reality only a fragment of the men and women of any country know anything at all about these men, and the admiration of most is an acceptance of the authority of others as to what it is proper to admire. Genuine admiration is in proportion to the intelligence and idealism of the admirer. And there are in this country a thousand intense admirers of Babe Ruth and his mighty baseball club to one who pours out his soul before the image of Pasteur. You may know a man (or woman) not by his lip-homage, but by what he genuinely admires, by that which evokes his real enthusiasm and praise. Judge by that and then note that the most constant admiration of the women of our country goes out to actresses, actors, professional beauties, with popular authors and lecturers a bad second, and that of the men is evoked by prize fighters, ball players and the rich. No wonder the problems of the world find no solution, for it is only by fits and starts that men and women admire real intelligence and real ability. The orator has more admirers than the thinker, and this is the curse of politics; the executive has more admirers than the research worker, and this is the bane of industry; the entertainer is more admired than the educator, and that is why Charlie Chaplin makes a million a year and President Eliot received only a few thousand. The race and the nation has its generous enthusiasms and its bursts of admiration for the noble, but its real admiration it gives to those whom it best understands. Fortunately the leaders of the race have more of generosity and fine admiration than have the mass they lead. Left to itself, the mass of the race limits its hero-worship to the lesser, unworthy race of heroes.

---

[56] The peasant type, greatly admired by the agricultural folk of Central Europe, is stout and ruddy. This is a better ideal of beauty than the lily-white, slender and dainty maid of the cultured, who very often can neither work nor bear and nurse children.

The school histories, which should emphasize the admirable as well as point out the reverse, have played a poor role in education. The hero they depict is the warrior, and they fire the hearts of the child with admiration and desire for emulation. They say almost nothing of the great inventors, scientists and philanthropists. The teaching of history should, above all, set up heroes for the child to study, admire and emulate. "When the half-gods go the gods arrive." The stage of history as taught is cluttered with the tin-plate shedders of blood to the exclusion of the greater men. [57]

When the object that confronts us is so superior, so vast, that we sink into insignificance, then admiration takes on a tinge of fear in the state or feeling of awe. All men feel awe in the presence of strength and mystery, so that the concept of God is that most wrapped up with this emotion, and the ceremonies with which kings and institutions have been surrounded strike awe by their magnificence and mystery into the hearts of the governed. We contemplate natural objects, such as mountains, mighty rivers and the oceans, with awe because we feel so little and puny in comparison, and we do not "enjoy" contemplating them because we hate to feel little. Or else we grow familiar with them, and the awe disappears. The popular and the familiar are never awe-full, and even death loses in dignity when one has dissected a few bodies. So objects viewed by night or in gloom inspire awe, though seen by day they are stripped of mystery and interest. To the adolescent boy, woman is a creature to be regarded with awe,—beautiful, strangely powerful and mysterious. To the grown-up man, enriched and disillusioned by a few experiences, woman, though still loved, is no longer worshiped.

Though the reverent spirit is admirable and poetic, it is not by itself socially valuable. It has been played upon by every false prophet, every enslaving institution. It prevents free inquiry; it says to science, "Do not inquire here. They who believe do not investigate. This is too holy a place for you." We who believe in science deny that anything can be so holy that it can be cheapened by light, and we believe that face to face with the essential mysteries of life itself even the most assiduous and matter-of-fact must feel awe. Man, the little, has probed into the secrets of the universe of which he is a part. What he has learned, what he can learn, make him bow his head with a reverence no worshiper of dogmatic mysteries can ever feel.

---

[57] Plutarch's Lives are an example of the praise and place given to the soldier and orator; and many a child, reading them, has burned to be an Alexander or a Caesar. Wells' History, with all its defects, pushes the "conquerors" to their real place as enemies of the race.

CHAPTER X
COURAGE, RESIGNATION, SUBLIMATION, PATIENCE, THE WISH, AND ANHEDONIA

In the preceding chapter we spoke of the feeling of energy and certain of the basic emotions—such as fear, anger, joy, sorrow, disgust, surprise and admiration. It is important to know that rarely does a man react to any life situation in which the feeling of energy is not an emotional constituent and governs in a general way that reaction. Moreover, fear, anger, joy and the other feelings described mingle with this energy feeling and so are built great systems of the affective life.

1. Courage is one of these systems. It is not merely the absence of fear that constitutes courage, though we interchange "fearless" with "courageous." Frequently it is the conquest of fear by the man himself that leads him to the highest courage. There is a type of courage based on the lack of imagination, the inability to see ahead the disaster that lurks around every corner. There is another type of courage based on the philosophy that to lose control of oneself is the greatest disaster. There are the nobly proud, whose conception of "ought," of "noblesse oblige," makes them the real aristocrats of the race.

The fierce, the predisposed to anger are usually courageous. Unrestrained anger tends to break down imagination and foresight; caution disappears and the smallest will attack the largest. In racial propaganda, one way to arouse courage is to arouse anger. The enemy is represented as all that is despicable and mean and as threatening the women and children, religion, or the flag. It is not sufficient to arouse hate, for hate may fear. While individuals of a fierce type may be cowards, and the gentle often enough are heroes, the history of the race shows that physical courage resides more with the fierce races than with the gentle.

Those who feel themselves superior in strength and energy are much more apt to be courageous than those who feel themselves inferior. In fact, the latter have to force themselves to courage, whereas the former's courage is spontaneous. Men do not fear to be alone in a house as women do, largely because men feel themselves equal to coping with intruders, who are sure to be men, while women do not. One of the early signs of chronic sickness is a feeling of fear, a loss of courage, based on a feeling of inferiority to emergencies. The Spartans made it part of that development of courage for which their name stands, to develop the physique of both their men and women. Their example, in rational measure, should be followed by all education, for courage is essential to nobility of character. I emphasize that such training should be extended to both male and female, for we cannot expect to have a timorous mother efficiently educate her boy to be brave, to say nothing of the fact that her own happiness and efficiency rest on courage.

Tradition is a mighty factor in the production of courage. To feel that something is expected of one because one's ancestors lived up to a high standard becomes a guiding feeling in life. Not to be inferior, not to disappoint expectation, to maintain the tradition that a "So-and-So" never shows the white feather, makes, heroes of the soldiers of famous regiments, of firemen and policemen, of priests, of the scions of distinguished families, aye, even of races. To every man in the grip of a glorious tradition it seems as if those back of him are not really dead, as if they stand with him, and speak with his voice and act in his deeds. The doctor who knows of the martyrs of his profession and knows that in the code of his calling there are no diseases he must hesitate to face, goes with equanimity where others who are braver in facing death of other kinds do not dare to enter.

Courage is competitive, courage is cooperative, as is every other phase of the mental life of men. We gather courage as we watch a fellow worker face his danger with a brave spirit, for we will not be outdone. Amour propre will not permit us to cringe or give in, though we are weary to death of a struggle. But also we thrill with a common feeling at the sight of the hero holding his own, we are enthused by it, we wish to be with him; and his shining example moves us to a fellowship in courage. We find courage in the belief that others are "with us," whether that courage faces physical or moral danger. To be "with" a man is to more than double his resources of strength, intelligence and courage; it is more than an addition, for it multiplies all his virtues and eliminates his defects. The sum total is the Hero. I wonder if there really ever has been a truly lonely hero, if always there has not been some one who said, "I have faith in you; I am with you!" If a man has lacked human backing, he has said to himself, "The Highest of all is with me, though I seem to stand alone. God gives me courage!"

In a profoundly intellectual way, courage depends on a feeling that one is useful, not futile. Men lose courage, in the sense of brave and determined effort, when it seems as if progress has ceased and their place in the world has disappeared. This one sees frequently in middle-aged men, who find themselves relegated to secondary places by younger men, who feel that they are slipping and soon will be dependents.

Hope, the foreseeing of a possible success, is necessary for most courage, though now and then despair acts with a courage that is largely pride. The idea of a future world has given more courage to man in his difficulties than all other conceptions together, for the essence of the belief in immortality is to transfer hope and success from the tangle of this world to the clear, untroubled heavenly other world.

2. Here we must consider other, related qualities. The office of intelligence is to adjust man to a complex world, to furnish pathways to a goal which instinct perhaps chooses. Suppose a goal reached,—say marriage is entered upon with the one that we think is to give us that satisfaction and happiness we long for. The marriage does not so result, either because we have expected too much, or because the partner falls

114

below a reasonable expectation, or because contradictory elements in the natures of the wedded pair cannot be reconciled. Unity is not reached; disunion results, almost, let us say, from the very start. What happens?

Many adjustments may take place. A crude one is that the pair, after much quarreling, decide to separate or become divorced, or on a still cruder, ignoble level, one or the other runs away, deserts the family. A common adjustment, of an anti-social kind, forms the basis of much of modern and ancient literature; the partners seek compensation elsewhere, enter into illicit love affairs and maintain a dual existence which rarely is peaceful or happy. Indeed, the nature of the situation, with outraged conscience and fear of exposure, prevents happiness.

But there are those who in such a situation do what is known as "make the best of it." They avoid quarrels, they keep up the pretense of affection, they seek to discover the good qualities in the mate; they are, as we say, resigned to the situation. To be resigned is to accept an evil with calmness and equanimity, but without energy. Resignation and courage are closely related, though the former is a rather pallid member of the family. The poor and the miserable everywhere practise this virtue; the church has raised it perforce to the most needed of qualities; it is a sort of policy of nonresistance to the evils of the world and one's own lot.

But resignation represents only one type of legitimate adjustment, of sublimation. By sublimation is meant the process of using the energy of a repressed desire and purpose for some "higher" end. Thus in the case of domestic unhappiness the man may plunge himself deeply into work and even be unconscious of the source of his energy. This type of adjustment is thus a form of compensation and is seen everywhere. In the case of many a woman who gives herself over to her children without stint you may find this sublimation against the disappearance of romance, even if no actual unhappiness exists. Where a woman is childless, perforce and not per will, an intense communal activity often develops, leading to good if that activity is intelligent, leading to harm if it is not. For sublimation develops the crank and pest as well as the reformer. In every half-baked reform movement you find those who are striving to sublimate for a thwarted instinct or purpose. [58]

Sublimation is the mark of the personality that will not admit defeat even to itself. The one who does admit defeat becomes resigned or seeks illicit compensation,—other men, other women, drink. Freud and his followers believe that the neurasthenic or hysteric is striving to find compensation through his symptoms or that he seeks to fly from the situation that way. I believe that the symptoms of the neurasthenic and hysteric often find a use in this way, but are not caused by an effort for compensation. That is, a neurasthenic may learn that his or her pains or aches give advantages in sympathy, relief from hard tasks or disagreeable situations; that they cover up or are an excuse for failure and inferiority,—

---

[58] The historian, Higginson, put it well when he said substantially, "There is a fringe of insanity around all reform."

but the symptoms arise originally from defects in character or because of the physical and social situation. Nevertheless, it is well to keep in mind, when dealing with the "nervous," that often enough their weaknesses are related to something they may gain through them. This I have called elsewhere "Will to power through weakness," and it is as old as Adam and Eve. The weak have their wills and their weapons as have the strong.

The highest sublimation, in the face of an insuperable obstacle to purpose or an inescapable life situation, finds a socially useful substitute in philanthropy, kindness, charity, achievement of all sorts; the lowest seeks it in a direct but illicit compensation for the self and in a way that merely increases the social and personal confusion; and a pathological sublimation in part, at least, manifests itself iii sickness. These are the three leading forms, but it must be remembered that there are no pure types in character; a man may sublimate nobly when his domestic happiness is threatened but cheat when his business purposes are blocked; a woman may compensate finely for childlessness but "go all to pieces" because hair is growing on her face and the beauty she cherishes must go. Contradictions of all sorts exist, and he is wise who does not expect too great consistency from himself or others.

3. "Man," says Hocking, "can prolong the vestibule of his desire through infinity." By the vestibule of desire this philosopher means the deferring of satisfaction for any impulse or desire. We love, but we can wait for love's fulfillment; we desire achievement, but we can work and watch the approach of our goal. Something we desire is directly ahead, almost in our reach,— fame, love, riches, vindication, anything you please from the sensuous to the sublime satisfaction; and then an obstacle, a delay, appears, and the vestibule is lengthened out. A man may even plan for the satisfaction he can never hope to have, and in his greatest ideal that vestibule reaches through eternity.

That quality which enables a man to work and wait, to stand the deferring of hope and desire, is patience. The classic figure of patience sitting on a monument is wrong, for she must sit on the eager desires of man. Nor is patience only the virtue of the good and farseeing, for we find patience in the rogue and schemer. Altruists may be patient or impatient, and so may be the selfish. Like most of the qualities, patience is to be judged by the company it keeps.

Nevertheless, the impatient are very often those of small purposes and are rarely those of great achievement. For all great purposes have to be spread over time, have to overcome obstacles, and these must be met with courage and patience. Impatience is fussiness, fretfulness and a prime breeder of neurasthenia. Patience is realistic, and though it may seek perfection it puts up with imperfection as a part of human life. But here I am drifting into an error against which I warned the reader,—of making an entity of a conception. People are patient or impatient, but not necessarily throughout. There are men and women who fuss and fume over trifles who never falter or fret when their larger purposes are blocked or deferred. Some cannot stand detail who plan wisely and with patience. Vice versa, there are meticulous folk, little people, whose petty obstacles are met with patience and cheerfulness, who revel in minute detail, but who want returns soon and cannot wait a long time. We are not to ask of any man whether he is patient but rather what does he stand or do patiently? What renders him impatient?

A form of impatience of enormous social importance is that which manifests itself in cure-alls. A man finds that his will overcomes some obstacles. Eager to apply this, he announces that will cures all ills. Impatient of evil, men seek to annihilate it by denying its existence or by loudly chanting that good thoughts will destroy it. These are typical impatient solutions in the sphere of religion; in the sphere of economics men urge nationalization, free trade, socialism or laissez faire, or some law or other to change social structure and human nature. War itself is the most impatient and consequently most socially destructive method of the methods of the treatment of evil.

While patience is a virtue, it may also be a vice. One may bear wrongs too patiently or defer satisfaction too long. One meets every day men and women who help injustice and iniquity by their patience. We are too patient, at least with the wrongs of others; perhaps we really do not feel this intensely or for any length of time. In fact, the difficulty with most of the preaching of life is its essential insincerity, for it counsels patience for that which it feels but little. We bear the troubles of others, on the whole, very well. Nevertheless, there are Griseldas everywhere whom one would respect far more if they rebelled against their tyrants and taskmasters. Organized wrong and oppression owe their existence mainly to the habitual patience of the oppressed. To be meek and mild and long-suffering in a world containing plenty of egoists and cannibalistic types is to give them supremacy. [59] We admire patience only when it is part of a plan of action, not when it is the mark of a passive nature.

4. Because man foresees he wishes. Rather than the reasoning animal, we might speak of the human being as the wishing animal. An automatically working instinct would produce no wish. The image of something which has been experienced arouses an excitement akin to the secretion of saliva at the thought of food. The wish which accompanies the excitement is a dissatisfaction, a tingling, an incomplete pleasurable emotional state which presses to action. Sensuous pleasure, power, conformity to the ideal, whatever direction the wish takes, are sought because of the wish. Right education is to train towards right wishing.

Because the wish is the prelude to action, it became all powerful in mythology and superstition. Certain things would help you get your wishes, others would obstruct them. Wishes became animate and had power,—power to destroy an enemy, power to help a friend, power to bring good to yourself. But certain ceremonies had to be observed, and certain

---

[59] Here the ideals of East and West clash. The East, bearing a huge burden of misery and essentially pessimistic, exhorts patience. The West, eager and full of hope, is impatient.

people, magicians and priests had to be utilized in order to give the wish its power. Wisdom and magic were mainly the ways of obtaining wishes. Childhood still holds to this, and prayer is a faith that your wish, if placed before the All-Mighty, will be fulfilled.

Since wishing brings a pleasurable excitement, it has its dangers, in the daydream where wishes are fulfilled without effort. Power, glory, beauty and admiration are obtained; the ugly Duckling becomes the Swan, Cinderella becomes the Princess, Jack kills the Giant and is honored by all men; the girl becomes the beauty and heroine of romance; the boy becomes the Hero, taking over power, wealth and beauty as his due. The world of romance is largely the wish-world, as is the most of the stage. The happy ending is our wish-fulfillment, and only the sophisticated and highly cultured object to it. Moulding the world to the heart's desire has been the principal business of stage, novel and song.

In the normal relations of life, the wish is the beginning of will, as something definitely related to a future goal. He who wishes finds his way to planning and to patient endeavor, IF training, circumstances and essential character meet. To wish much is the first step in acquiring much,—but only the first step. For many it is almost the only step, and in the popular phrase these have a "wishbone in the place of a backbone." They are the daydreamers, the inveterate readers of novels, who carry into adult life what is relatively normal in the child. The introspective are this latter type; rarely indeed do the objective personalities spend much time in wishing. Undoubtedly it is from the introspective that the wish as a symbol and worker of power gained its influence and meaning. This transformation of the wish to a power is found in all primitive thought, in the power of the blessing and the curse, in the delusions of certain of the insane who build up the belief in their greatness out of the wish to be great; and in our days New Thought and kindred beliefs are modernized forms of this ancient fallacy.

It is a comforting thought to those who seek an optimistic point of view that most men wish to do right. Very few, indeed, deliberately wish to do wrong. But the difficulty lies in this, that this wish to do right camouflages all their wishes, no matter what their essential character. Thus the contestants on either side of any controversy color as right their opposing wishes, and cruelties even if they burn people at the stake for heresy, kill and ruin, degrade and cheat, lie and steal. Thus has arisen the dictum, "The end justifies the means." The good desired hallows the methods used, and all kinds of evil have resulted. Practical wisdom believes that up to a certain point you must seek your purpose with all the methods at hand. But the temptation to go farther always operates; a man starts to do something a little underhanded in behalf of his noble wish and finds himself committed to conduct unqualifiedly evil.

5. There are certain other emotional states associated with energy and the energy feeling of great interest. What we call eagerness, enthusiasm, passion, refers to the intensity of an instinct, wish, desire or purpose. In childhood this energy is quite striking; it is one of the great

charms of childhood and is a trait all adults envy. For it is the disappearance of passion, eagerness and enthusiasm that is the tragedy of old age and which really constitutes getting old. Youth anticipates with eagerness and relishes with keen satisfaction. The enthusiasm of typical youth is easily aroused and sweeps it on to action, a feature called impulsiveness. Sympathy, pity, hope, sex feeling—all the self-feelings and all the other feelings—are at once more lively and more demonstrative in youth, and thus it is that in youth the reform spirit is at its height and recedes as time goes on. What we call "experience" chills enthusiasm and passion, but though hope deferred and a realization of the complexity of human affairs has a moderating, inhibiting result, there is as much or more importance to be attached to bodily changes. If you could attach to the old man's experience and knowledge the body of youth, with its fresher arteries, more resilient muscles and joints, its exuberant glands and fresh bodily juices,—desire, passion, enthusiasm would return. In the chemistry of life, passion and enthusiasm arise; sickness, fatigue, experience and time are their antagonists.

This is not to deny that these energy manifestations can be aroused from the outside. That is the purpose of teaching and preaching; the purpose of writer and orator. There is a social spread of enthusiasm that is the most marked feature of crowds and assemblies, and this eagerness makes a unit of thousands of diverse personalities. Further, the problem of awakening enthusiasm and desire is the therapeutic problem of the physician and especially in the condition described as anhedonia.

In anhedonia, as first described by Ribot, mentioned by James, and which has recently been worked up by myself as a group of symptoms in mental and nervous disease, as well as in life in general, there is a characteristic lack of enthusiasm in anticipation and realization, a lack of appetite and desire, a lack of satisfaction. Nothing appeals, and the values drop out of existence. The victims of anhedonia at first pass from one "pleasure" to another, hoping each will please and satisfy, but it does not. Food, drink, work, play, sex, music, art,—all have lost their savor. Restless, introspective, with a feeling of unreality gripping at his heart, the patient finds himself confronting a world that has lost meaning because it has lost enthusiasm in desire and satisfaction.

How does this unhappy state arise? In the first place, from the very start of life people differ in the quality of eagerness. There is a wide variability in these qualities. Of two infants one will call lustily for whatever he wants, show great glee in anticipating, great eagerness in seeking, and a high degree of satisfaction when his desire is gratified. And another will be lackadaisical in his appetite, whimsical, "hard to please" and much more difficult to keep pleased. Fatigue will strip the second child of the capacity to eat and sleep, to say nothing of his desires for social pleasures, whereas it will only dampen the zeal and eagerness of the first child. There is a hearty simple type of person who is naively eager and enthusiastic, full of desire, passion and enthusiasm, who finds joy and satisfaction in simple things, whose purposes do not grow stale or monotonous; there is a finicky type, easily displeased and dissatisfied, laying weight on trifles, easily made anhedonic, victims of any reduction in their own energy (which is on the whole low) or of any disagreeable event. True, these sensitive folk are creators of beauty and the esthetic, but also they are the victims of the malady we are here discussing.

Aside from this temperament, training plays its part. I think it a crime against childhood to make its joys complex or sophisticated. Too much adult company and adult amusements are destructive of desire and satisfaction to the child. A boy or girl whose wishes are at once gratified gets none of the pleasure of effort and misses one of the essential lessons of life.—that pleasure and satisfaction must come from the chase and not from the quarry, from the struggle and effort as well as from the goal. Montaigne, that wise skeptic, lays much homely emphasis on this, as indeed all wise men do. But too great a struggle, too desperate an effort, exhausts, and as a runner lies panting and motionless at the tape, so we all have seen men reach a desired place after untold privation and sacrifice and who then found that there seemed to be no energy, no zeal or desire, no satisfaction left for them. The too eager and enthusiastic are exposed, like all the overemotional, to great recessions, great ebbs, in the volume of their feeling and feel for a time the direst pain in all experience, the death in life of anhedonia.

After an illness, particularly influenza, when recovery has seemingly taken place, there develops a lack of energy feeling and the whole syndrome of anhedonia which lasts until the subtle damage done by the disease passes off. Half or more of the "nervousness" in the world is based on actual physical trouble, and the rest relates to temperament.

When a great purpose or desire has been built up, has drained all the enthusiasm of the individual and then suddenly becomes blocked, as in a love affair, or when a business is threatened or crashes or when beauty starts to leave,—then one sees the syndrome of anhedonia in essential purity. A great fear, or an obsessive moral struggle (as when one fights hopelessly against temptation), has the same effect. The enthusiasm of purpose and the eagerness of appetite go at once, in certain delicate people, when pride is seriously injured or when a once established superiority is crumbled. The humiliated man is anhedonic, even if he is a philosopher.

The most striking cases are seen in men who have been swung from humdrum existence to the exciting, disagreeable life of war and then back to their former life. The former task cannot be taken up or is carried on with great effort; the zest of things has disappeared, and what was so longed for while in the service seems flat and stale, especially if it is now realized that there are far more interesting fields of effort. In a lesser degree, the romances that girls feed on unfit them for sober realities, and the expectation of marriage built up by romantic novel and theater do far more harm than good. The triangle play or story is less mischievous than the one which paints married life as an amorous glow.

One could write a volume on eagerness, enthusiasm and passion, satisfaction and dissatisfaction. Life, to be worth the living, must have its enthusiasms, must swing constantly from desire to satisfaction, or else seems void and painful. Great purposes are the surest to maintain enthusiasm, little purposes become flat. He who hitches his wagon to a star must risk indeed, but there is a thrill to his life outweighing the joy of minor success.

To reenthuse the apathetic is an individual problem. When the lowered pressure of the energy feeling is physical in origin, then rest and exercise, massage hydrotherapy, medicines (especially the bitter tonics), change of scene are valuable. And even where the cause is not in illness, these procedures have great value for in stimulating the organism the function of enthusiasm is recharged. But one does not neglect the value of new hopes, new interests, friendship, physical pleasure and above all a new philosophy, a philosophy based on readjustment and the nobility of struggle. Not all people can thus be reached, for in some, perhaps many cases, the loss of these desires is the beginning of mental disease, but patient effort and intelligent sympathetic understanding still work their miracles.

CHAPTER XI

THE EVOLUTION OF CHARACTER WITH ESPECIAL REFERENCE TO THE GROWTH OF PURPOSE AND PERSONALITY

There have been various philosophies dealing with the purposes of man. Man seeks this or that—the eternal good, beauty, happiness, pleasure, survival—but always he is represented as a seeker. A very popular doctrine, Hedonism, now somewhat in disfavor, represents him as seeking pleasurable, affective states. The difficulty of understanding the essential nature of pleasure and pain, the fact that what is pleasure to one man is pain to another, rather discredited this as a psychological explanation. I think we may phrase the situation fairly on an empirical basis when we say that seeking arises in instinct but receives its impulse to continuity by some agreeable affective state of satisfaction. Man steers towards pleasure and satisfaction of some type or other, but the force is the unbalance of an instinct.

When we speak of man as a seeker, we are not separating him from the rest of living things. All life seeks, and the more mobile a living thing is the more it seeks. A sessile mussel chained to a rock seeks little but the fundamentals of nutrition and generation and these in a simple way. An animal that builds habitations for its young, courts its mate, plays, teaches and fights, may do nothing more than seek nutrition and generation, but it seeks these through many intermediary "end" points, through many impulses, and thus it has many types of satisfaction. When a creature develops to the point that it establishes all kinds of rules governing conduct, when it establishes sanctions that are eternal and has purposes that have a terminus in a hereafter which is out of the span of life of the planner, it becomes quite difficult to say just what it is man seeks. In fact, every man seeks many things, many satisfactions, and whatever it may be that Man in the abstract seeks, individual men differ very decidedly not only as to what they seek but as to what should be sought.

Our viscera, our tissues, as they function, change by the using up of energy and the breaking down of materials. That change brings about sensory disturbances in our body which are not unpleasant in moderation, which we call hunger, thirst and fatigue. To relieve these three primitive states we seek food, drink and rest; we DESIRE food, drink and rest. Desire then is primitive, organic, arising mainly in the vegetative nervous system, and it awakens mechanisms that bring us food, drink and rest. A feeling which we call satisfaction results when the changes in the viscera and tissues are readjusted or on the way to readjustment. Here is the simplest paradigm for desire seeking satisfaction, but it is on a plane rarely found in man, because his life is too complicated for such formulae to work.

Food must be bought or produced, and this involves cooperation, competition, self-denial, thrift, science, finance, invention. It involves ethics, because though you are hungry you must not steal food or give improper value for it. Moreover, though you are hungry, you have developed tastes, manners, etc., and you cannot, must not eat this or that (through religion); you mast eat with certain implements), and would rather die than violate the established standards in such matters. [60] Thus to the simple act of eating, to the satisfaction of a primitive desire set up by a primitive need, there are any number of obstacles set up by the complexities of our social existence. The sanction of these obstacles, their power to influence us, rests in other desires and purposes arising out of other "needs" of our nature. What are those needs? They are inherent in what has been called the social instincts, in that side of our nature which makes us yearn for approval and swings us into conformity with a group. The group organizes the activities of its individuals just as an individual organizes his activities. The evolutionists explain this group feeling as part of the equipment necessary for survival. Perhaps this is an adequate account of the situation, but the strength of the social instincts almost lead one to a more mystical explanation, a sort of acceptance of the group as the unit and the individual as an incomplete fragment.

What is true of hunger is true of thirst and fatigue. Desires in these directions have to accommodate themselves, in greater or lesser degrees, to the complexities in which our social nature and customs have involved us. It is true that desires upon which the actual survival of the individual depend will finally break through taboo and restriction if completely balked. That is, very few people will actually starve to death, die of thirst or keep awake indefinitely, despite any convention or taboo. Nevertheless there are people who will resist these fundamental desires, as in the case of MacSwiney, the Irish republican, and as in the case of martyrs recorded in the history of all peoples. It may be that in some of these we are dealing with a powerful inhibition of appetite of the kind seen in anhedonia.

The elaboration of the sex impulses and desires into the purposes of marriage, the repression into lifelong continence and chastity, forms one of the most marvelous of chapters in the psychological history of man. The desire for sex relationship of the crude kind is very variable both in force, time of appearance and reaction to discipline and unquestionably arises from the changes in the sex organs. Both to enhance and repress it are aims of the culture and custom of each group, and the lower groups have given actual sexual intercourse a mystical supernatural value that has at times and in various places raised it into the basis of cults and religions. Repressed, hampered, canalized, forbidden, the sex impulses have

---

[60] The Sepoy Rebellion had its roots in a food taboo, and Mussulman, Hebrew and Roman Catholic place a religious value on diet. Most of the complexities of existence are of our own creation.

profoundly modified clothes, art, religion, morals and philosophy. The sex customs of any nation demonstrate the extreme plasticity of human desires and the various twists, turns and customs that tradition declares holy. There have been whole groups of people that have deemed any sexual pleasure unholy, and the great religions still deem it necessary for their leaders to be continent. And the absurdities of modesty, a modified sex impulse, have made it immoral for a woman to show her leg above the calf while in her street clothes, [61] though she may wear a bathing suit without reproach.

Whatever a desire is basically, it tends quickly to organize itself in character. It gathers to itself emotions, sentiments, intelligence; it plans and it wills, it battles against other desires. I say IT, as if the desire were an entity, a personality, but what I mean is that the somatic and cerebral activities of a desire become so organized as to operate as a unit. A permanent excitability of these nervous centers as a unit is engendered, and these are easily aroused either by a stimulus from the body or from without. Thus the sex impulse arises directly from tensions within the sex organs but is built up and elaborated by approval of and admiration for beauty, strength and intelligence, by the desire for possession and mastery, by competitive feeling, until it may become drawn out into the elaborate purpose of marriage or the family.

What is the ego that desires and plans? I do not know, but if it is in any part a metaphysical entity of permanent nature in so far it does not become the subject matter of this book. For as a metaphysical entity it is uncontrollable, and the object of science is to discover and utilize the controllable elements of the world. I may point out that even those philosophers and theologians to whom the ego is an entity of supernatural origin deny their own standpoint every time they seek to convince, persuade or force the ego of some one to a new belief or new line of action; deny it every time they say, "I am tired and I shall rest; then I shall think better and can plan better." Such a philosopher says in essence, "I have an entity within me totally and incommensurably different from my body," and then he goes on to prove that this entity operates better when the body is rested and fed than otherwise!

For us the ego is a built-up structure and has its evolution from the diffuse state of early infancy to the intense, well-defined state of maturity; it is elaborated by a process that is in part due to the environment, in part to the inherent structure of man. We may postulate a continuous excitement of nerve centers as its basis, and this excitement cognizes other excitement in some mysterious manner, but no more mysterious than life, instinct or intelligence are. These excitements struggle for the possession of an outlet in action, and this is what we call competing desires, struggle against temptation, etc.

Sometimes one desire is identified with the ego as part of itself, sometimes the desire is contrasted with the ego and we say, "I struggled

---

[61] This is, of course, not quite so true in 1921 as in 1910.

with the desire but it overcame me." Common language plainly shows the plurality of the personality, even though the man on the street thinks of himself as a united "I," even an invisible "I."

One of the fundamental desires, nay the fundamental desire, is the expansion of the self, i. e., increased self-esteem. When the infant sprawls in his basket after his arrival in this world, it is doubtful if he has a "me" which he separates from the "non-me." Yet that same infant, a few years later, and through the rest of his life, believes that in his personality resides something immortal, and has as his prime pleasure the feeling of worth and growth of that personality, and as his worst hurt the feeling of decay and inferiority of that personality.

Let us watch that infant as it sprawls in its little bed, the darling of a pair of worshiping parents. In that relationship the child is no solitary individual; society is there already, watching him, nourishing and teaching him. Already he is in the, hands of his group who, though seeking his happiness, are nevertheless determined that he shall obtain it their way. And from then to the end of his life that group will in large measure offer him the criteria of values, and his self-esteem will, in the majority of cases, rest upon his idea of their esteem of him. In the brooding mother, in the tender father lie dormant all the judgments of the time on the conduct and guiding motives of the little one.

The baby throws his arms about, kicks his legs, rolls his eyes. In these movements arising from internal activities which, we can only state, relate to vascular distribution, neuronic relations, visceral and endocrinic activities, is the germ of the impulse to activity which it is the function of society and the individual himself to shape into organized useful work. Thus is manifested a native, inherent, potentiality, which we may call the energy of the baby, the energy of man, a something which the environment shapes, but which is created in the laboratory of the individual. The father and mother are delighted with the fine vigorous movements of the child, and there is in that delight the approval that society always gives or tends to give to manifestations of power. We tend involuntarily to admire strength, even though misdirected. The strong man always has followers though he be a villain, and in fact the history of man is to a large extent based on the fact that the strong man evokes enthusiasm and obedience.

This impulse to activity is an unrest, and its satisfaction lies in movement; in other words there is a pleasure or a relief in mere activity. The need of discharging energy, the desire to do so, the pleasure and satisfaction in so doing constitute a cornerstone of the foundation of life and character. This desire for activity, as we shall call it henceforth, is behind work and play; it fluctuates with health and disease, with youth and old age; it becomes harnessed to purpose, it is called into being by motives or inhibited by conflict and indecision and its organization is the task of society. Men differ in regard to the desire for activity, with a range from the inert whose energy is low to the dynamic types that are ever busy and ever seeking more to do.

The child's first movements are aimless, but soon the impressions it

125

receives by striking hands and feet against soft and hard things bring about a dim knowledge of the boundaries of itself, and the kinesthetic impulses from joints and muscles help this knowledge. The outside world commences to separate itself from the "me," though both are vague and shadowy. Soon it learns that one part of the outside world is able to satisfy its hunger, to supply a need, and it commences to recognize the existence of benevolent outside agencies; and it also learns little by little that its instinctive cries bring these agencies to it. I do not mean that the baby has any internal language corresponding to the idea of outside agency, benevolence, etc., but it gets to know that its cries are potent, that a breast brings relief and satisfaction. At first it cries, the breast comes, there is relief and satisfaction, and it makes no connection or no connection is made between these events of outer and inner origin. But the connection is finally made,—desire becomes definitely articulate in the cry of the baby, which thus becomes a plea and a summons. Anticipation of good to come appears and with it the germ of hope and forward looking, and there is realization or disappointment, joy or anger or sorrow. Thus desire is linked up with satisfaction in a definite way, ideas and feelings of demand and supply begin to appear and perhaps power itself, in the vague notion, "I can get milk," commences to be felt. Social life starts when the child associates the mother with the milk, with the desire and the satisfaction. In the relationship established between mother and baby is the first great social contact; love, friendship, discipline, teaching and belief have their origin when, at the mother's breast, the child separates its mother from the rest of the things of the world. And not only in the relief of hunger is the mother active, but she gets to be associated with the relief from wet and irritating clothes, the pleasant bath, and the pleasure of the change of position that babies cry for. Her bosom and her arms become sources of pleasure, and the race has immortalized them as symbolic of motherhood, in song, in story and in myth.

Not only does he associate the mother with the milk but her very presence brings him comfort, even when he is not hungry. It is within the first few months of life that the child shows that he is a gregarious [62] animal,—gregarious in the sense that he is unhappy away from others. To be alone is thus felt to be essentially an evil, to be with others is in itself a good. This gregarious feeling is the sine qua non of social life: when we punish any one we draw away from him; when we reward we get closer to him. All his life the child is to find pleasure in being with people and unhappiness when away from them, unless he be one of those in whom the gregarious instinct is lacking. For instincts may be absent, just as eye pigment is; there are mental albinos, lacking the color of ordinary human feeling. Or else some experience may make others hateful to him, or he may have so intellectualized his life that this instinct has atrophied. This gregarious feeling will heighten his emotions, he will gather strength from

---

[62] One of my children would stop crying if some one merely entered his room when he was three weeks old. He was, and is, an intensely gregarious boy

the feeling that "others are with him," he will join societies, clubs, organizations in response to the same feeling that makes sheep graze on a hillside in a group, that makes the monkeys in a cage squat together, rubbing sides and elbows. The home in which our child finds himself, though a social institution, is not gregarious; it gives him only a limited contact, and as soon as he is able and self-reliant he seeks out a little herd, and on the streets, in the schoolroom and playground, he really becomes a happy little herd animal.

Let us turn back to the desire for activity. As the power to direct the eyes develops, as hands become a little more sure, because certain pathways in brain and cord "myelinize," [63] become functional, the outside world attracts in a definite manner and movements become organized by desires, by purpose. It's a red-letter day in the calendar of a human being when he first successfully "reaches" something; then and there is the birth of power and of successful effort. All our ideas of cause and effect originate when we cause changes in the world, when we move a thing from thither to yon. No philosopher, though he becomes so intellectualized that he cannot understand how one thing or event causes another, ever escapes from the feeling that HE causes effects. Purpose, resistance, success, failure, cause, effect, these become inextricably wound up with our thoughts and beliefs from the early days when, looking at a dangling string, we reached for it once, twice, a dozen times and brought it in triumph to our mouth. And our idea that there were forbidden things came when the watchful mother took it out of our mouth, saying, "No, no, baby mustn't!"

At any rate, the organization of activity for definite purposes starts. The little investigator is apparently obsessed with the idea that everything it can reach, including its fingers and toes, are good to eat, for everything reached is at once brought to the mouth, the primitive curiosity thus being gustatory. In this research the baby finds that some few things are pleasant, many indifferent and quite a few disgusting and even painful, which may remain as a result not far different from that obtained by investigation in later years. The desire for pleasant things commences to guide its activities. Every new thing is at once an object for investigation, perhaps because its possibilities for pleasure are unknown. That curiosity may have some such origin is at least a plausible statement. At any rate, desire of a definite type steps in to organize the mere desire for activity; and impulse is controlled by purpose.

The child learns to creep, and the delight in progression lies in the fact that far more things are accessible for investigation, for rearrangement, for tasting. It is no accident that we speak of our "tastes" that we say, "I want to taste of experience." That is exactly what the child creeping on the floor seeks,—to taste of experience and to anticipate, to

---

[63] At birth, though most of the great nervous pathways are laid down, they are non-functional largely because the fibers that compose them are unclothed, non-myelinated. The various kinds of tracts have different times for becoming "myelinated" as was the discovery of the great analogist, Flechsig.

realize, to learn. Out of the desire for activity grows a desire for experience born of the pleasure of excitement that we spoke of previously. This desire for experience becomes built up into strange forms under teaching and through the results of experience. It is very strong in some who become explorers, roues, vagabonds, scientists as a result, and it is very weak in others who stay at home and seek only the safe and limited experience. You see two children in one room,—and one sits in the middle of the floor, perhaps playing with a toy or looking around, and the other has investigated the stove and found it hotter than he supposed, has been under the table and bumped his head, has found an unusually sweet white lump which in later life he will call sugar. The good child is often without sufficient curiosity to be bad, whereas the bad child may be an overzealous seeker of experience.

So our child reaching out for things develops ideas of cause, effect and power, commences to have an idea of himself as a cause and likes the feeling of power. As he learns to walk, the world widens, his sense of power grows, and his feeling of personality increases. Meanwhile another side of his nature has been developing and one fully as important.

The persons in his world have become quite individual; mother is now not alone, for father is recognized with pleasure as one who likewise is desirable. He carries one on his shoulder so that a pleasurable excitement results; he plays with one, holds out strings and toys and other instruments for the obtaining of experience. Usually both of these great personages are friendly, their faces wear a smile or a tender look, and our little one is so organized that smiles and tender looks awaken comfortable feelings and he smiles in return. The smile is perhaps the first great message one human being sends to another; it says, "See, I am friendly, I wish you well." Later on in the history of the child, he will learn much about smiles of other kinds, but at this stage they are all pleasant. Though his parents are usually friendly and give, now and then they deprive, and they look different; they say, "No, no!" This "no, no" is social inhibition, it is backed up by the power of deprivation, punishment, disapproval; it has its power in a something in our nature that gives society its power over us. From now there steps in a factor in the development of character of which we have already spoken, a group of desires that have their source in the emotional response of the child to the parent, in the emotional response of an individual to his group. Out of the social pressure arises the desire to please, to win approval, to get justification, and these struggle in the mind of the child with other desires.

We said the child seeks experience,—but not only on his own initiative. The father stands against the wall, perhaps with one foot crossing the other. Soon he feels a pressure and looks down; there is the little one standing in his imitation of the same position. Imitation, in my belief, is secondary to a desire for experience. The child does not imitate everything; he is equipped to notice only simple things, and these he imitates. Why? The desire to experience what others are experiencing is a basic desire; it expresses both a feeling of fellowship and a competitive feeling. We do not feel a strong tendency to imitate those we dislike or despise, or do not respect, we tend to imitate those we love and respect, those for whom we have a fellow feeling. Part of the fellow feeling is an impulse to imitate and to receive in a positive way the suggestion offered by their conduct and manners.

Analogous to imitation, and part of the social instinct, is a credulity, a willingness to accept as if personally experienced things stated. Part of the seeking of experience is the asking of questions, because the mind seeks a cause for every effect, a something to work from. Indeed, one of the main mental activities lies in the explaining of things; an unrest is felt in the presence of the "not understood" which is not stilled until the unknown is referred back to a thing understood or accepted without question. The child finds himself in a world with laid-down beliefs and with explanations of one kind or another for everything. His group differs from other groups in its explanations and beliefs; his family even may be peculiar in these matters. He asks, he is answered and enjoined to believe. Without credulity there could be no organization of society, no rituals, no ceremonials, no religions and customs,—but without the questioning spirit there could be no progress. Most of the men and women of this world have much credulity and only a feeble questioning tendency, but there are a few who from the start subject the answers given them to a rigid scrutiny and who test belief by results. Let any one read the beliefs of savages, let him study the beliefs of the civilized in the spirit in which he would test the statement of the performance of an automobile, and he can but marvel at man's credulity. Belief and the acceptance of authority are the conservative forces of society, and they have their origin in the nursery when the child asks, "Why does the moon get smaller?" and the mother answers, "Because, dear, God cuts a piece off every day to make the stars with." The authorities, recognizing that their power lay in unquestioning belief, have always sanctified it and made the pious, non-skeptical type the ideal and punished the non-believer with death or ostracism. Fortunately for the race, the skeptic, if silenced, modifies the strength of the belief he attacks and in the course of time even they who have defended begin to shift from it and it becomes refuted. Beliefs, as Lecky [64] so well pointed out, are not so often destroyed as become obsolete.

It may seem as if imitation were a separate principle in mental growth, and there have been many to state this. As is well known Tarde made it a leading factor in human development. It seems to me that it is linked up with desire for experience, desire for fellowship, and also with a strongly competitive feeling, which is early manifest in children and which may be called "a want of what the other fellow has." Children at the age of a year and up may be perfectly pleased with what they have until they see another child playing with something,—something perhaps identical with

---

[64] Lecky: "History of European Morals." As he points out, the belief in witchcraft never was disproved, it simply died because science made it impossible to believe that witches could disorganize natural laws.

their own. They then betray a decided, uncontrollable desire for the other child's toy; they are no longer content with their own, and by one means or another they seek to get it,—by forcible means, by wheedling or coaxing, or by tormenting their parents. The disappearance of contentment through the competitive feeling, the competitive nature of desire, the role that envy plays in the happiness and effort of man, is a thesis emphasized by every moralist and philosopher since the beginning of things. In the strivings of every man, though he admit it or not, one of the secret springs of his energy is this law of desire, that a large part of its power and persistence is in the competitive feeling, is in envy and the wish to taste what others are experiencing.

A basic law of desire lies in an observation of Lotze, elaborated by William James. We may talk of selfishness and altruism as if they were entirely separate qualities of human nature. But what seems to be true is that one is an extension of the other, that is, we are always concerned with the ego feeling, but in the one case the ego feeling is narrow and in the other case it includes others as part of the ego. Lotze's observations on clothes shows that we expend ego feeling in all directions, that we tend to be as tall as our top hats and as penetrating as our walking sticks, that the man who has a club in his hand has a tactile sense to the very end of the club. James in his marvelous chapter on the various selves points out that a man's interests and affections are his selves, and that they enclose one another like the petals of a rose. We may speak of unipetalar selves, who include only their own bodies in self-feeling; of bipetalar selves who include in it their families, and from there on we go to selves who include their work, their community, their nation, until we reach those very rare souls whose petals cover all living things. So men extend their self-feeling, if ambitious, to their work, to their achievements,—if paternal to their children; if domestic, to wife and home; if patriotic to the nation, etc. Development lies in the extension of the self-feeling and in the increase of its intensity. But the obstacle lies in the competitive feelings, in that dualism of man's nature that makes him yearn not only for fellowship, but also for superiority. These desires are in eternal opposition, but are not necessarily antagonistic, any more than are the thumb and the little finger as they meet in some task, any more than are excitation and inhibition. Every function in our lives has its check and balance, and fellowship, yearning and superiority urge one another.

From the cradle to the grave, we desire fellowship as an addition to our gregarious feeling. We ask for approval, for we expand under sympathy and contract under cold criticism. Nothing is so pleasant as "appreciation," which means taking us at our own valuation or adding to it,, and there is no complaint so common as, "They don't understand me," which merely means, "They blame me without understanding that I really seek the good, that I am really good, though perhaps I seem not to be." The child who hurts its thumb runs to its mother for sympathy, and the pain is compensated for, at least in part, by that sympathy. Throughout life we desire sympathy for our hurts, except where that sympathy brings with it a feeling of inferiority. To be helped by others in one way or another is the practical result of this aspect of fellowship.

(There is a convincing physical element in the feelings and desires of man, evidenced in language and phrase. Superiority equals aboveness, inferiority equals beneathness; sympathy equals the same feeling. To criticize is to "belittle" and to cause the feeling of littleness; to praise is "to make a man expand," to enlarge him. Blame hurts one's feelings,—"He wounded me," etc.)

At the same time we are strangely affected by the condition of others. Where no competitive-jealousy complex is at work, we laugh with other people in their happiness, we are moved to tears by suffering; we admire vigor, beauty and the fine qualities of others; we accept their purposes and beliefs; we are glad to agree with the stranger or the friend and hate to disagree. We establish within ourselves codes and standards largely because we wish to accept and believe and act in the same way as do those we want as fellows. Having set up that code as conscience or ideals, it helps us to govern our lives, it gives a stability in that we tend at once to resist jealousy, envy, the "wrong" emotions and actions. "Helping others" becomes a great motive in life, responding to misery with tears, consolation and kindness, reacting to the good deeds of others with praise. To be generous and charitable becomes method for the extension of fellowship.

Asking for help in its varied form of praise, appreciation and kindness, giving help as appreciation and kindness, are the weak and strong aspects of the fellowship feelings. It is a cynical view of life, perhaps, but it is probably true that the weak phase is more common and more constant than the second. Almost everybody loves praise and appreciation, for these enlarge the ego feeling, and some, perhaps most, like to be helped, though here, as was above stated, there is a feeling of inferiority aroused which may be painful. Relatively there are few who are ready to praise, especially those with whom they are in close contact and with whom they are in a sort of rivalry. The same is true of genuine appreciation, of real warm fellow feeling; the leader, the hero, the great man receives that but not the fellow next door. As for giving, charity, kindness, these are common enough in a sporadic fashion, but rarely are they sustained and constant, and often they have to depend on the desire "not to be outdone," not to seem inferior,—have, as it were, to be shamed into activity. For there is competition even in fellowship.

There are people, especially among the hysterics, who are deeply wounded when sympathy is not given, when appreciation and praise is withheld or if there is the suggestion of criticism. They are people of a "tender ego," not self-sustaining, demanding the help of others and reacting to the injury sustained, when it is not given, by prolonged emotion. These sensitive folk, who form a most difficult group, do not all react alike, of course. Some respond with anger and ideas of persecution, some with a prolonged humiliation and feeling of inferiority; still others develop symptoms that are meant to appeal to the conscience of the one who has wounded them. On the other hand, there are those whose feeling of self sustains them in the face of most criticism, who depend largely upon the established mentor within themselves and who seek to conform to the rulings of that inward mentor. Such people, if not martyred too soon, and if possessed of a fruitful ideal, lay new criteria for praise and blame.

Contrasting with the desires and purposes of fellowship we find the desires and purposes of superiority and power. Primarily these are based on what McDougall calls the instinct of self-display, which becomes intellectualized and socialized very early in the career of the child. In fact, we might judge a man largely by the way he displays himself, whether by some essentially personal bodily character, some essentially mental attribute or some essentially moral quantity; whether he seeks superiority as a means of getting power or as a means of doing good; whether he seeks it within or without the code. One might go on indefinitely, including such matters as whether he seeks superiority with tact or the reverse and whether he understands the essential shallowness and futility of his pursuit or not. To be superior is back of most of striving, and it is the most camouflaged of all human motives and pleasures. For this is true: that the preaching of humility, of righteous conduct, of service, of self-sacrifice, by religion and ethics have convinced man that these are the qualities one ought to have. So men seek, whenever they can, to dress their other motives and feelings in the garb of altruism.

Camouflage of motive as a means of social approval has thus become a very important part of character; we seek constantly to penetrate the camouflage of our rivals and enemies and bitterly resist any effort to strip away our own, often enough hiding it successfully from ourselves. There are few who face boldly their own egoism, and their sincerity is often admired. Indeed, the frank child is admired because his egoism is refreshing, i. e., he offers no problem to the observer. Out of the uneasiness that we feel in the presence of dissimulation and insincerity has arisen the value we place on sincerity, frankness and honesty. To be accused of insincerity or dishonesty of motive and act is fiercely resented.

The desire for power and superiority will of course take different directions in each person, according to his make-up, teaching and the other circumstances of his life. Property as a means of pleasure, and as a symbol of achievement and of personal worth, is valued highly from the earliest days of the child's life. Very early does the child show that it prizes goods, shows an acquisitive trend that becomes finally glorified into a goal, an ambition. Money and goods become the symbol and actuality of power, triumph, superiority, pleasure, safety, benevolence and a dozen and one other things. Men who seek money and goods may therefore be seeking very different things; one is merely acquisitive, has the miser trend; another loves the game for the game's sake, picks up houses, bonds, money, ships, as a fighter picks up trophies, and they stand to him as symbols of his superiority. Some see in property the fulcrum by which they can apply the power that will shift the lives of other men and make of themselves a sort of God or Fate in the destinies of others. For others, and for all in part, there is in money the safety against emergencies and further a something that purchases pleasure, whether that pleasure be of body, or taste or spirit. Wine and women, pictures and beautiful things, leisure for research and contemplation,—money buys any and all of these, and as the symbol of all kinds of value, as the symbol of all kinds of power, it is sought assiduously by all kinds of men.

There are many who start on their careers with the feeling and belief that money is a minor value, that to be useful and of service is greater than to be rich. But this idealistic ambition in only a few cases stands up against the strain of life. Unless money comes, a man cannot marry, or if he marries, then his wife must do without ease and leisure and pretty things, and he must live in a second-rate way. Sooner or later the idealist feels himself uneasily inferior, and though he may compensate by achievement or by developing a strong trend towards seclusiveness, more often he regrets bitterly his idealism and in his heart envies the rich. For they, ignorant and arrogant, may purchase his services, his brains and self-sacrifice and buy these ingredients of himself with the air of one purchasing a machine. So the idealist finds himself condemned to a meager life, unless his idealism brings him wealth, and he drifts in spirit away from the character of his youth. It is the strain of life, the fear of old age and sickness, the silent pressure of the deprivations of a man's beloved ones, the feeling of helplessness in disaster and the silent envious feeling of inferiority that makes inroads in the ranks of the idealists so that at twenty there are ten idealists to the one found at forty.

I remember well one of my colleagues, working patiently in a laboratory, out of sight of the world and out of the stream of financial reward, enthused by science and service, who threw up his work and went into the practice of medicine. "Why?" I asked him. "Because when one of my brothers took sick and was in dire need, I who loved him could not help. I had no money, and all my monographs put together could not help him buy a meal. There is a cousin of ours, who has grown rich running a cheap moving-picture house, where the taste of the community is debauched every day. He lent my brother two thousand dollars out of his superfluities; it involved no sacrifice to him, for he purchased a third car at the same time—and yet HE is our savior. Love alone is a torture. I am going to get money."

The world is built up on the sacrifices of the idealists, and eternally it crucifies them. Wealth and power are to him who has a marketable commodity, and one cannot complain when true genius becomes rich. But the genius to make money may be and often is—an exploiting type of ability, a selfishly practical industry, which neither invents nor is of great service. The men who now do the basic work in invention and scientific work in laboratories are poorly paid and only now and then honored. Every year in the United States hundreds of them leave their work in research and seek "paying jobs," to the impoverishment of the world, but to their own financial benefit. Countries where the scramble for wealth is not so keen, where the best brains do not find themselves pressed into business, produce far more science, art and literature than we do, with all our wealth. We will continue to be a second-rate nation in these regards, still looking for our great American novel and play, still seeking real singers and artists, until our idealism can withstand the pressure of our practical civilization.

For here is a great division in people. There are those who become enthused by the noble aims of life, by the superiority and service that come in the work of teacher, priest, physician, scientist, philosopher and philanthropist, and those that seek superiority and power in wealth, station and influence. Those who, will fellowship and those who will power is a short way of putting it, the idealists and the practical is another. Fellowship is built up on sympathy, pity, friendliness and the desire to help others; it is essentially democratic, and in it runs the cooperative activities of man. For it is not true that "competition is the life of trade"; cooperation is its life. Men dig ore in mines, others transport their produce, others smelt it and work it into shape, according to the designs and plans of still other men; then it is transported by new groups and marketed by an endless chain of men whose labors dovetail to the end that mankind has a tool, a habitation or an ornament. The past and present cooperate in this labor, as do the remote ends of the earth. Competition is the SPUR of trade; its mighty sinews, its strong heart and stout lungs are cooperative.

Power is aristocratic, and elaborates and calls into play competitive spirit. In all men the desire for power and the desire for fellowship blend and interplay in their ambitions and activities; in some fellowship predominates, in others power. If a man specializes in fellowship aims, without learning the secret of power, he is usually futile and sterile of results; if a man seeks power only and disregards fellowship, is hated and is a tyrant, cruel and without pity. To be an idealist and practical is of course difficult and usually involves a compromise of the ideal. Some degree of compromise is necessary, and the rigid idealist would have a better sanction for his refusal to compromise if he or any one could be sure of the perfection of his ideal.

The practical seek their own welfare or the welfare of others through direct means, through exerting the power and the influence that is money and station. Rarely do they build for a distant future, and their goal is in some easily and popularly understood good. What they say and what they do applies to getting rich or healthy, to being good in a conventional way; success is their goal and that success lies in the tangibles of life. They easily become sordid and mean, since it is not possible always to separate good and evil when one is governed by expediency and limited idea of welfare. This is also true,—that while the practical usually tend to lose idealism entirely, and find themselves the tools of habits and customs they cannot break from, now and then a practical man reaches a high place of power and becomes the idealist.

Though all men seek power and fellowship, we have a right to ask what are a man's leading pursuits. And we must be prepared to tear off a mask before we understand the most of our fellows, for society and all of life is permeated with disguise. Now and then one seeks to appear worse than he is, hates fuss and praise, but this rare bird (to use slang and Latin in one phrase) is the exception that proves the rule that men on the whole try to appear better than they are. Rarely does a man say, "I am after profit and nothing else," although occasionally he does; rarely does the scientist say, "I seek fame and reward," even though his main stimulus may be this desire and not the ideal of adding to the knowledge of the world. Behind the philanthropist may lurk the pleasure in changing the lives of others, behind the reformer the picture of himself in history. The best of men may and do cherish power motives, and we must say that to seek power is ethically good, provided it does not injure fellowship. One must not, however, be misled by words; duty, service, fellowship come as often to the lips of the selfish as the unselfish.

We spoke of power as a form of superiority. Since all superiority is comparative, there are various indirect ways of seeking superiority and avoiding inferiority. One of these is by adverse criticism of our fellows. The widespread love of gossip, the quick and ever-present tendency to disparage others, especially the fortunate and the successful, are manifestations of this type of superiority seeking. Half the humor of the world is the pleasure, produced by a technique, of feeling superior to the boor, the pedant, the fool, the new rich, the pompous, the over-dignified, etc. Half, more than half, of the conversation that goes on in boudoir, dining room, over the drinks and in the smoking room, is criticism, playful and otherwise, of others. There are people in whom the adversely critical spirit is so highly developed that they find it hard to praise any one or to hear any one praised—their criticism leaps to the surface in one way or another, in the sneer, in the "butt," in the joke, in the gibe, in the openly expressed attack. This way of being superior may be direct and open, more often it is disguised. Many a woman (and man) who denounces the sinner receives from her contemplation of that sinner the most of her feeling of virtue and goodness. The more bitterly the self-acknowledged "saint" denounces the sinner, the more, by implication, he praises himself.

People seek the strangest roads to the feeling of superiority. From that classical imbecile who burnt down the Temple of Diana to the crop of young girls who invent tales of white slavery in order to stand in the public eye as conspicuous victims, notoriety has been mistaken for fame by those desperate for public attention. To be superior some way, even if only in crime and foolishness, brings about an immense amount of laughable and deplorable conduct to which only a Juvenal could do justice. The world yields to superiority such immense tribute that to obtain recognition as superior becomes a dominant motive. How that superiority is to be reached presents great difficulties, and the problem is solved according to the character of the individual.

At the same time that we seek superiority we seek to be liked, to be esteemed, to be respected. These are not the same things, but are sufficiently alike in principle to be classed together. With some the desire to be liked becomes a motive that ruins firmness of purpose and success, as in the well-known "good fellow,"—accommodating, obliging and friendly, who sacrifices achievement to this minor form of fellowship. On a larger plane there is the writer or artist who sacrifices his best capacities in order to please the popular fancy, seeks popularity rather than greatness, for it is seldom that the two coincide. Back of many a man's "respectability" is the fear of being disliked or discredited by his group. TO BE RESPECTABLE, TO LIVE SO THAT NEITHER THE NEIGHBORS NOR ONE'S OWN RATHER UNCRITICAL CONSCIENCE CAN CRITICIZE, IS PERHAPS THE MOST COMMON AIM IN LIFE. There are some who are all things to all men, merely out of the desire to be agreeable, who find it easy to agree with any opinion, because they have not the courage to be disliked. Even the greatest men yield to the desire to be admired and liked, though the test of greatness is unpopularity.

For there never can be a real and lasting democ-racy in belief, opinion and ideal. The mass must always lag behind the leaders, since it takes a generation or two for the ideas of the old leaders to permeate any society. Now and then a great leader finds a great following in his own lifetime, but his leadership rarely involves a new principle. There will always be a few ground breakers, behind them a few straggling followers, and far, far behind, the great mass of mankind.

This digression aside, to be popular, agreeable and entertaining are both aims and weapons. Most of us would infinitely rather be liked than disliked, and with some it is a passion and a weakness. But to be popular, to be a good fellow, is an extraordinarily useful trait when combined with firm purposes and good intelligence. The art of life is to please, though its business is achievement and success, and here the art may further the business. Manners, courtesy and certain of the abilities, such as musical talent, story telling and humor are cultivated largely, though not wholly, out of the desire to please.

Manners and courtesy are really standardized methods of behavior, which are to adjust us in a pleasing way to our superiors, equals and inferiors, and to the various conventional situations of life. Naturally these will vary greatly in different ages and different countries. A democracy acknowledging in theory no superiors will insist that every man be called "sir" and every woman "madam," whereas an aristocracy laughs at that. In reality there is no democracy anywhere, and so we address differently the woman of the mansion and the woman of the hovel, The mistress of the house calls her maid by her first name but would wonder what the world is coming to if the maid became as familiar. In a limited sense, manners and courtesy are conventional ways of doing things, as the way of living, the tipping of the hat, the form of greetings, the way of eating, but these conventions have great value to the majority of people as evidencing breeding and training or the lack (superiority or inferiority), and also as removing doubt and choice, so that things run smoothly and without contradiction. In a more noble sense, manners and courtesy prescribe conduct in order to proscribe offense to the self-valuation of others. Convention says, "Address people as if they were your equals at least; don't contradict brusquely because that implies their inferiority or stupidity; avoid too controversial topics since bitterness and humiliation may thus arise; do not notice defects or disabilities for the same reason; do not brag or be too conspicuous, since to boast of superiority is to imply the inferiority of others, and they will dislike you," etc. We tend to dislike and hate those who make us feel inferior, except under those special circumstances where sex-love, awe and admiration enter to make a certain inferiority desirable or befitting. So a large part of manners and courtesy concern themselves with the formulae of conduct which avoid this result to others, and we are also enjoined to conduct ourselves so that others will not regard us as inferior. We speak of a man as a "low person" if he eats with his knife, and very few things so humiliate us as the knowledge that we have behaved in an unmannerly way. One of the great purposes, then, is to be conventional, to behave, dress and "look" according to an accepted standard, one that is laid down for age, sex and social station. There are people to whom convention is truly almost holy, and true to our principle of variability, there are others who hate convention.

Because many writers have shot shafts of satire and ridicule at convention and custom, and because of the enormous reading public, the artificial nature of convention has been emphasized to that large part of the community that desires to be different merely for the sake of being different, and there is built up a conventional unconventionality. It has become the mark of the artist, the great in spirit, to be unconventional (at least in novels), and so there are a hundred "unconventional" poseurs to one genuinely free in spirit. Anything that becomes a dogma or a cult is not unconventional, for it is the standard or the custom of a group. Most Bohemians, so-called, are poseurs and conventionalized to their marrow. And most of the really unconventional are "freaks," "odd sticks" whose grotesque individualities cannot conform. But in the mass of the unconventional one finds here and there, like nuggets of gold in sand, the true reformers of the world.

The "poseurs" in custom have their analogies in the pompous, over-dignified and over-important; the affected, in a word. Affectation is felt to be a disharmony between the pose and the inner values or an attempt to win superiority or "difference" of a superior kind by acting. In either case it excites ridicule, hatred or disgust, and shafts at it form part of the stock in trade of the satirist, humorist and indeed every portrayer of life. What men demand of each other is sincerity, and even where the insincerity is merely a habitual pose it arouses hostile feeling which expresses itself all the way from criticism to the overt act.

Since to feel superior is so highly prized in social relationships of all kinds, part of the technique of those seeking some advantage or other—economic, social, personal—from those who must be influenced is to give them the feeling of superiority. Flattery, cajolement, humble supplication and the finer maneuvers of tact, all have this in mind. These however are palatable to the intelligent only when felt to be sincere and when emanating from some one more or less esteemed, though there are plenty who "fall" for the grossest flattery from almost any one, whose ego feeling is easily inflated with a corresponding shrinking in judgment and common sense. In the relations of men and women, flattery in one shape or another plays an enormous role —from the effect on women of the statement or implication in a subtle or gross way that they are charming, and the effect on men of acknowledged superiority in strength courage or intelligence. Of course, in both cases the effect is partly in the physical attractiveness of the flatterer and tends to become ridiculous when he or she is without charm. The simpering language that is irresistible when uttered by a starry-eyed maid of eighteen loses somewhat in beauty and effect when emanating from the lips of bespectacled forty. The power to use and the power to resist flattery in any of its forms have played almost as great a role in the history of the race as strength, beauty or intelligence.

It would be futile to elaborate in detail the various ways of seeking superiority or resisting inferiority. Two directions of this impulse need some attention, as they lead to personality traits of great importance. "Having one's way" becomes a dominant desire with many people, and much of the clashing that occurs in families, organizations and the council chambers of nations arises from a childish, egoistic seeking of superiority. People enter into the most heated and sterile arguments, often coming to blows, if the course of conduct they desire to have followed is modified or blocked. Even when secretly convinced that they are wrong, husbands and wives will continue to insist on victory, for too often the domestic relationship is a struggle for leadership and dominance rather than a partnership and a conference. Two heads are better than one when the intelligence within the heads is of good grade and when the desire for superiority does not take trivial directions. And the effect of yielding to the whims of children is to develop an irritable, domineering egoism bent on having its own way, resisting reasonable compromise or correction. The greatest benefit of discipline and above all of contact with equals to a child is in the effect on this phase of egoism, i. e., that cooperation means compromise; to be reasonable implies listening with respect to others' plans and to accept better ways of doing things, even if they have originated with others; in other ways the subordinating of trivial egoism. The large families of other days offered the conflict of wills and its consequent lesson within the home; to-day the solitary child, or the one whose brother or sister is three, four or five years younger or older must go into the streets to obtain this discipline or else go without. The indulged have this form of inferior egoism more than do those who have been roughly handled, and so it is more common in women of the better-to-do classes and in men who have always exercised authority. It is of course found in what is known as the stubborn person, —he whose will is law to himself and who seeks to make it law to others. Ordinarily the stubborn person is merely a nuisance, but also, if he couples that stubbornness with intelligence and some especial ability, he may reach great heights, though he is seldom popular.

A sub-form of having one's own way is the adherence to one's own "opinion." The clash of opinions is in its noblest aspect the basis of knowledge; the correction of opinion that results when man meets man is the growth of tolerance and urbanity. Wide reading, travel and experience teach us that our opinions can never be absolutely right, and we grow to look upon them in a detached sort of way. In fact, the prime result of the growth of intelligence and of experience is to make one, as it were, objective toward oneself, to view one's own thoughts, beliefs and emotions with some humor and skepticism. But the uncultured, the narrow, the inexperienced, the young and the strongly egotistic never detach themselves from their opinions, and their opinions are themselves. Attack an opinion, contradict or amend it,—and a sort of fighting spirit is aroused. Argument differs from discussion in that it seeks all means to win— ridicule, sophistry, and personal attack —and it is by far the more common. There was a time when opinion was entirely enslaved, when only the ruler might venture on a new belief or its expression; then there came a time when the right to freedom of opinion and its expression was conceded, and now, with huge forces confronting one another, freedom of opinion [65] is again threatened. But that is an issue larger than our subject.

You may judge a man by his type of argument and his reaction to the opinions of others. One should hold to his own beliefs and opinions, but only if they withstand the assaults of reason. To build ego feeling into opinions is to make ignorance sacred. For most of us there are certain opinions that we will not tolerate, and there are others to which we are indifferent. There are those who feel it incumbent on themselves to contradict any opinion, even if they agree fundamentally with it. The mere fact that some one else gave it utterance arouses a sort of jealousy. Then there are others who will not permit any opinion of their own to be discussed, to whom it is a personal affront to do this. What we call urbanity is tolerance of other opinions; what we call reasonableness is the willingness to change opinions if convinced. What we call vacillation is to have no fixed opinion, to be influenced at once by the opinions of others. The pleasure sought in argument is a victory for our opinions and thus for ourselves.

Here Montaigne's wisdom aptly expresses itself: "We deride ourselves a hundred times when we mock our neighbor." He is stubborn and unreasonable who does not agree with us. "Be reasonable," cry the unreasonable as they argue. "How stubborn and pigheaded you are," say those inaccessible to reason. The difficulty in reaching a true estimate of the world, ourselves and our neighbors lies in the egoism which permeates our beliefs and opinions.

A second direction of the impulse to superiority is personal beauty. Not only does the young girl (or any other, male or female) dress and adorn herself to attract those whose good opinion she seeks, but also she

---

[65] The most profound contribution to the subject of discussion and freedom of opinion in recent years has been written by Walter Lippman in the Atlantic Monthly, September, 1920.

seeks superiority over her competitors. Her own self-valuation increases with the admiration of some and the discomfiture of others. To be beautiful, attractive or pretty becomes thus a goal to many aims of the personality; it offers a route to success in obtaining power, riches, etc.; it yields the longed-for admiration, and it gives the satisfaction of superiority. It rarely has in it any ideal of service or of help, though beauty in the abstract is an ideal of high value. To desire to be beautiful physically as a leading aim usually leads to selfishness and petty vanity. As a subsidiary aim it balances character, but unfortunately, as we have before seen, it is inculcated as a primary aim early in the life of a girl. True, men seek to be beautiful in a masculine way, but the goal of masculine beauty is strength, which is directly serviceable. This is not to say that there are no men who are vain of their good looks, for there are many. But only occasionally does one find a man who organizes his life efforts to be beautiful, who establishes criteria of success or failure on complexion, hair, features of face and lines of figure. So long, therefore, as woman can obtain power through beauty and sex appeal, so long may we expect a trivial trend in her character.

We have lost track of our hypothetical child in the history of his character development, lost sight of him as he struggles in a morass of desires and purposes of power, fellowship and superiority. His situations become still more complex as we watch him seek to unify his life around permanent purposes, against a pestering, surging, recurring, temporary desire. He desires, let us say, to conform to the restriction in sex, but as he approaches adolescence, within and without stimuli of breathless ardor assail him. He must inhibit them if he proposes to be chaste, and his continent road is beset with never-resting temptations. He calls himself a fool at times for resisting, and his mind pictures the delights he misses—if not from direct experience, from information he gathers in books and from those who know—and if he yields, then self-reproach embitters him. But correctly to portray the situation is to drop our hypothetical adolescent, for here is where individual reaction and individual situations are too varied to be met with in one case. Some do not inhibit their sex desires at all; others resist now and then, others yield occasionally; still others remain faithful to the ideal. Some drop the conventional ideal and replace with unconventional substitutes, some resist at great cost to themselves, and others find no difficulty in resisting what is no temptation at all to them. Passion, resistance, opportunity, training and sublimation differ as remarkably as nuns differ from prostitutes.

A similar situation is found in the work purposes. To work steadily, with industry and unflagging effort, at something perhaps not inherently attractive is not merely a measure of energy,—it is a measure of inhibition and will. For there are so many more immediate pleasures to be had, even if offering only variety and relaxation. There is the country, there is the lake for fishing; there is the dance hall where a pretty girl smiles as your arm encircles her waist; there is the ball field where on a fine day you may go and forget duty and strained effort in the swirl of an enthusiasm that emanates from the thousands around you as they applaud the splendid athletes; there is the good fellowship and pleasure that beckon as you bend to a task. To shut these out, to inhibit the temporary "good" for the permanent good, is the measure of character.

These sex and work situations we must take up in detail in separate chapters. What is important is that as life goes on, necessity, the social organization and gradual concentration of energy canalize the purposes, reduce the power of the irrelevant and temporary desires. Habit and custom bring a person into definite relationship with society; the man becomes husband, father, worker in some definite field of industry; ambition becomes narrowed down to the possibilities or is entirely discarded as hopeless. The character becomes a collection of habits, with some controlling purpose and some characteristic relaxations. This at least is true of the majority of men. Here and there are those who have not been able to form a unification even along such simple lines; they are without steady habits, derelicts morally, financially and socially, or if with means independent of personal effort they are wastrels and idlers. And again there are the doers and thinkers of the world, the fortunate, whose lives are associated with successful purposes, whose ambitions grow and grow until they reach the power of which they dreamed. There are the reformers living in a fever heat of purpose, disdaining rest and relaxation, dangerously near fanaticism and not far from mental unbalance, but achieving through that unbalance things the balanced never have the will to attempt. He who works merely to get rich or powerful or to provide food for his family cannot understand the zealots who see the world as a place where SOMETHING MUST happen,—where slavery MUST be abolished, women MUST have votes, children MUST go to school until sixteen, prostitution MUST disappear, alcohol MUST be prohibited, etc. Such people miss the pretty, pleasant relaxing joys of life, but they gain in intensity of life what they lose in diffuseness.

This war of the permanent unified purposes versus the temporary scattering desires—the power of inhibition —is involved in the health and vigor of the person. Disease, fatigue and often enough old age show themselves in lowered purpose, in the failure of the will (in the sense of the energy of purpose), in a scattering of activity. Indeed, in the senile states one too often sees the disappearance of moral control where one least expected it. And one of the greatest tragedies of our times occurred when an elderly statesman, on the brink of arterial disease of the brain, lost the strength and firmness of purpose that hitherto had characterized him. One of the worst features of the government of nations is the predominance of old men in the governing bodies. For not only are they apt to have over-intellectualized life, not only have they become specialists in purpose and therefore narrow, but the atrophy of the passions and desires of youth and middle life has rendered them unfit to legislate for the bulk of the race, who are the young and middle-aged. It is no true democracy where old age governs the rest of the periods of life.

Unification of purpose often goes too far. Men lose sight of the duties they owe to wife and family in their pursuit of wealth or fame; they forget that relaxation and pleasure-seeking are normal and legitimate aims. They deify a purpose; they attach it to themselves so that it becomes more essentially themselves than their religion or their family. They speak of their work as if every letter were capitalized and lose sympathy and interest in the rest of the wide striving world. Men grow hard, even if philanthropists, in too excessive a devotion to a purpose, and soon it is their master, and they are its slaves. Happy is he who can follow his purpose efficiently and earnestly, but who can find interest in many things, pleasure in the wide range of joys the world offers and a youthful curiosity and zest in the new.

Every human being, no matter how civilized and unified, how modern and social in his conduct, has within him a core of uncivilized, disintegrating, ancient and egoistic desires and purposes. "I feel two natures struggling within me" is the epitome of every man's life. This is what has been called conflict by the psychoanalysts, and my own disagreement with them is that I believe it to be distinctly conscious in the main. A man knows that the pretty young girls he meets tempt him from his allegiance to his wife and his desires to be good; a woman knows that the prosaic husband no longer pleases, and why he does not please,—only if you ask either of them bluntly and directly they will deny their difficulties. The organic activities of the body, basic in desire of all kinds, are crude and give rise to crude forbidden wishes, but the struggle that goes on is repressed, rebelled against and gives rise to trains of secondary symptoms,—fatigue, headache, indigestion, weariness of life and many other complaints. It is perfectly proper to complain of headache, but it is a humiliation to say that you have chosen wrongly in marriage, or that you are essentially polygamous, or that an eight-hour day of work at clerking or bookkeeping disgusts and bores you. People complain of that which is proper and allows them to maintain self-respect, but they hide that which may lower them in the eyes of others. Gain their confidence, show that you see deeper than their words and you get revelations that need no psychoanalytic technique to elicit and which are distinctly conscious.

This brings me to the point that the constant inhibition, blocking and balking of desires and wishes, though in part socially necessary and ethically justifiable, is decidedly wearisome, at times to all, and to many at all times. It seems so easy and pleasant to relax in purposes, in morals, in thought, to be a vagrant spirit seeking nothing but the pleasures right at hand; to be like a traditional bee flitting from the rose to rose of desire. (Only the bee is a decidedly purposive creature, out for business not pleasure.) "Why all this striving and self-control?" cries the unorganized in all of us. "Why build up when Death tears down?" cries the pessimist in our hearts. Great epochs in history are marked by different answers to these questions, and in our own civilization there has grown up a belief that bodily pleasure in itself is wrong, that life is vanity unless yoked to service and effort. The Puritan idea that we best serve God in this way has been modified by a more skeptical idea that we serve man by swinging our efforts away from bodily pleasure and toward work, organized to some good end; but essentially the idea of inhibition, control, as the highest virtue, remains. Such an ideal gains force for a time, then grows too wearisome, too extreme, and a generation grows up that throws it off and seeks pleasure frankly; paints, powders, dances, sings, develops the art of "living," indulges the sense; becomes loose in morals, and hyperesthetic and over-refined in tastes. Then the ennui, boredom and disgust that always follow sensual pleasures become diffuse; happiness cannot come through the seeking of pleasure and excitement and anhedonia of the exhausted type arises. Preachers, prophets, seers and poets vigorously proclaim the futility of pleasure, and the happiness of service; inhibition comes into its own again and a Puritan cycle recommences. Stoic, epicurean; Roman republic, Roman empire; Puritan England, Restoration; Victorian days, early twentieth century; for to-day we are surging into an era of revolt against form, custom, tradition; in a word against inhibition.

As with periods, so with people; self-indulgence, i. e., indulgence of the passing desires, follows the idealism of adolescence. Youth sows its wild oats. Then the steadying purposes appear partly because the pleasure of indulgence passes. Marriage, responsibility, straining effort mark the passing of ten or a dozen years; then in middle life, and often before, things get flat and without savor, monotony creeps in and a curiosity as to the possibilities of pleasure formerly experienced is awakened. (I believe that most of the sexual unfaithfulness in men and women over thirty springs not from passion but from curiosity.)

There occurs a dangerous age in the late thirties and early forties, one in which self-indulgence makes itself clamorous. The monotony of labor, the fatigue of inhibition make themselves felt, and at this time men (and women) need to add relaxation and pleasure of a legitimate kind. Golf, the fishing trip, games of all kinds; legitimate excitement which need not be inhibited is necessary. This need of excitement without inhibition is behind most of the gambling and card playing; it explains the extraordinary attraction of the detective story and the thrilling movies; it gives great social value to the prize fight and the ball game where you may see the staid and the sober giving vent to an excitement that, may fatigue them for a time but which clears the way for their next day's inhibitions.

Unfortunately too many mistake excitement for happiness. The forms of relief from inhibition—card playing, sports, the theater, the thrilling story and the movie—grow to be habits and lose their exciting value. They can give no permanent relief from the pain of repression; only a philosophy of life can do that. A philosophy of life! One might write a few volumes on that (and there are so many great philosophers already on the market), and yet such a philosophy would only state that strenuous purpose must alternate with quiet relaxation; excitement is to be sought only at periods and never for any length of time; relief from inhibitions can only be found in legitimate ways or self-reproach enters. Play, sports, short frequent vacations rather than long ones, freedom from ceremony as a rule—but now and then a full indulgence in ceremonials—and a realization that there is no freedom in self-indulgence.

I remember one Puritanically bred young woman who fled from her restrictions and inhibitions and joined a "free love" colony in New York. After two years she left, them and came back to New England. Her statement of the situation she found herself; it summarizes all attempts at "freedom." "It wasn't freedom. You found yourself bound to your desires, a slave to every wish. It grew awfully tiresome and besides, it brought so many complications. Sometimes you loved where you weren't loved—and vice versa. Jealousy was there, oh, so much of it—and pleasure disappeared after a while. It wasn't conscience—I still believe that right and wrong are arbitrary matters —but I found myself envying people who had some guide, some belief, some restrictions in themselves! For it seemed to me they were more free than I."

The fact is, for most men and women inhibition is no artificial phenomenon, despite its burdensomeness. It is not only inevitable, it is desirable. A feeling of power appears when one resists; there is mental gain, character growth as a result. Life must be purposive else it is vain and futile, and the feeling of no achievement and failure is far more disastrous than a thousand inhibitions.

Though man battles and compromises with himself, he also battles and compromises with his fellows and circumstances. That is to say, he must continually adjust himself to the unforeseen, the obstacle, the favoring circumstance; the possible and impossible; the certain and uncertain. Adjustment to reality is what the neurologists call it, but they do not define reality, which indeed cannot be defined. It is not the same thing for any two persons. For some reality is success, for others it is virtue. The scientist smiles at the reality of the love-sick girl, and she would think his reality a bad dream. The artist says, "Beauty is the reality"; the miser says, "Cash"; the sentimentalist answers, "None of this but Love"; and the philosopher, aloof from all these, defines reality as "Truth." And the skeptic asks, "What is Truth?" We gain nothing by saying a man must adjust himself to reality; we say something definite when we say he must adjust his wishes to his abilities, to the opposing wills, wisher, and abilities of others; to the needs of his family and his country; to disease, old age and death; to the flux of the river of life. In the quickness of adjustment we have a great character factor; in the farsightedness of adjustment (foreseeing, planning) we have another. Does a man take his difficulties with courage and good cheer does he make the "best of it" or is he plunged into doubt and indecision by obstacles or complications? Is he calm, cool, collected, well poised, in that he watches and works without too much emotion and maintains self-feeling against adversity? We say a man is self-reliant when he finds in himself resources against obstacles and does not call on his neighbors for help. We would do well to extend the term to the one whose fund of courage, hope, energy and resource springs largely from within himself; who resists the forces that reduce courage, hope and energy. A higher sort of man not only supplies himself with the energetic factors of character, but he inspires, as we say, others; he is a sort of bank of these qualities, with high reserves which he gives to others. Contrast him with those whose cry constantly is "Help, help." Charming they may be as ornaments, but they deplete the treasury of life for their associates and are only of value as they call out the altruism of others.

There is no formula for adjustment. Intelligence, insight into one's powers and capacities, caution, boldness, compromise, firmness, aggressiveness, tact,—these and a dozen other traits and qualities come into play. It is a favorite teaching of optimistic sentimentalists, "Will conquers everything—it is omnipotent." God's will is,—but no one else's. What happens when two will and pray for diametrically opposing results? "Then God is on the side of the heaviest battalions," said Napoleon. Victory comes to the best prepared, the most intelligent, the least hampered and the luckiest. Outside of metaphysics and theology there is no abstract will; it is a part of purpose, intelligence and instinct and shares in their imperfections and limitations. To will the impossible is to taste failure, although it may be difficult to know what is impossible. Fight hard, be brave, keep your powder dry and have good friends is the best counsel for adjustment. But learn resignation and cultivate a sense of humor.

No inspiration in that? Well, I must leave inspiration to others who have an infallible formula. The best I can offer in adjustment is the old prayer, "Lord, make me love the chase and not the quarry! Lord, make me live up to my ideals!"

Out of the welter of conflicts into which the individual is plunged through his own nature and the nature of the life around him, out of the experience of the race and the teaching of its leaders come ideals. Good, Beauty, Justice,—these are good deeds, beautiful things, true and non-contradictory expressions, just acts raised to the divine and absolute, and therefore worshiped. And their opposite, arising from evil deeds, ugly and disgusting things, misleading experiences and suffering, become unified into various forms of Evil. Life becomes divided into two parts, Good and Evil, and personified (by the great majority) into God and the Devil. Man seeks the Good, hates Evil, esteems himself when he conforms to the ideal, loathes himself when he violates it. He cannot judge himself; he wishes to know the judgment of others and accepts or rejects that judgment.

We say man seeks pleasure, satisfaction, the Good. True. But it is important to know that essentially he seeks a higher self-valuation, seeks to establish his own dignity and worth and has his highest satisfaction when that valuation is reached through conformity with absolute standards.

CHAPTER XII
THE METHODS OF PURPOSE—
WORK CHARACTERS

Having asked concerning any person, "What are his purposes?" whether of power or fellowship, whether permanent or transitory, whether adjustable or not, we next ask, "How does he seek their fulfillment?"

"He who wills the end wills the means" is an old saying, but men who will the same end may will different means. There have been those who used assassination to bring about reform, and there are plenty who use philanthropy to hasten their egoistic aims. The nihilist who throws a bomb to bring about an altruistic state is own cousin to the ward heeler who gives coal to his poor constituents so that his grafting rule may continue.

1. There are those who use the direct route of force to reach their goal of desire and purpose. They attempt to make no nice adjustments of their wishes to the wishes of others; the obstacle, whether human or otherwise must get out of their way or be forcibly removed or destroyed. "A straight line is the shortest distance between two points," and there is only one absolute law,—"the good old rule, the simple plan that they may take who have the power and they may keep who can." The individuals who react this way to obstacles are choleric, passionate, egoistic and in the last analysis somewhat brutal. This is especially true if they seek force at first, for with nearly all of us extreme provocation or desperation brings direct-action measures.

Conspicuously those accustomed to arbitrary power use this method. They have grown accustomed to believing that their will or wish is a cause, able to remove obstacles of all kinds. When at all opposed the angry reaction is extreme, and they tend to violence at once. The old-fashioned home was modeled in tyranny, and the force reaction of the father and husband to his children and wife was sanctioned by law and custom. The attitude of the employer to employee, universally in the past and still prominent, was that of the master, able in ancient times to use physical punishment and in our day to cut off a man's livelihood if he showed any rebellion. In a larger social way War is crude brute force, and those who delude themselves that the God of victory is a righteous God have read history with a befoozled mind. Force, though the world rests on it, is a terrible weapon and engenders brutality in him who uses it and rebellion, hate and humiliation in him upon whom it is used. It is an insult to the dignity and worth of the human being. It must be used for disciplining purposes only,—on children, on the criminal, and then more to restrain than to punish. It cannot disappear from the world, but it should be minimized. Only the sentimentalized believe it can disappear entirely, only the brutal rejoice in its use. Force is a crude way of asserting and obtaining superiority; the gentle hate to use it, for it arouses their sympathy for their opponent. Whoever preaches force as the first weapon in any struggle is either deluded as to its value or an enemy of mankind.

As a non-inhibited response, force and brutality appear in the mentally sick. General paresis, cerebral arterio-selerosis, alcoholic psychoses present classical examples of the impatient brutal reaction, often in men hitherto patient and gentle.

2. Strategy or cunning appears as a second great method of obtaining the fulfillment of one's purposes. We all use strategy in the face of superior or equal power, just as we tend to use force confronted by inferiority. There is of course a legitimate use of cunning, but there is also an anti-social trend to it, quite evident in those who by nature or training are schemers. The strategist in love, war or business simulates what he does not feel, is not frank or sincere in his statements and believes firmly that the end justifies the means. He uses the indirect force of the lie, the slander, insinuation —he has no aversion to flattery and bribery—he uses spies and false witnesses. He is a specialist in the unexpected and seeks to lull suspicion and disarms watchfulness, waiting for the moment to strike. Sometimes he weaves so tangled a web that he falls into it himself, and one of the stock situations in humor, the novel and the stage is where the cunning schemer falls into the pit he has dug for others. In his highest aspect he is the diplomat; in his lowest he is the sneak. People who are weak or cowardly tend to the use of these methods, but also there is a group of the strong who hate direct force and rather like the subtler weapons.

The strategist tends to be quite cynical, and his effect on his fellow men is to increase cynicism and pessimism. They who have suffered through the schemer grow to suspect their fellows under any guise. They become suspicious and hard, determined never to trust any one again. Indeed, practical wisdom to a large extent is the wisdom of strategy and is full of mottoes and proverbs inculcating non-generous ideals. When people have been "fooled" or misled, the most valuable of the social cementing qualities, faith in one's fellows, is weakened. Despite the disintegrating effect of unscrupulous shrewdness, it is common enough to hear men say of a successful votary of the art, "Well, I give him credit. He is a very clever fellow, and he has brought home the bacon." Success is so highly prized and admired that the means of obtaining it becomes secondary in the eyes of the majority.

3. The role of speech in the relationships of human beings is of course too great to be over-estimated. Speech becomes the prime weapon in swaying and molding the opinions and acts of others. It is the medium of the threat of force and the stratagem of cunning, but also it enters human life as the medium of persuasion and conviction. The speech ability, the capacity to use words in attaining purpose, shows as striking variations as any other capacity.

Though a function of intelligence, the power to speak (and write) convincingly and easily, is not at all related to other phases of intelligence.

Though it can be cultivated, good verbalism is an innate ability, and a most valuable one. The power to speak clearly so as to express what is on one's own mind is uncommon, as any one can testify who has watched people struggling to express themselves. "You know" is a very frequent phrase in the conversation of the average man, and he means that, "My words are inadequate, but you know what I mean." The delight in the good writer or speaker is that he relieves other people's dissatisfaction in their own inadequate expression by saying what they yearn to say for themselves, thus giving them a vicarious achievement.

But the power of clear expression is not at all the power of persuasion, although it may be a part of it. One may clearly express himself and antagonize others. The persuader seeks to discover the obstacles to agreement with him in the minds of others and to remove or nullify them. He may seek to do this by a clear exposition of his wishes and desires, by showing how these will benefit the others (or at least not harm them), by meeting logically or otherwise the objections and demonstrating their futility. This he will attempt, if he is wise and practical, only in a limited group or among those who are keen-minded and open to reason. Even with them he will have to kindle and maintain their interest, and he must arouse a favorable emotional state.

This latter is the principal goal in persuasion. Every good speaker or writer who seeks to reach the mass of people needs the effect of the great feelings—of patriotism, sympathy and humor—needs flattery, gross or subtle, makes people laugh or smile or feel kindly disposed to him before he attempts to get their cooperation. He must place himself on their level, be regarded as one of them; fellowship and the cooperative tendencies must be awakened before logic will have value.

The persuader cuts his cloth to suit his case. He is a psychologist of the intuitive type. He may thunder and scold if he finds in his audience, whether numbering one or a million, a tendency to yield to authority, and he then poses as that authority, handing out his dicta in an awe-inspiring fashion. He will awaken the latent trend to ridicule and scoffing by pointing out inconsistency in others, or he may awaken admiration for his fairness and justice by lauding his opponent, taking care not to overdo it.

Persuasion is often a part of scheming, rarely is it used by the forceful, except in the authoritative way or to arouse anger against the opponent. It is the weapon of those who believe in democracy, for all exposition has persuasion as its motive. A statement must not only be true to others,—to the mass. Therefore persuasion as applied to the great mass of people is rarely closely knit or a fine exposition of truth and historical evolution; that one must leave for the highbrow book or treatise. It is passionate and pleading; it thunders and storms; it has wit and humor; it deals with symbols and analogies, it plays on the words of truth, justice, ideals, patriotism. It may be honest and truthful, but it cannot be really accurate or of high intellectual value.

And the persuasion that seeks private ends from private audiences "sizes" up its audience as a preliminary. The capacity to understand others and to sway them, to impress them according to their make-up, is a trait of great importance for success or failure. It needs cultivation, but often it depends on a native sociability, a friendliness and genuine interest, on a "good nature" that is what it literally purports to be,—good nature. Though many of the persuasive kind are insincere and selfish, I believe that on the whole the taciturn and gruff are less interested in their fellows than the talkative and cordial.

The persuasive person has a touch of the fighting spirit in the trait called aggressiveness. He is rarely shy or retiring. To do well, he must be prepared for rebuffs, and he is possessed of a species of courage and resistance against refusal and humiliation. In the highest form the persuader is a teacher and propagandist, changing the policy of peoples; in the commonest form he is a salesman, seeking to sell a commodity; in the lowest he is the faker, trying to hoodwink the credulous.

4. The strong, the crafty, the talkers each seek fulfillment of purpose from an equal or higher level than their fellows. But power and fulfillment may be reached at from a lower level, from the beggar's position, from the place of weakness. There are some whose existence depends upon the response given to their supplications, who throw themselves directly on the charity and tender-heartedness of society. Inefficient, incapable of separate existence, this parasitic class is known to every social service group, to every rich or powerful man who helps at least in part to maintain them. I do not mean those who are physically or intellectually unable to cope with the world; these are merely unfortunate. I mean those whose energy and confidence is so low, or whose lack of pride is such that they are willing to ask for help continually rather than make their own way.

There is, however, a very interesting type of person who uses weakness as a weapon to gain a purpose, not support. The tears of many women have long been recognized as potent in that warfare that goes on between the sexes; the melting of opposition to the whim or wish when this manifestation of weakness is used is an old story. The emotional display renders the man uncomfortable, it disturbs him, he fears to increase it lest the opponent become sick, his conscience reproaches him, and he yields rather than "make a fuss." Tears can be replaced by symptoms of a hysteric nature. I do not mean that these symptoms are caused by the effort to win, but they become useful and are made habitual. Nor is this found only in woman; after an accident there are men in plenty whose symptoms play a role in securing compensation for themselves, not necessarily as malingerers. It is in human nature to desire the sympathy of others, and in some cases this sympathy is sought because through sympathy some other good will be forthcoming,—a new dress, a lump sum of money, or merely securing one's own way. Very noticeably do children tend to injure themselves if crossed; anger tends to turn on itself, and the effect on the other party is soon realized, and often utilized. A child may strike its head against the floor without any other motive than that arising from hopeless anger, but if this brings the parents to their knees, [66] the association is made and the experience becomes part of the working technique of the child.

5. There is in man an urge to activity independent of reward save in the satisfaction that comes from that activity. This current is organized into work, and the goal becomes achievement. The most powerful factor in discharging the energies of man is the desire for achievement. Wealth, superiority, power, philanthropy, renown, safety and pleasure enormously reinforce this purpose, but behind the GOOD work of the world is the passion to create, to make something, to mold the resisting forces of nature into usefulness and beauty. Handicraftsman, artist, farmer, miner, housewife, writer,—all labor contradicts the legend that work is a curse. To gain by work, to obtain desires through labor, is a method of attainment that is a natural ideal of man.

This makes opportune a discussion of the work-traits. Since ours is an industrial society, in which the work of a member is his means of obtaining not only respect, but a living, these traits are largely those by which he is judged and by which he judges himself.

Since work for some is their life and for others their means of obtaining a living, it is obvious that the work-traits may be all the traits of the individual, or only a few of them. Certain traits are especially important, and to these we must limit ourselves.

The energy of the individual. Some are so constituted that they can constantly discharge their energy at a high rate. These are the dynamics, the hyperkinetic, the Rooseveltian—strenuous—the busy people, always able to do more. The modern American life holds this type as an ideal, though it is quite questionable whether these rather over-busy people do not lose in reflective and creative ability. The rushing stream turns the wheels of the mills, but it is too strenuous for stately ships. This type however achieves things, is seen often in the fine executive and usually needs no urging.

There is another fine type not so well adapted to our civilization, which is easily exhausted, but can accomplish very much in a short time; in other words discharges energy intermittently at a high rate. Charles Darwin was of this kind—intermittently hyperkinetic —obliged to rest after an hour's labor, but by understanding this, WILLING to rest. Unfortunately, unless one is a genius or rich, industry does not make allowances for this type. Industry is organized on steadiness of energy discharge,—eight hours every day, six days a week.

The commonest type is the "average" person who is capable of moderately intense but constant activity. This is the steady man and woman; it is upon this steadiness that the whole factory—shop system—is based. That this steadiness deadens, injures vivacity and makes for restlessness, is another matter.

---

[66] This turning of anger upon itself is a factor in self-destruction. It is seen, so the naturalists say, in the snake and the asp, and it is common in human relations.

A distinctly pathological type is found in some feebleminded and some high mentalities. This unfortunate discharges energy at a low rate is slow in action and often intermittent as well as hypokinetic. The loafer and the tramp are of this type. Around the water front of the seaports one can find the finest specimens who do odd jobs for as much as will pay for lodging and food and drink. Perhaps the order of the desired rewards should be reversed. Every village furnishes individuals of this group, either unable or unwilling to work consecutively or with energy. Often purposeless day-dreamers or else bereft of normal human mentality, these are the chronically unemployed of our social- industrial system.

It must be remembered that to work steadily every day and in the same place is not an innate circumstance of man's life. For the untold centuries before he developed into an agriculturist and a handicraftsman, he sought his food and his protection in the simplest way and with little steady labor. Whether as hunter or fisher or nomad herdsman, he lived in the open air, slept in caves or in rudely constructed shelters and knew nothing of those purposes that keep men working from morning till night. It's a long way from primitive man and his occupations, with their variety and their relaxations, to the factory hand, shut up in a shop all day and doing just one thing year in and year out, to the housewife with her multitudinous, never-ending tasks within four walls, to the merchant engrossed with profit and loss, weighing, measuring, buying, selling and worrying without cessation. The burden of steadiness in labor is new to the race, and it is only habit, necessity and social valuation that keeps most men to their wheel.

We would, I think, be oversentimental in our treatment of this subject if we omitted two hugely important factors in work character. Two powerful motives operate,—the necessity of working and work as an escape from ourselves.

Not much need be said of the pressure of necessity. "To eat one must work." This sentence condenses the threat behind most of the workers of the world. They cannot stop if they would—for few are those, even in prosperous communities, who have three months of idleness in their savings. The feeling of insecurity this fact brings makes a nightmare out of the lives of the many, for to the poor worker the charity organization is part of the penalty to be paid for sickness or unemployment. To my mind there are few things more pathetic than a good man out of a job, and few things for which our present society can be so heartily damned. Few even of the middle class can rest; their way of living leaves them little reserve, and so they plug along, with necessity as the spur to their industry.

To escape ourselves! Put any person of adult age, or younger, in a room with nothing to do but think, and you reduce him to abject misery and restlessness. Most of our reading, entertainment, has this object, and if necessity did not spur men on to work steadily, the tedium of their own thoughts would. To reflect is pleasant only to a few, and the need of a task is the need of the average human being. Perhaps once upon a time in some idyllic age, some fabled age of innocence, time passed pleasantly without

151

work. To-day, work is the prime way of killing time, adding therefore to its functions of organizing activity, achievement and social value of recreation.

Yet contradictory as it seems, though many of us love work for its own sake, most of us do not love our own work. That is because few of us choose our work; it is thrust upon us. Happy is he who has chosen and chosen wisely!

Industry, energy, steadiness are parts of the work-equipment; enthusiasm, eagerness, the love of work, in short, is another part. Love of work is not a unitary character; it is a resultant of many forces and motives. Springing from the love of activity, it receives its direction from ambition and is reinforced by success and achievement. Few can continue to love a work at which they fail, for self-love is injured and that paralyzes the activity. Here and there is some one who can love his work, even though he is half-starved as a result,—a poet, a novelist, an inventor, a scientist, but these dream and hope for better things. But the bulk of the half-starved labor of the world, half-starved literally as well as symbolically, has no light of hope ahead of it and cannot love the work that does not offer a reward. It is easy for those who reap pleasure and reward from their labors to sing of the joy of work; business man, professional man, artist, handicraftsman, farmer,—these may find in the thing they do the satisfaction of the creative desires and the reward of seeing their product; but the factory is a Frankenstein delivering huge masses of products but eating up the producers. The more specialized it becomes the less each man creates of the unit, machine or ornament; the less he feels of achievement. Go into a cotton mill and watch the machines and their less than human attendants at their over-specialized tasks. Then ask how such workers can take any joy in work? Let us say they are paid barely enough to live upon. What food does the desire for achievement receive? What feeds the love of the concrete finished product of which a man can proudly say, "I did it!" The restlessness of this thwarted desire is back of much of that social restlessness that puzzles, annoys and angers the better-to-do of the world. As the factory system develops, as "efficiency" removes more and more of the interest in the task, social unrest will correspondingly increase. One of the great problems of society is this:

How are we to maintain or increase production and still maintain the love of work? To solve this problem will take more than the efficiency expert who works in the interest of production alone; it will take the type of expert who seeks to increase human happiness.

Native industry, the love of work are variables of importance. No matter what social condition we evolve, there will be some who will be "slackers," who will regard work as secondary to pleasure, who will take no joy or pride in the finished product, who will feel no loyalty to their organization; and vice versa, there will be those working under the most adverse conditions who will identify themselves, their wishes and purposes with "the job" and the product. Nowhere are the qualities of persistent effort and interest of such importance as in industry, and nowhere so well rewarded.

In the habits of efficiency we have a group of mechanically performed actions and stereotyped reactions essential for work. Except in certain high kinds of work, which depend upon originality and initiative, method, neatness and exactness are essential. "Time is money" in most of the business of the world; in fact time is the great value, since in it life operates. The unmethodical and untidy waste time as well as offend the esthetic tastes, as well as directly lose material and information. The habits in this sense are the tools of industry, though exactness may be defined as more than a tool, since it is also part of the final result. He whose work-conscience permits him to be inexact, permits himself to do less than his best and in that respect cheats and steals.

The work-conscience is as variably developed as any other type of conscience. There are those who are rogues in all else but not in their work. They will not turn out a bad piece of work for they have identified the best in them with their work. Contrariwise, there are others who are punctilious in all other phases of morality who are slackers of an easy standard in their work efforts. This is as truly a double standard of morals as anything in the sex sphere,—and as disastrous.

There is on every second wall in America the motto typical of our country, "Do it now!" To it could be added a much better one, "Do it well!" The energy of work and its promptness are only valuable when controlled by an ideal of service and thoroughness. A great part of the morals of the world is neglected; part of the responsibility is not felt, in that a code of work is yet to be enunciated in an authoritative way. I would have it shown graphically that all inefficiency is a social damage with a boomerang effect on the inefficient and careless, and in the earliest school, teaching the need of thoroughness would be emphasized. Our schools are tending in the other direction; the curriculum has become so extensive that superficiality is encouraged, the thorough are penalized, and "to get away with it" is the motto of most children as a result.

In an ideal community every man and woman will be evaluated as to intelligence and skill, and a place found accordingly. Since we live a few centuries too soon to see that community, since jobs are given out on a sort of catch-as-catch-can plan, it would be merely a counsel of perfection to urge some such method.

Nevertheless ambitious parents, whose means or whose self-sacrifice enable them to plan careers for their children, should take into solemn account, not their own ambitions, but the ability of the child. A man is apt to see in his son his second self and to plan for him as for a self that was somehow to succeed where he failed. But every tub in the ocean of human life must navigate on its own bottom, and a father's wishes will not make a poet into a banker or a fool into a philosopher. Nothing is so disastrous to character as to be misplaced in work, and there is as much social inefficiency in the high-grade man in the low-grade place as when the low-grade man occupies a high-grade place. We have no means of discovering originality, imagination or special ability in our present-day psychological tests, and we cannot measure intensity of purpose, courage and the quality of interest. Yet watching a child through its childhood and its adolescence ought to tell us whether it is brilliant or stupid, whether it is hand-minded or word-minded, whether it is brave, loyal, honest, a leader or a follower, etc. Moreover, the child's inclinations should play a part in the plans made. A man who develops a strong will where his desires lead the way will hang back and be a slacker where dissatisfaction is aroused.

To that employer of labor who seeks more than dividends from his "hands," who has in mind that he is merely an agent of the community, and is not obsessed with the idea that he is "boss," I make bold to make the following suggestions:

Any plan of efficiency must be based on sympathy and human feeling. To avoid unnecessary fatigue is imperative, not only because it increases production, but because it increases happiness. Fatigue may have its origin in little matters,—in a bad bench, in a poor work table, or an inferior tool. Chronic fatigue [67] alters character; the drudge and slave are not really human, and if your workers become drudges, to that degree have you lapsed from your stewardship. Men react to fatigue in different ways: one is merely tired, weak and sleepy —a "dope," to use ordinary characterization—but another becomes a dangerous rebel, ready to take fire at any time.

More important than physical fatigue (or at least as important) is the fatigue of monotony. If your shop is organized on a highly mechanical basis, then the worker must be allowed to interrupt his labors now and then, must have time for a chat, or to change his position or even to lie down or walk. Monotony disintegrates mind and body—disintegrates character and personality—brings about a fierce desire for excitement; and the well-known fact that factory towns are very immoral is no accident, but the direct result of monotony and opportunity. It's bad enough that men and women have to become parts of the machine and thus lowered in dignity, worth and achievement; it is adding cruelty to this to whitewash windows, prohibit any conversation and count every movement. Before you may expect loyalty you must deserve it, and the record of the owners of industry warrants no great loyalty on the part of their employees. Annoying restrictions are more than injuries; they are insults to the self-feeling of the worker and are never forgotten or forgiven.

That a nation is built on the work of its people—their steadiness, energy, originality and intelligence, is trite. That anything is really gained by huge imports and exports when people live in slums and have their creative work impulses thwarted is not my idea of value. Factories are necessary to a large production and a large population, but the idea of quantity seems somehow to have exercised a baleful magic on the minds of men. England became "great" through its mills, and its working people were starved and stunted, body and soul. Of what avail are our Lawrences

---

[67] The Gilbreths have written an excellent little book on this subject. Doctor Charles E. Myers' recent publication, "Mind and Work," is less explicit, but worth reading.

and Haverhills when we learn that in the draft examinations the mill towns showed far more physical defects, tuberculosis and poor nutrition than the non-factory towns?

Work is the joy of life, because through it we fulfill purposes of achievement and usefulness. Society must have an organization to fit the man to his task and his task to the man; it must organize its rewards on an ethical basis and must find the way to eliminate unnecessary fatigue and monotony. The machine which increases production decreases the joy of work; we cannot help that, therefore society must at least add other rewards to the labor that is robbed of its finest recompense.

A counsel of perfection! The sad part is that books galore are written about the ways of changing, but meanwhile the law of competition and "progress" adds machines to the world, still further enslaving men and women. We cannot do without machines,—nor can we do without free men and women. The fact is that competition is a spur to production and to industrial malpractice, since the generous employer must adopt the tactics of his competitors whether in a Southern mill town or in Japan.

I must confess to a feeling of disgust when I read preachments on the joys of work, on consecrating one's self to one's task. I can do that, because I do about what I please and when I please, and so do you, Mister Preacher, and so do the exceptional and the able and the fortunate here and there and everywhere. But this is mathematically and socially impossible for the great majority, and unless a plan of life fits that majority it is best to call the plan what it is,—an aristocratic creed, meant for the more able and the more fortunate.

CHAPTER XIII
THE QUALITIES OF THE LEADER
AND THE FOLLOWER

The social group, in its descent from the herd, has become an intensely competitive, highly cooperative organization. There are two sets of qualities essential to those phases of society that concern us as students of character.

Out of the mass there come the leaders, those who direct and organize the thought and action of the group. The leader, in no matter what sphere he operates, excels in some quality: strength, courage, audacity, wisdom, organizing ability, eloquence,—or in pretension to that quality. The leader is a high variable and somehow is endowed with more of a desired or desirable character than others. As fighter, thinker or preacher he has made the history of man. A dozen million common men did not invent the wheel; it was one aboriginal genius who played with power and saw that the rolling log might transport his goods. The shadow may have interested in a mild way every contemporary and ancestor of the one who discovered that it moved regularly with the sun. And when a group is confronted by an unknown danger, it is not the half-courage of the crowd that adds up to bravery and fearless fighting spirit; it is the one man who responds to the challenge with courage and sagacity who inspires the rest with a similar feeling. The leaders of the world stand on each other's shoulders, and not on the shoulders of the common man. Democracy does not lie in an equal estimate of men's abilities and worth; it is in the recognition that the true aristocrat or leader may arise anywhere; that he must be allowed to develop, no matter who his ancestors and what his sex or color may be; and that he has no privileges but those of service and leadership.

The leadership qualities will always be determined by the character of the group that is to be led and the task to be performed. Obviously he who is to lead a warrior group of small numbers in a fray needs be agile, quick of mind, strong and fearless, whereas a general who sits in a chair at a desk ten miles from the fighting front and controls a million men fighting with airships, guns and bayonets must be a technical engineer of executive ability and experience. The leader whose task is to exhort a group into some plan of action—the politician, the popular speaker—needs mainly to appeal to the sympathies and stir the emotions of his group; his desire to please must be efficiently yoked with qualities that please his group, and those qualities will not be the same for a group of East Side immigrants as for a select Fifth Avenue assemblage. In the one instance an uncouth, unrestrained passion, fiercely emphasized, and a bold declaration of ideals of an altruistic type will be necessary; in the second all that will be ridiculous, but passion hinted at with suave polished speech and a careful outline of practical plans are essential. The labor leader, the leader of a capitalist group, will be different in many qualities, but they will be alike in their vigor and energy of purpose, in their aggressive fighting spirit, their proneness to anger at opposition but controlled when necessary by tact and diplomacy. They will impress the group they lead as being sincere, honest, able, knowing how to plan, choose and fight. These last three qualities are those which the members of the group demand; the leader must know how to plan, choose and fight for them. Nor, if he is to succeed easily, must he be too idealistic; he must not seek too distant purposes; the group must understand him, and though he must keep them in some awe and fear of him, yet must they feel that he represents an understandable ideal. The leader who preaches things out of comprehension arouses the kind of opposition which finally crucifies him.

The leader must feel superiority to his group, and whether he proclaims it or not, he usually does. Now and then he is a cold, careful planner, an actor of emotions he does not feel, a cynic playing on passions and ideals he does not share. Usually he is deeply emotional, sometimes deeply intellectual, but not often; generally he has his ears to the ground and listens for the stir that tells the way men wish to be led. Then he mounts his horse, literally or figuratively, brandishes his sword and shouts his commands.

A leader springs up in every group, under almost all kinds of circumstances. Let ten men start out for a walk, and in ten minutes one of them, for some reason or another, is giving the orders, is choosing and commanding. Often enough the leadership falls to social rank and standing rather than to leadership qualities. In fact, that is the chief defect in a society which builds up rank and social station; leadership falls then to men by virtue of birth, financial status or some non-relevant distinction. All one has to do is to read of the misfit leaders England's "best" turned out to be in the early part of the late war to realize how inefficient and untrustworthy such leadership may be. One meaning of democracy is that no man is a leader by virtue of anything but his virtues, and that opportunity must be given to the real leader to come into his own.

Leadership means neither selfishness nor altruism, nor does it connote wisdom. A leader may be rankly egoistic and careless of the welfare of his people—Alexander, Napoleon—or he may be imbued with a mission which is altruistic but unwise. Such, in my opinion, was Peter the Hermit who started the Crusades. The wise men of the world lead only indirectly,—by a permeation of their thoughts, slowly, into the thought of the leaders of the race and from them downwards. Adam Smith exerted a great influence. But how many read his books? The leaders of thought did, and they extended his teachings into the community, but certainly not as Adam Smith taught. Christ made an upheaval in Jerusalem and its vicinity; a few leaders taught revisions of His doctrines, and as the doctrines passed along, they became institutionalized and dogmatized into a total, made up as much of paganism as of Christ's teachings. It is the tragedy of those whose names exercise authority in the world that their teachings are often without great influence. For all of Christ's teachings, the Christian nations plunge into great wars and repudiate His doctrines as applicable neither to industry nor international relations.

If the leader needs certain qualities, the follower needs others. He must be capable of attachment to the leader or his institution; he must possess that quality called loyalty. Loyalty is the transference of the ego-feeling to the group, an institution or an individual. It has in it perhaps the self-abasement principle of McDougall, but perhaps it is just as well to say that admiration, respect and confidence are basic in it. Loyalty differs from love only in that there is a sort of inferiority denoted in the first. If you feel yourself superior to the person or institution claiming your loyalty, you are not loyal in feeling, though you may be in act; you are bound by honor or love and not by loyalty.

Loyalty in the inferior may be awakened by many things, but to be permanent the follower must sooner or later feel himself a part of the program. He must have not only duties and responsibilities but benefits, and he must be given a visible symbol of membership. A child becomes loyal when he is given a badge or title, and so do men. This is the meaning of uniforms, badges, titles and privileges; they are symbols of "belonging" and so become symbols of loyalty. From the higher intellects loyalty can only be won if they have a share in conference, in the exertion of power and in identification with the institution in a privileged way. Though cash and direct benefit do not insure loyalty, they go a long way toward getting it. Many a man who is a rebel as a workman is loyal as a foreman, and while here and there is one who is loyal and leal{sic} whether the wind blows good or ill, the history and proverbs of men tell very plainly that loyalty usually disappears with the downfall of the leader, or when benefits of one kind or another are too long delayed. A man may be loyal to the leader or institution powerful and splendid in his youth (usually pride is as much involved as loyalty), but his children never are.

Disciplinability is a quality of the follower. He must be willing to sacrifice his freedom of action and choice and turn it over to another. Rules and regulations are necessary for efficiency. In a larger sense, they become laws, and the law-abiding are the disciplined, ready to obey whatever law. Thus the reformers do not come from the law-abiding in spirit; it is the rebel who changes laws. Without the law-abiding, disciplined spirit there would be only anarchy, and though men have obeyed frightful laws and still do, this is better than no social discipline. A revolution occurs when the discipline, i.e., the rules and regulations and the rulers and regulators, have not kept pace with the new ideas that have permeated society. Men are willing to be governed; nay, they demand it, but there must be at least a rude conformity between the governed and the laws by which they are governed. In other words, discipline of any kind is welcome if the disciplined believe it to be right and just. Men accept punishment for infraction of a law if they believe themselves to be rightfully punished, but rebel against unjust discipline.

There are those who deny either openly or covertly the right of society to regulate their lives or desires. In modern literature this type of rebel is quite favor, ably depicted, although he is usually represented as finally punished in one way or another. Where a man rebels against a specific type of restriction but favors another kind he is a reformer; if however he favors merely the removal of restriction and regulation [68] he is an anarchist and, in my opinion, without real knowledge of life. While the rebel who denies the right of discipline exists, he is rare; the commonest rebel does not deny society's right to regulate but either will not or cannot keep his rebel desires in conformity. Most criminals are of this type, and the inability to conform may arise from many defects in training or original character.

In fact, though we may rebel against discipline and its various social modifications, most of us are quite anxious that others shall be disciplined and raise the hue and cry at once when they rebel. Behind this dislike of the rebel is certainly the feeling that he predicates a superiority for himself by so doing, and this injures our self-esteem. Of course there is and may be a genuine belief that he menaces society and its stability, but those who raise this cry the loudest are usually themselves menaced either in authority and power or in some more direct cashable value.

The qualities which are now to be briefly discussed are in the main great inhibitions. The moral code is in great part and by the majority of men understood as inhibition and prohibition. A man is held to be honest if he does not steal and truthful if he does not lie. In reality this conception is largely correct, and it is as we extend our ideas of stealing and lying that we grow in morality.

Honesty, in relation to property, is the control of the acquisitive impulses and instincts and is wrapped up with the idea of private property. The acquisitive impulses are very strong in most people but not necessarily in all, and we find great variability here as elsewhere in human character. One child desires everything he sees, wants it for his own and does not wish others even to touch it, while another gives away everything he has. The covetous, the indifferent, the generous, the hoarders, the spenders,— these are a few of the types one finds every day in relation to the property and acquisitive feelings.

The spirit of "mine" needs on the whole little encouragement, though the ways to achieve "mine" are part of education. Mainly the spirit of "thine" needs encouragement, and most of our law, as differentiated from religion and ethics, has been built up on settling disputes in this

---

[68] Watch a busy crossing when the traffic policeman is at work, regulating and disciplining. Everything is orderly, smooth-working, and no one complains. Let him step away for a moment; at once there is confusion, danger and the intensely competitive spirit of the drivers comes out, with the skillful and reckless and selfish invading the rights of the less skilled, timid and considerate. The policeman's return is welcomed by the bulk of the drivers. There are very many points of similarity between society and the busy crossing which need no elaboration on my part.

matter. In its primary form, honesty in relation to property is the willingness to conform to society's rulings in this matter, e.g., the belief in ownership as sacred and that to acquire something desired one must (ethical must) go through certain recognized procedures. The whole conception rests on the social instinct's inhibitions of the acquisitive instinct and in the growth and strength of feelings of conscience and duty as previously described. Social heredity and tradition operate very powerfully in the matter of this kind of honesty; to steal, as we see it, from neighboring tribes is ethical for savage races, and even to steal such property as women. Throughout the ages the booty of war was one of the recognized rights of warriors, and even though to-day we have conventions protecting the private property of the enemy, this is one of those rules definitely understood as made to be broken.

Stealing is very common among children, who find their desire for good things too strong to be inhibited. But very quickly the average child learns control in so far as certain types of stealing are concerned. Some, however, never cease to steal, and in my opinion and experience this is true of those who become thieves later on. In very few cases do those who are eventually pickpockets and second-story men first develop their art in adolescence or youth; they have stolen from earliest childhood. Those who steal for the first time in adult life are usually those exposed to great temptations and occupying a position of trust, such as the bank officer or the trusted employee. Here the stress of overexpensive tastes, of some financial burden or the desire to get rich quick through speculation overcome inhibition, especially as it is too often assumed by the speculator that he will be able to return the money.

How widespread petty stealing is will be attested to by the hotel keeper and high-grade restaurant owner, whose yearly losses of linen, silver and bric-a-brac are enormous. The "best" people do not think it really wrong to do this, especially if the things taken have a souvenir value. Farmers whose fruit trees adjoin a public thoroughfare will also state that the average automobilist has quite a different code of morals for apples and pears than for money and gasoline.

"Caveat emptor"—let the buyer beware! This has been the motto of the seller of merchandise since the beginning of trade. It has made for a lot of cheating of various kinds, some of which has persisted as part of the practice of at least many merchants up to this day. Cheating in weight or quantity led to laws; and there cannot be any relaxation in these laws, or false scales and measures immediately appear. Cheating in quality led to adulterations in food stuffs which were veritably poisonous, so that it became necessary for each great nation to pass stringent laws to prevent very respectable and very rich men from poisoning their customers. Cheating in fabrics still flourishes and in unsuspected quarters, not always those of the small dealer. And, misrepresentation flourished in advertising openly and blatantly until very recently. It is true that advertising has changed its tastes and uses dignified and high-flown language, protesting the abnormally virtuous ideal of service of the article advertised; but can it be true that the makers of every car believe it to be so remarkable in performance and appearance?

To the credit of American merchants let it be stated that a widespread improvement has taken place in these matters, and that on the whole there never was a more unanimous determination to render service as at present. Yet while the goal of business is profit, and the goal of the buyer is the bargain, so long will there be a mutual over-reaching that does not fall far short of dishonesty.

There are types that are scrupulously honest in that they will not take a penny of value not obtained in the orthodox way of buying, trading or earning, who will take advantage of necessity, whose moral code does not include that fine sense of honor that spurns taking advantage of adversity. These are the real profiteers, and in the last analysis they add to their dishonesty an essential cruelty, though often they are pillars of the church.

I have dwelt on the dishonest; the types of honest men and women who give full value in work and goods to all whom they deal with are of course more numerous. The industrial world revolves around those who resist temptation, who work faithfully, who give honest measure and seek no unfair advantage. But that business is no brotherhood is an old story, and poor human nature finds itself forced by necessity and competition into ways that are devious and not strictly honest. It's the system that is at fault, for men have formed a scheme of creating and distributing values that severely tries and often weakens their ideals.

Truth in the sense of saying what is true and truth in the sense of getting at ultimate relations are two different matters. The first kind of truth is the basis of social intercourse, the second kind the goal of philosophic efforts.

Speaking the truth invariably is not an easy matter and in the strictest sense is quite questionable as to value. The white lie, so-called, the pleasant, assumed interest, the untruth intended to smooth social relations are shock absorbers and are part of the courtesy technique.

In a more technical sense, the untruth told to obtain some advantage or to escape the disagreeable in one form or another is held to be dishonorable, but is very widely practiced. People are enraged at being deceived if the deception is the work of an outsider or one not liked; they are shocked if deceived, lied to, by one they love. The lie stands as the symbol of weakness, but to be "taken in" has more than the material hurt the lie inflicts; it wounds vanity and brings doubt and suspicion into social relations, all of which are very disagreeable. It is held by ethical teachers to be worse to lie about faults than to have committed the faults, though this may be modified to mean only the minor faults.

All judges and lawyers will testify that "the truth, the whole truth and nothing but the truth" is very seldom told in court. Controversy is the enemy of truth, and when the fighting spirit is aroused, candor disappears. Where any great interest is involved, where the opponent is seeking to dispossess or to evade payment, or where legal punishment may be felt, the truth must be forced from most people. Moreover, passion blinds, and the natural and astonishing inaccuracy in observation and reporting [69] that every psychologist knows is multiplied wherever great emotions are at work. If perjury were really punished, the business of the courts would be remarkably increased.

All this is normal lying,—not habitual but occurring under certain circumstances. As clearly motivated is the lying of the braggart, the one who invents stories that emphasize his exceptional qualities. The braggart however is a mere novice as compared with the "pathological liar," who does not seem able to tell the truth, who invents continually and who will often deceive a whole group before he is found out. The motive here is that curious type of superiority seeking which is the desire to be piteously interesting, to hold the center of the stage by virtue of adverse adventures or misfortunes. Hence the wild white-slave yarns and the "orphan child" who has been abused. Every police department knows these girls and boys, as does every social service agency.

I am afraid we all yield to the desire to be interesting or to make artistic our adventures. To tell of what happens to us, of what we have seen or said or done exactly as it was, is difficult, not only because of faulty memory, but because we like to make the tale more like a story, because, let us say, of the artist in us. Life is so incomplete and unfinished! We so rarely retort as we should have! And a bald recital of most events is not interesting and so,—the proportions are altered, humor is introduced, the conversation becomes more witty, especially our share, and the adventure is made a little more thrilling. And each who tells of it adds little or much, and in the end what is told never happened. "The Devil is the father of lies," runs the old proverb. If so, we have all given birth to some of his children.

Though direct lying is held to be harmful and socially disastrous, and evidence of either fear and cowardice or malevolence, the essential honesty of people is usually summed up in the term sincerity. The advance of civilization is marked by the appearance of toleration, the recognition that belief is a private right, especially as concerns religion, and that sincerity in belief is more important than the nature of belief. What is really implied by sincerity is the absence of camouflage or disguise, so that it becomes possible to know what a man believes and thinks by his words and his acts. As a matter of fact, that ideal is neither realized nor desirable, and it is as wise and natural to inhibit the expression of our beliefs and feelings as it is to inhibit our actions. To be frank with a man, to tell him sincerely that we believe he is a scoundrel, and that we hate him and to show this feeling by act, would be to plunge the world into barbarism. We must disguise hate, and there are times when we must disguise love. Sincerity is at the best only relative; we ought to be sincere about love,

---

[69] Not only is this true in law but in all controversy, whether theological, scientific, social or personal, the ego-feeling enters in its narrowest and blindest aspects to defeat honor, justice and truth.

religion and the validity of our purposes, but in the little relationships sincerity must be replaced by caution, courtesy and the needs of efficiency. In reality we ask for sincerity only in what is pleasant to us; the sincere whose frankness and honesty offend we call boors.

Sincere self-revelation, if well done, is one of the most esteemed forms of literary production. Montaigne's preface to his "Essays" is a promise that he lived up to in the sincerity and frankness of his self and other analysis. "Pepy's Diary" charms because the naked soul of an Englishman of the seventeenth century is laid before us, with its trivialities, lusts, repentance and aspirations. In the latter nineteenth century, Mary MacLane's diary had an extraordinary vogue because of the apparent sincerity of the eager original nature there revealed. We love young children because their selfishness, their curiosity, their "real" nature, is shown to us in their every word and act. In their presence we are relaxed, off our guard and not forced to that eternal hiding and studying that the society of our equals imposes on us.

We all long for sincerity, but the too sincere are treated much as the skeptic of Bjoriasen's tale, who was killed by his friends. As they stood around his body, one said to the other, "There lies one who kicked us around like a football." The dead man spoke, "Ah, yes, but I always kicked you to the goal." The sincere of purpose must always keep his sincerity from wounding too deeply; he must always be careful and include his own foibles and failings in his attack, and he must make his efforts witty, so that he may have the help of laughter. But here the danger is that he will be listed as a pleasant comedian, and his serious purpose will be balked by his reputation.

Sincerity, thus, is relative, and the insincere are those whose purposes, declared by themselves to be altruistic, are none the less egoistic, whose attachments and affections, loudly protested, are not lasting and never intense, and whose manners do not reflect what they themselves are but what they think will be pleasing and acceptable to others. The relatively sincere seek to make their outer behavior conform, within the possibilities, to their inner natures; they are polite but not gushing, devoted to their friends at heart and in deed, but not too friendly to their enemies or to those they dislike, and they believe in their own purposes as good. The unhappiest state possible is when one starts to question the sincerity and validity of one's own purposes, from which there results an agonizing paralysis of purpose. The sincere inspire with faith and cooperation, if there is a unity of interest, but it must not be forgotten that others are inspired to hatred and rivalry, if the sincerity is along antagonistic lines. We are apt to forget that sincerity, like love, faith and hope, is a beautiful word, but the quality of sincerity, like the other qualities, may be linked with misguided purpose. No one doubts the sincerity of the Moslem hordes of the eighth century in desiring to redeem the world for Mahomet, but we are quite as sincerely glad that sturdy Charles Martel smashed them back from Europe. Their very sincerity made them the more dangerous. In estimating any one's sincerity, it is indispensable to inquire with what other qualities is this sincerity linked,—to what nouns of activity is it a qualifying adjective?

Honesty, truthfulness and sincerity are esteemed because there is in our social structure the great need that men shall trust one another. The cynic and the worldly wise, and also the experiences of life, teach "never trust, always be cautious, never confide in letter or speech," curb the trusting urge in our nature. The betrayal of trust is the one sin; all other crimes from murder down may find an excuse in passion or weakness, but when the trusting are deceived or injured, the cement substance of our social structure is dissolved and the fabric of our lives threatened. To trust is to hand over one's destiny to another and is a manifestation of the mutual dependence of man. It is in part a judgment of character, it is in part an original trait, is an absence of that form of fear called suspicion and on its positive side is a form of courage.

Since it is in part a judgment of character in the most of us, it tends to grow less prominent as we grow older. The young child is either very trusting or entirely suspicious, and when his suspicions are overcome by acquaintance and simple bribes, he yields his fortunes to any one. (It is a pleasant fiction that children and dogs know whom to trust, by an intuition.) But as life proceeds, the most of us find that our judgment of character is poor, and we hesitate to pin anything momentous on it. Only where passion blinds us, as in sex love, or when our self-love and lust for quick gain [70] or hate has been aroused do we lose the caution that is the antithesis of trust. The expert in human relations is he who can overcome distrust; the genius in human relations is he who inspires trust.

For the psychopathologist an enormous interest centers in a group of people whom we may call paranoic. In his mildest form the paranoic is that very common "misunderstood" person who distrusts the attitude and actions of his neighbors, who believes himself to be injured purposely by every unintentional slight, or rather who finds insult and injury where others see only forgetfulness or inattention. Of an inordinate and growing ego, the paranoic of a pathological trend develops the idea or delusion of persecution. From the feeling that everything and every one is against him, he builds up, when some major purpose becomes balked, a specific belief that so and so or this or "that group is after me." "They are trying to injure or kill me" because they are jealous or have some antagonistic purpose. Here we find the half-baked inventor, whose "inventions" have been turned down for the very good reason that they are of no value, and who concludes that some big corporations are in league with the Patent Office to prevent him from competing with them; here we have the "would-be" artist or singer or writer whose efforts are not appreciated, largely because they are foolish, but who believes that the really successful (and he often

---

[70] All the great swindlers show how the lust for gain plus the wiles of the swindler overcome the caution and suspicion of the "hard-headed," The Ponzi case is the latest contribution to the subject.

names them) hate and fear him, or that the Catholics are after him, or perhaps the Jews or the Masons.

In its extreme form the paranoic is rare just as is the extremely trusting person of saintly type. But in minor form every group and every institution has its paranoic, hostile, suspicious, "touchy," quick to believe something is being put over on him and quick to attribute his failure to others. In that last is a cardinal point in the compass of character. Some attribute their failure to others, and some in their self-analysis find the root of their difficulties and failures in themselves.

Under the feeling of injustice a paranoid trend is easily aroused in all of us, and we may misinterpret the whole world when laboring under that feeling, just as we may, if we are correct, see the social organization very clearly as a result. Therein is the danger of any injustice and seeming injustice, As a result condemnation is extreme, wrongly directed and with little constructive value. We become paranoid, see wrong where there is none and enemies in those who are friendly.

The over-trusting, over-confidential are the virtuous in excess, and their damage is usually localized to themselves or their families. They tell their secrets to any one who politely expresses an interest, they will hand over their fortunes to the flattering stranger, to the smooth-tongued. Sometimes they are merely unworldly, absorbed in unworldly projects, but more often they are merely trusting fools.

Man the weak, struggling in a world whose forces are pitiless, whose fairest face hides grim disaster, has sought to find some one, some force, he might unfailingly trust. He raises his hands to heaven; he cries, "There is One I can trust. Though He smite me I shall have faith."

CHAPTER XIV
SEX CHARACTERS AND DOMESTICITY

Originally reproduction is a part of the function of all protoplasm; and in the primitive life-forms an individual becomes two by the "simple process" of dividing itself into halves. Had this method continued into the higher forms most of the trouble as well as most of the pleasure of human existence would never occur. Or had the hermaphrodite method of combining two sexes in the one individual, so frequent in the plant world, found its way into the higher animals, the moral struggles of man would have become simplified into that resulting from his, struggles with similar creatures. Literature would not flourish, the drama would never have been heard of, dancing and singing would not need the attention of the uplifter, dress would be a method of keeping warm, and life would be sane enough but without the delicious joys of sex-love.

Why are there two sexes? [71] I must refer the reader to the specialists in this matter, but can assure him that no one knows. With the rise of Mandel's theory of heredity, it has been assumed that such a scheme offers a wider variety of possible character combinations. At present it is safe to say that no one can give a valid reason for the existence of male and female, and that while this elaboration of the reproducing individual into two parts may be necessary for some purpose, at first glance it appears like an interesting but mysterious complication.

I refer the reader to textbooks in anatomy and embryology, and to the specialists on sex like Krafft-Ebbing, Havelock Ellis and Ploss for details as to the differences between man and woman. There are first the essential organs of generation, differing in the two sexes, the ovary furnishing the egg, the testes furnishing the seed or sperm; then the organs of sexual contact; the secondary sex characteristics, such as stature, distribution of hair, deposits of fat, shape of body and especially of the pelvis, the voice, smoothness of skin, muscular development, etc. There is an orderly evolution in the development of sex characters which starts with earliest embryo life and goes on regularly until puberty, when there is an extraordinary development of latent characters and peculiarities. After puberty maturity is reached by easy stages, and then comes involution or the recession of sex characters. This is reached in woman rather suddenly and in man more gradually. The completely differentiated man differs from his completely differentiated mate in the texture of his hair, skin, nails; in the width and mobility of pupils, in the color of his sclera, etc., as well as in the more essential sex organs.

Indeed there are very essential bodily differences that are obviously important though not well understood. One is that the bodily temperature

---

[71] See Lloyd Morgan's book on sex.

of man is slightly higher than that of woman, and that he has five million red blood corpuscles to every cubic millimeter of his blood, while she has four and a half million; that his brain weighs considerably more but is not heavier proportionately; that her bodily proportions resemble those of the child-form [72] more than do his, which some interpret as a point of superiority for her, while others interpret it as a sign of inferiority. On the whole, the authorities consider that man is made for the discharge of energy at a high rate for a short time, he is the katabolic element, while woman stores up energy for her children and represents the anabolic element of the race.

As a corollary to the above, it is necessary to know that each human being (and also each higher animal) starts out with the potential sex organs of both sexes, and that each individual becomes sexually differentiated at about the eleventh week of intra-uterine life. Moreover every male has female organs, and every female has male organs, though in the normal conditions these are mere vestiges and play no part in the sex life of the person. Yet this indicates that the separation of male and female is not absolute, and logically and actually a male may have female characters, physically and mentally, and vice versa a female may resemble the male in structure and character.

The sex relations have in the racial sense reproduction as their object, but it is wise to remember that in the whole living world only man knows this, and he has known it for only a relatively short time. Furthermore, in youth, when the sexual life is at its intensest, this fact, though known, is not really realized, and in the individual's plans and desires parenthood figures only incidentally, if at all. Society, in its organization, places its emphasis on child-bearing, and so indirectly reproduction becomes a great social aim rather than an individual purpose.

1. The feeling of parenthood is, as every one knows, far stronger in woman than in man. But here again generalizations are of no use to us, since there are women who develop only a weak maternal feeling, while there are men whose intensity of response to children is almost as great as any woman's. Undoubtedly occupation in other than the traditional woman's field is weakening the maternal feeling or is at least competing with it in a way that divides the modern mother's emotions and purposes and is largely responsible for her restless nervousness. This I think may safely be stated: that industry, athleticism, education, late marriage, etc., are not making for better physical motherhood. [73] On the contrary, the modern woman has a harder time in bearing her children, and worst of all she is showing either a reluctance or an inability to nurse them. Small families are becoming the rule, especially among the better to do. On the other hand, the history of the home is the gradual domestication of the man, his greater devotion to the children and to his wife. The increase in

---

[72] See Havelock Ellis.
[73] "The Nervous Housewife."

167

divorce has its roots in social issues too big to be discussed with profit here, but perhaps the principal item is the emancipation of woman who is now freer to decline unsatisfactory relations with her mate.

2. The sex passion, as a direct feeling, is undoubtedly stronger in the male, as it is biologically necessary it should be, since upon him devolves the active part in the sex relationship. [74] The sexologists point out two types of sex feeling, one of which is supposed to be typically male, the other typically female.

The male feeling is called sadism, after an infamous nobleman who wrote on the subject. It is a delight in power, especially in cruelty, and shows itself in a desire for the subjection of the female. In its pathological forms it substitutes cruelty for the sexual relation, and we have thus the horrible Jack the Rippers, etc. The Freudians go to the extreme of seeing in all love of power a sadism, but the truth is that the sadistic impulse is the love of power, cruelly or roughly expressed in sex. The cave man of the stories is a sadist of a type, and one generally approved of, at least in theory. A little of sadism is shown in the delight in pinching and biting so often seen; and the expression "I'd like to eat you up" has a playful sadism in it.

The opposite of sadism is masochism. This is a delight in being roughly used, in being the victim of aggression. The typical female is supposed to rejoice in the power and strength of the male as exerted on her. The admiration women often give to the uncouthly strong, their praise of virility, is masochistic in its origin. The desire of the peasant woman to be beaten as a mark of man's love is supposed to be masochistic, a pleasure in pain, which is held to be a primitive female reaction.

Sex psychopathology discloses innumerable cases where extreme sadism and masochism exist in both sexes; that is, not only males but females are sadistic, and so not only females but males are masochistic. Undoubtedly in minor degree both qualities express themselves in male and female; undoubtedly the male is more frequently a sadist than is the female. Though the majority of women may thrill in the strength and power of the lover, there are relatively few American women who will tolerate real roughness or cruelty. As a matter of fact the basic feelings in sex love, aside from the sexual urge itself, are tenderness and admiration. Naturally men desire to protect, and this becomes part of their tenderness; they admire and love the beauty of women and are attracted by the essential (or supposed essential) feminine qualities. And as naturally women desire to be protected; this enhances their tenderness, and their admiration is elicited by the peculiar male characters of strength, hardihood and aggressiveness, as well as by beauty and human qualities generally. Though the love of conquest is a part of sex feeling, it is neither male nor female, but is that feeling of superiority and power so longed for in all relations. Men like to conquer the proud, reserved, haughty woman because she piques them, and women often set out to "win" the reserved

---

[74] See Havelock Ellis, Krafft-Ebbing, Freud.

"woman hater" for the same reason. Thus tenderness and sex passion, with sadism and masochism in lesser degree, are basic in sex feeling, but other qualities enter so largely that any complete analysis is almost impossible. The belief, engendered by romance and teaching, that happiness lies in love, spurs youth on. Admiration for achievement, love of beauty, desire for the social standing that winning some one gives, desire for home and perhaps even for children are some of the factors of love.

Sex passion varies enormously in people. In some men it is an almost constant desire, obsessive, and is relatively uncritical and unchoosing. Occasionally, though much more rarely, the same condition is found in women. Such abnormal individuals are almost certain of social disaster, and when married their conduct usually leads to divorce or desertion. Then there is a wide range of types down to the almost sexless persons, [75] the frigid, who are much more commonly found among women than men. In fact, with many women active sex desire may never occur, and for others it is a rarity, while still others find themselves definitely desirous only after pregnancy. Not only are women less passionate, but their desire is more "finicky," more in need of appropriate circumstances, the proper setting and the chosen mate than with man. In other words, sex desire is more physical and urgent in the man and more psychical and selective in the woman.

A curious by-product of the sexual feeling is fetichism. To do it justice, fetichism is found in all feeling toward others, but is most developed in sex relation. The fetich is a symbol of the desired person, thus the handkerchief and glove of the woman or the hat of the man. Pathologically any part of the dress—the shoe or the undergarments—may become so closely associated with sexual feeling as to evoke it indiscriminately or even to displace it. Normal fetich formation may become a bit foolish and sentimental but never becomes a predominant factor in sex relationship.

The history of modesty is the history of the sex taboo. As pointed out, the sex feelings are the most restricted of any of the instincts. I despair of giving an adequate summary of this, but it may be best stated by declaring that all the restrictions we hold as imperative have, at one time or another in some place, been regarded as sacred and desirable. Brother and sister marriages were favored by Egyptian royalty, prostitution was a rite in Phoenician worship, phallic worship frankly held as a symbol that which to-day we hold profane (in a silly way), plural marriage was and is countenanced in a large part of the world to-day, marriage for love is held as foolish in most countries, even now. The practice of child restriction now prevalent in Europe and America would be looked at with horror in those countries where children of ten or eleven are allowed to marry.

---

[75] Some claim that the "frigid" woman is such because her mate is ignorant of the art of love. This is true of some frigid women. Instruction to men and women about to be married on the technique of sexual life might well take a fine place in the curriculum of life.

Exogamy, endogamy, monogamy, polygamy,—all these are customs and taboos, and though in our day and country monogamy has the social and religious sanction, there is nothing to indicate that this is a permanent resting place for marriage. Certainly the statistics of divorce indicate a change in the permanent status of marriage.

What this is meant to emphasize is the social nature of sexual modesty. Modesty of other kind rests either on a moderate self-valuation or a desire to avoid offense by not emphasizing one's own value, or it is both. However sexual modesty originated, practically it consists in the concealing of certain parts of the body, avoiding certain topics of conversation, especially in the presence of the other sex, and behaving in such fashion as to restrict sexual demonstration. There is a natural coyness in women which has been socially emphasized by restrictions in dress, conduct and speech to a ridiculous degree. Thus it was immodest in our civilization for women to show their legs, and the leg became the symbol of the femaleness of the woman or girl, as also did the breast. [76] The body became taboo, and at present, when women are commencing to dress so that the legs are shown, the arms are bare, and the back and shoulders visible, the cry of immodesty, immorality and social demoralization is raised, as if real morality rested in these ridiculous, barbaric taboos.

But no matter how much one emphasizes the arbitrary nature of modesty, of the restrictions placed on dress, speech and conduct, it still remains true that their function is at present to act as inhibitors. Ridiculous as it is to believe that morality resides in the length of the skirt or in the degree of paint and powder on the face, the fact is that usually they who depart too widely from the conventional in these matters are uninhibited and are as apt to depart from the conventional in deed as they are in deportment. There are those who say that we would be far more moral if we went about naked; that clothes suggest more than nakedness reveals. This is true of some kinds of clothes—the half nakedness of the stage or the ballroom, or the coquettish additions to clothes represented by the dangling tassels —but it is not true of the riding breeches, or the trim sport clothes, or the walking suit. The dress of men, though ugly, is useful, convenient and modest, and there is no doubt that a generation of free women, determined to become human in appearance, could evolve a modest and yet decorative costume. All of the present-day extravagance in female attire, with its ever-changing fashion, is a medley of commercial intrigues, female competition and sex excitement. Though the modesty restrictions are absurd, the motive that obscurely prompts it is not, and the transgressors either seek notice in a risky way, are foolish, to speak bluntly, or else are inviting actual sexual advances.

Though we may actually restrict the sex life so that some men and women become pure in the accepted sense, it will always be true that men

---

[76] All the anthropologists, Tyler, McLennan, Ellis and especially Frazier, deal at length with this fascinating subject. The psychopathologists relate the most extraordinary stories of fetich love.

and women will be vaguely or definitely attracted to each other. Like the atmospheric pressure which though fifteen pounds to the square inch at the sea level is not felt, so there exists a sex pressure, excited by men and women in each other. There is a smoldering excitement always ready to leap into flame whenever the young and attractive of the sexes meet. The conventions of modesty tend to restrict the excitement, to neutralize the sex pressure, but they may be swept aside by immodesty and the suggestive. The explanation of the anger and condemnation felt by the moral man in the presence of the "brazen" woman lies in the threat to his purposes of respectability and faithfulness; he is angered that this creature can arouse a conflict in him. The bitterness of the "saint" against the wanton originates in the ease with which she tempts him, and his natural conclusion is that the fault lies with her and not with his own passions. The respectable woman inveigles against her more untrammeled sister, not so much through her concern for morality, as through the anger felt against an unscrupulous competitor who is breaking the rules.

In so far as women are concerned, the sex pressure on them is increased in many ways. For two years I examined, mentally, the girls who were listed as sex offenders by the various social agencies of Boston. As a result of that experience, plus that of a physician and citizen of the world, a few facts of importance stand out in my mind.

1. There is a group of men whom one may call sex adventurers. These are not all of one kind in education, social status and age, but they seek sex experiences wherever they go and are always alert for signs that indicate a chance to become intimate. They take advantage of the widespread tendency to flirt and haunt the places where the young girls tend to parade up and down (certain streets in every large city), the public dance halls, the skating resorts, the crowded public beaches, etc. They regard themselves as connoisseurs in women and think they know when a girl is "ripe"; they are ready to spend money and utilize flattery, gifts and bold wooing, according to their nature and the way they size up their prey.

2. The female sex adventurer is not so common, except in the higher criminal classes where the effort to ensnare rich men calls forth the abilities of certain women. In a limited way the prostitute, professed or clandestine, is a sex adventurer, but ordinarily she is merely supplying a demand and has only to exert herself physically, rarely needing to conquer men's inhibitions. We omit here the schemes of conquest of girls and women seeking marriage as too complex for any one but a novelist, and also because the moral code regards them as legitimate. Women who are ready to accept sexual advances are common enough in the uninhibited girl, the dissatisfied married woman, the young widow, the drug habitue; but aside from the woman who has capitalized her sex, the sex adventurer is largely male.

What attracts him? For he rarely pesters the good woman, and ordinarily the average woman is not solicited.

The girl usually "picked up" dresses immodestly or in the extreme of style, even though she is essentially shabby and poorly clad. To-day business sees to it that fripperies are within the reach of every purse.

She usually corresponds to a type of prettiness favored in the community, often what is nowadays called the chicken type. Plump legs and fairly prominent bosom and hips are symbols of those desired among all grades of men, together with a pretty face. The homely girl finds it much easier to walk unmolested.

If she appears intelligent and firm, the above qualities will only entitle her to glances, respectful and otherwise. The sex adventurer hates to be rebuffed, and he is not desperately in love, so that he will not risk his vanity. If she appears of that port vivacious type just above the moron level—in other words if she is neither bright nor really feeble-minded—then sex pressure is increased. The feeble-minded girl of the moron type, or the over-innocent and unenlightened girl, is always in danger.

There is further the sexually excited or the uninhibited girl. We must differentiate between those who attempt no control, and those whose surge of desire is beyond the normal limits. The uninhibited of both sexes are a large group, and the bulk of the prostitutes are deficient in this respect rather than in intelligence. Sometimes inhibition arrives late, after sexual immorality has commenced. In men this is common, but unfortunately for women, society stands in their way when this occurs with them. "Youth must have its fling" is a masculine privilege denied to feminine offenders.

The desire for a good time plays havoc with the uninhibited girl. Unable to find interest in her work, which too often is uninteresting, desiring good clothes and excitement, she discovers that these are within her reach if she follows her instincts. What starts out as a flirtation ends in social disaster, and a girl finds out that some men who give good times expect to be paid for them.

Since our study is not a pathological treatise, we must omit further consideration of the offender and dismiss without more comment the whole range of the perverter. It suffices to say that the perverted are often such congenitally, in which case nothing can be done for them, and others are the results of certain environments, which range all the way from girls' boarding-schools to the palaces of kings.

In ancient times, and in many countries to-day, certain perversions were so common as to defy belief, and we are compelled to associate with some of the greatest names, practices [77] that shock us. These same ancients would denounce as unnatural in as hearty terms the increasing practices of child-limitation among us.

The sex desires and instincts struggle with, overcome or harmonize with the social instincts. It would be impossible to portray even the simplest sex life from the mental standpoint. The chastest woman who is unconscious of sex desire is motivated by romance and the sex feelings and customs of others in her ideas of happiness and right behavior. The cynical

---

[77] I pass over as out of the range of this book the question raised by Freud, whether or not we are all of us homosexual as well as heterosexual.

profligate, indulging every sensual urge, in so far as he can, must guide himself by the resistance of society, by the necessity of camouflage, the fear of public opinion and often the impediment of his own early training. Men and women start out perhaps as romantic idealists, enter marriage, and in the course of their experiences become almost frankly sensual. And in the opposite direction, men and women wildly passionate in youth develop counter tendencies that swing them into restraint and serene self-control. There are those to whom sex is mere appetite, to be indulged and put out of the way, so as not to interfere with the great purposes of success; there are those to whom it is a religion, carried on with ceremonials and rites; there are those to whom it is an obsession, and their minds are in a sexual stew at all times. There are the under-inhibited, spoken of above, and there are the over-inhibited, Puritanical, rebelling at the flesh as such, disguising all their emotions, reluctant to admit their humanness and the validity of pleasure.

The romantic ideal, glorifying a sort of asexual love of perfect men and women, asceticism which permits sex only as a sort of necessary evil and sensuality which proclaims the pleasure of sex as the only joy and scoffs at inhibition influence the lives of us all. The effect of the forbidden, the tantalizing curiosity aroused and the longing to rise above the level of lust make the sex adjustment the most difficult of all and produce the queerest results. Sex is a road to power and to failure, a road to health and sickness. As in all adjustments, there are some who are conscious of but few difficulties, who are moral or immoral without struggle or discontent. Contrasted with these are the ones who find morality a great burden, and those who, yielding to desire, find continuous inner conflict and dissatisfaction and lowered self-valuation as a result.

Our society is organized on chastity and continence prior to marriage, purity and constancy after marriage. That noble ideal has never been realized; the stories of Pagan times, of the Middle Ages and of the present day, as well as everyday human experience, show that the male certainly has not lived up to his part of the bargain. Legalized prostitution in most countries, illegal prostitution in the United States and England, in addition to the enormous amount of clandestine relationships, are a sufficient commentary on the results. The increasing divorce rate, the feminist movement, the legalizing of the "illegitimate" child in Norway and Sweden and the almost certain arrival of similar laws in all countries indicate a softer attitude toward sex restrictions. The rapidly increasing age of marriage means simply that continence will be more and more difficult, for I am not one of those who believe that the repression of this vital instinct is without harm. Continence is socially necessary, but beyond a certain age it is physically and mentally harmful. Man is thus placed on the horns of a dilemma from which it will take the greatest wisdom and the finest humanity to extricate him. But I cannot lay claim to any part of the knowledge and ability necessary to formulate the plan. Let us at least be candid; let us not say grandiloquently that the sexual urge can be indefinitely repressed without harm to the average individual. We may safely assert that there are people, men and women both, to whom the sex impulses are vague and of little force, but to the great majority, at least of men, sex desire is almost a hunger, and unsatisfied it brings about a restlessness and dissatisfaction that enters into all the mental life. On what basis society will meet this situation I do not pretend to know, but this is certain,—that all over the civilized world there is apparent an organizing rebellion against the social impediment to sexual satisfaction.

For it must be remembered that sexual satisfaction is not alone naked desire. It is that—but sublimated into finer things as well. It is the desire for stability of affection, for a sympathetic beloved, an outlet for emotion, a longing for respectable unitary status. The unit of respectable human life is the married couple; the girl wants that social recognition, and so does her man. Both yearn to cast off from their old homes and start a new one, as an initial step in successful living. The thought of children—a little form in a little bed, and the man and woman gazing in an ecstasy of pride and affection upon it—makes all other pleasures seem unworthy and gives to the ache for intimacy a high moral sanction.

This brings us to the point where we must consider those characteristics that make up domesticity and homekeeping. Early impressions and the consistent teaching of literature, stage, press and religion have given to the home a semi-sacred character, which is one of the great components of the desire to marry, especially for women. The home is, in the minds of most of those who enter into marriage, a place owned, peculiarly possessed, and it offers freedom from the restraints of society and the inhibitions of ceremony and custom. Both the man and woman like to think that here is the place where their love can find free expression, where she will care for him and he will provide for her, and where their children can grow in beauty, intelligence and moral worth under their guidance. But this is only the sentimental side of their thought, the part they give freest expression to because it is most respectable and "nice." In the background of their minds is the desire for ownership, the wish to say, "This is mine and here I rule." Into that comes the ideal that the stability of society is involved and the homekeeper is its most important citizen, but when we study the real evolution of the home, study the laws pertaining to the family, we find that the husband and father had a little kingdom with wife and children as subjects, and that only gradually has there come from that monarchical idea the more democratic conception cherished to-day.

Men and women may be considered as domestic or non-domestic. The domestic type of man is ordinarily "steady" in purpose and absorbed more in work than in the seeking of pleasure, is either strongly inhibited sexually or else rather easily satisfied; cherishes the ideal of respectability highly; is conventional and habituated, usually has a strong property feeling and is apt to have a decided paternal feeling. He may of course be seclusive and apt to feel the constraints of contact with others as wearying and unsatisfactory; he is not easily bored or made restless. All this is a broad sketch; even the most domestic find in the home a certain amount of tyranny and monotony; they yearn now and then for adventure and new romance and think of the freedom of their bachelor days with regret over their passing. They may decide that married home life is best, but the choice is not without difficulty and is accompanied by an irrepressible, though hidden dissatisfaction. On the whole, however, the domestic man finds the home a haven of relief and a source of pleasurable feeling.

The non-domestic man may be of a dozen types. Perhaps he is incurably romantic and hates the thought of settling down and putting away for good the search for the perfect woman. Perhaps he is uninhibted sexually or over-excitable in this respect, and is therefore restless and unfaithful. He may be bored by monotony, a restless seeker of new experiences and new work, possessed by the devils of wanderlust. He may be an egoist incapable of the continuous self-sacrifice and self-abnegation demanded by the home,—quarrelsome and selfish. Sometimes he is wedded to an ideal of achievement or work and believes that he travels best who travels alone. Often in these days of late marriage he has waited until he could "afford" to marry and then finds that his habits chain him to single life. Or he may be an unconventional non-believer in the home and marriage, though these are really rare. The drinker, the roue, the wanderer, the selfish, the nonconventional, the soarer, the restless, the inefficient and the misogynist all make poor husbands and fathers and find the home a burden too crippling to be borne.

One of the outstanding figures of the past is the domestic woman, yearning for a home, assiduously and constantly devoted to it, her husband and her numerous children. Fancy likes to linger on this old-fashioned housewife, arising in the early morning and from that time until her bedtime content to bake, cook, wash, dust, clean, sew, nurse and teach; imagining no other career possible or proper for her sex; leading a life of self- sacrifice, toil and devotion. Poet, novelist, artist, and clergyman have immortalized her, and men for the most part cherish this type as their mother and dream of it as the ideal wife.

Perhaps (and probably) this woman rebelled in her heart against her drudgery and dreamed of better things; perhaps she regretted the quickly past youth and dreaded the frequent child-bearing. Whether she did or not, the appearance of a strongly non-domestic type is part of the history of the latter nineteenth century and the early twentieth.

The non-domestic women are, like their male prototypes, of many kinds, and it would be idle to enumerate them. There is the kind of woman that "has a career," using this term neither sarcastically nor flatteringly. The successful artist of whatever sort—painter, musician, actress—has usually been quite spoiled for domesticity by the reward of money and adulation given her. Nowhere is the lack of proportion of our society so well demonstrated as in the hysterical praise given to this kind of woman, and naturally she cannot consent to the subordination and seclusion of the home. Then there is the young business woman, efficient, independent, proud of her place in the bustle and stir of trade. She is quite willing to marry and often makes an admirable mother and wife, but sometimes she finds the menial character of housework, its monotony and dependence too much for her. The feminist aglow with equality and imbued with too vivid a feeling of sex antagonism may marry and bear children, but she rarely becomes a fireside companion of the type the average man idealizes. Then the vain, the frivolous, the sexually uncontrolled,—these too make poor choice for him who has set his heart on a wife who will cook his meals, darn his stockings and care for the children. To be non-domestic is a privilege or a right we cannot deny to women, nor is there condemnation in the term,—it is merely a summary characterization.

Though to remain single is to be freer than to be married and domestic, yet the race will always have far more domestic characters. These alone will bear children, and from them the racial characters will flow rather than from the exceptional and deviate types, unless the home disappears in the form of some other method of raising children. After all, the home is a costly, inefficient method of family life unless it has advantages for childhood. This it decidedly has, though we have bad homes aplenty and foolish ones galore. Yet there is for the child a care, and more important, an immersion in love and tender feeling, possible in no other way. We should lose the sacred principles of motherhood and fatherhood, the only example of consistent and unrewarded love, if the home disappeared. The only real altruism of any continuous and widespread type is there found. It is the promise and the possibility of our race that we see in the living parents. We know that unselfishness exists when we think of them, and the idealist who dreams of a world set free from greed and struggle merely enlarges the ideal home.

But we must be realistic, as well as idealistic. A silent or noisy struggle goes on in the home between the old and the new, between a rising and a receding generation. An orthodox old generation looks askance on an heretical new generation; parents who believe that to play cards or go to theater is the way of Satan find their children leaving home to do these very things. Everywhere mothers wonder why daughters like short skirts, powder and perhaps rouge, when they were brought up on the corset, crinoline and the bustle; and they rebel against the indictment passed out broadcast by their children. "You are old-fashioned; this is the year 1921." When children grow up, their wills clash with their parents', even in the sweetest, and most loving of homes. Behind many a girl's anxiety to marry is the desire for the unobstructed exercise of her will. Parents too often seek in their children a continuation of their own peculiarities, their own characters and ideals, forgetting that the continuity of the generations is true only in a biological sense, but in no other way. And children grown to strength, power and intelligence think that each person must seek his experiences himself and forget that true wisdom lies in what is accepted by all the generations.

Just as we have the types of husbands and the types of wives, so we judge men and women by the wisdom, dignity and faithfulness of their parenthood; so we judge them by the kind of children they are to their parents. In this last we have a point in character of great importance and one upon which the followers of Freud have laid much—over-much—stress.

The effect of too affectionate a home training, too assertive parenthood, is to dwarf the individuality of the child and make him a sort of parasite, out of contact with his contemporaries, seclusive and odd. There is a certain brand of goody-goody boy, brought up tied to his mother's apron strings, who has lost the essential capacities of mixing with varied types of boys and girls, who is sensitive, shy and retiring, or who is naively boorish and unschooled in tact. According to some psychiatrists this kind of training breeds the mental disease known as Dementia Praecox, but I seriously doubt it. One often finds that the goody-goody boy of fifteen becomes the college fullback at twenty,—that is, once thrown on the world, the really normal get back their birthright of character. I think it likely that now and then a feeling of inferiority is bred in this way, a feeling that may cling and change the current of a boy's life. The real danger of too close a family life, in whatever way it manifests itself, is that it cuts into real social life, narrows the field of influences and sympathies, breeds a type of personality of perhaps good morals but of poor humanity.

The home must never lose its contact with the world; it should never be regarded as the real world for which a man works. It is a place to rest in, to eat in, to work in; in it is the spirit of family life, redolent of affection, mutual aid and self-sacrifice; but more than these, it is the nodal point of affections, concerns and activity which radiate from it to the rest of the world.

CHAPTER XV
PLAY, RECREATION, HUMOR AND PLEASURE SEEKING

One of the great difficulties in thought is that often the same word expresses quite different concepts. Some superficial resemblance has taken possession of the mind and expressed itself in a unifying word, disregarding the fundamental differences.

Take the word "play." The play of childhood is indeed a pleasurable activity to the child, but it is really his form of grappling with life, a serious pursuit of knowledge and a form of preparation for his adult activities. It is not a way of relaxation; on the contrary, in play he organizes his activities, shuffles and reshuffles his ideas and experiences, looking for the new combinations we call "imaginations." The kitten in its play prepares to catch its prey later on; and the child digging in a ditch and making believe "this is a house" and "this is a river" is a symbol of Man the mighty changing the face of Nature. The running and catching games like "Tag" and "I spy," "Hide and go seek," "Rellevo" are really war games, with training in endurance, agility, cool-headedness, cooperation and rivalry as their goals. Only as the child grows older, and there is placed on him the burden of school work, does play commence to change its serious nature and partake of the frivolous character of adult life.

For the play of adult life is an effort to find pleasure and relaxation in the dropping of serious purposes, in the "forgetting" of cares and worries, by indulging in excitement which has no fundamental purpose. The pleasure of play for the adult is in the release of trends from inhibition, exactly as we may imagine that a harnessed horse, pulling at a load and with his head held back by a check-rein, might feel if he were turned loose in a meadow. This is the kind of play spirit manifested in going out fishing, dressed in old clothes, with men who will not care whatever is said or done. There is purpose, there is competition and cooperation and fellowship, but the organization is a loose one and does not bear heavily. So, too, with the pleasure of a game of ball for the amateur who plays now and then. There is organization, control and competition; but unless one is a poor loser, there is a relaxed tension in that the purpose is not vital, and one can shout, jump up and down and express himself in uninhibited excitement. Whether this excitement has a value in discharging other excitement and feelings that are inhibited in the daily work is another matter; if it has such a value, play becomes of necessary importance. In outdoor games in general, the feeling of physical fitness, of discharging energy along primordial lines and the happy feeling that comes merely from color of sky and grass and the outdoor world, bring a relief from sadness that comes with the work and life of the city man.

178

Often the play is an effort to seek excitement and thus to forget cares, or it is a seeking of excitement for its own sake. Thus men gamble, not only for the gain but because such excitement as is aroused offers relief from business worries or home difficulties. The prize fights, the highly competitive professional sports of all kinds are frequented and followed by enormous numbers of men, not only because men greatly admire physical prowess, but because the intense excitement is sought. I know more than one business and professional man who goes to the "fights" because only there can he get a thrill. There is a generalized mild anhedonia in the community, which has its origin in the fatigue of overintense purposes, failure to realize ideals and the difficulties of choice. People who suffer in this way often seek the sedentary satisfaction of watching competitive professional games.

Indeed, the hold of competition on man exists not alone in his rivalry feeling toward others; it is evidenced also in the excitement he immediately feels in the presence of competitive struggle, even though he himself has little or no personal stake. Man is a partisan creature and loves to take sides. This is remarkably demonstrated by children, and is almost as well shown in the play of adults. A recent international prize fight awakened more intense interest than almost any international event of whatever real importance. That same day it passed practically unnoticed that America ended a state of war with Germany.

A law of excitement, that it lies in part in a personal hazard accounts for the growth of betting at games. The effort to gain adds to the interest, i. e., excitement. That it adds tension as well and may result in fatigue and further boredom is not reckoned with by the bettor or gambler. To follow the middle of the road in anything is difficult, and nowhere is it more beset with danger than in the seeking of excitement.

Games of skill of all kinds, whether out of doors or within; baseball, cricket, billiards, and pool afford, then, the pleasure of exertion and competition in an exciting way and yet one removed from too great a stake. Defeat is not bitter, though victory is sweet; a good game is desired, and an easy opponent is not welcomed. The spirit of this kind of play has been of great value to society, for it has brought the feeling of fair play and sportsmanship to the world. Primitive in its origin, to take defeat nobly and victory with becoming modesty is the civilizing influence of sportsmanship. In the past women have lacked good-fellowship and sportsmanship largely because they played no competitive-cooperative games.

I shall not attempt to take up in any detail all the forms of pleasure-excitement seeking. Dancing, music, the theater and the movies offer outlets both for the artistic impulses and the seeking of excitement. In the theater and the movies one seeks also the interest we take in the lives of others, the awakening of emotions and the happy ending. Only a few people will ever care for the artistic wholesale calamity of a play like "Hamlet," and even they only once in a while.

Men and women seek variety, they seek excitement in any and all directions, they want relief from the tyranny of purpose and of care. But also,—they hate a vacuum, they can usually bear themselves and their thoughts for only a little while, because their thoughts are often basicly melancholy and full of dissatisfaction. So they seek escape from themselves; they try to kill time; reading, playing and going to entertainments. In fact, most of our reading is actuated by the play spirit, and is an effort to obtain excitement through the lives of others.

Humor [78] is a form of pleasure seeking and giving, but depends on a certain technique, the object of which is to elicit the laugh or its equivalent. The laugh is a discharge of tension, and while usually it accompanies pleasure, it may indicate the tension of embarrassment or even complex emotional states. But the laugh or smile of humor has to be elicited in certain ways, chief of which are to bring about a feeling of expectation, and by some novel arrangement of words, to send the mind on a voyage of discovery which suddenly ends with a burst of pleasure when the "point" is seen. The pleasure felt in humor arises from the feeling of novelty, the pleasure of discovering a hidden meaning and the pleasure in the "point" or motive of the story, joke or conduct.

Usually, the humorous pleasure has these motives: it points at the folly and absurdity of other people's conduct, thought, logic and customs. It gives a feeling of superiority, and that is why all races love to poke fun at other races: certain characteristics of Jew, Irishman, Yankee, Scot, etc., are presented in novel and striking fashion, in a playful manner.

It points out the weak and absurd side of people and institutions with which we have trouble; and this brings in marriage, business, mothers-in-law, creditors, debtors, as those whose weakness is exposed by the technique of humor.

Humor likes to explode pretension, pedantry, dignity, pomposity; we get a feeling of joy whenever those who are superior come a cropper, which is increased when we feel that they have no right to their places. So the humorous technique deals with the get-rich-quick folk, the foolish nobleman, the politician, the priest (especially in the Middle Ages), etc.

Not only does humor seek to obtain pleasure from an attack on others and thus to feel superior or to compensate for inferiority, but also it reaches its highest form in exposing man himself, including the humorist. The humorist, seeking his own weaknesses and contradictions, his falsities, strips the disguise from himself in some surprising way. Bergson points out that to strip away a disguise is naturely humorous unless it reveals too rudely the horrible. The humorist takes off the mask from himself and others, and in so far as we can detach ourselves from pride and vanity, we laugh. The one who cannot thus detach himself is "hurt" by humor; the one who somehow has become a spectator of his own strivings can laugh at himself. Thus humor, in addition to becoming a compensation and a form of entertainment, is a form of self-revelation and self-understanding carried on by a peculiar technique. On the whole this technique depends

---

[78] I use this term to include wit, satire and even certain phases of the comic.

upon a hiding of the real meaning of the story or situation under a disguise of the commonplace. The humorist phrases his words or develops his situation so as to send the thoughts of the listener flying in several directions. There is a brief confusion, an incongruity is felt, then suddenly from under a disguise the point becomes clear and the laugh is in part one of triumph, in part one of pleased surprise.

I shall not attempt an analysis of the psychology of humor, for illustrious writers and thinkers have stubbed their intellectual toes on this rock for centuries. In later years the analyses of Freud and Bergson are noted, but there is a list of writers from Aristotle down whose remarks and observations have brought out clearly certain trends. For us the direction that any one's humor takes is a very important phase in the study of character.

Humor is a weapon, and the humorist has two ends in view: the one to please his audience and to align them on his side, the second to attack either playfully or seriously some person or institution with the technique of humor. Certain trends are seen in humor, one to seek a feeling of superiority by revealing the inferiority of others in a surprising way, another to release a burdensome [79] inhibition, a third to play with and in a sense mock the disagreeable features of life, and the fourth to seek detachment from one's self, to seek relief from sorrow, disappointment and deprivation by viewing the self as from afar.

So there is a sarcastic humor which points out the foibles and weaknesses of others either grossly or delicately. Usually these others are those differing from one's own group—the Irish, Jew, farmer, Negro—and the jokes either deal with their personal appearance (a low humor) or their characteristic expressions, points of view and actions. The audience is convulsed at their quaintness or folly, though often enough on the stage the comic figure delivers a sort of wisdom mingled with his foolishness, and this adds to the humorous explosion. The sarcastic humor in its highest form reaches satire, where under a disguise powerful institutions or the habit and ways of life of a group are criticized. In polite society people are continually attacking each other in a kind of warfare called repartee, in which the tension is kept just without the bounds of real hostility, while the audience sides with the one whose shaft is the most telling. In the lower ranks this interchange, which is surprisingly frequent, is coarse and insulting. It is supposed to be a test of character to be able to "stand" these attacks with equanimity and even to join in the laugh against oneself. To "kid" and take "kidding" is thus an important social trait.

Humor is often used to expose the folly of the pretentious. Much of the stock in trade of the humorist lies in his attack on the pedant, the pompous, the great, the new-rich, the over-important of one kind or another. To find them less than they pretend to be gives two especial kinds of pleasure to the audience; the first the stripping away of disguise

---

[79] In this way humor is an effort for freedom; through humor one tastes of experiences otherwise forbidden.

(Bergson), and the second the relief of our own feeling of inferiority in their presence by showing how inferior they really are.

Since inhibition wears on us, the great inhibitions are directly attacked by the humorist. Thus sex forms one of the great subjects of humor, and from the obscene story told by those on whom the sex inhibitions rest lightly to the joke about clothes, etc., told by those who mock the opposite sex, the whole idea is to bring about pleasure in the release of inhibitton and the play of the mind around the forbidden. Freud has some interesting remarks on this type of humor, which he regards largely as sexual aggression. It is necessary to say that the release of inhibition is always that of an inhibition not too strongly felt or accepted. A really modest person, one to whom the sex code is a sacred thing, does not find pleasure in a crude sex joke. Similarly with the inhibition surrounding marriage, which is a stock subject of humor. The overearnest person dislikes this type of humor and reacts against it by calling it "in bad taste." In the Middle Ages (and to-day among those opposed to the Catholic church), the priest and nun were slyly or coarsely attacked by the humorist, and in all times those somewhat skeptical find in religion, its ceremonials and customs, a field for joke and satire.

The most interesting of the types of humor flirts with the disagreeable. Man is the only animal foreseeing death and disaster, and he not only quakes in the knowledge of misfortune, but also he jokes about it. It may be that the excitement of approaching in spirit the disagreeable is pleasant, and perhaps there is pleasure in attacking disaster, even in a playful way. The ability to joke about other people's misfortunes is not, of course, a measure of gallantry or courage and usually indicates a feeling of superiority such as we all tend to feel in the presence of the unfortunate, even where no element of weakness has caused their mishap. But to joke about one's own troubles, danger and disaster at least indicate a sense of proportion, an ability to stand aloof from oneself.

This propensity is remarkably manifest in hospitals, in war and wherever disaster or danger is present. The soldiers nickname in a familiar way all their troubles and all their dangers. The popular phrases for dying illustrate this,—croaked, flew up the spout, turned up the toes, etc. In the war the different kinds of guns and missiles had nicknames, and puns were made on the various dreaded results of injury. It was declared by the soldiers that no missile could injure any man unless it has his name and address on it, which is, of course, a poetical, humorous comparison of the missile to a longed-for letter. I heard a wounded man say the only trouble was that the postoffice department mistook him for another fellow. Grim humor always is evident in grim situations; it is a way of evasion and escape, and also it is a challenge.

When one objectifies himself so that he sees himself, his purposes and his weaknesses in the light in which others might see him and find him "funny," then he has reached the heights in humor. Certain people are notoriously lacking in this quality of detachment, and they cannot laugh at themselves or find any humor in a situation that annoys, mortifies or hurts them. Others have it to a remarkable degree, and if they possess at the same time the art of telling the humorous story about themselves, they become very popular. This popularity accounts for a good deal of seeming modesty and humorous self-depiction; it is a sort of recompense for the self-confessed foible and weakness; it is a way of seeking the good opinion and applause of others and is sometimes sought to a ridiculous extreme.

The character and the state of culture stand revealed in the type of humor enjoyed. If a man laughs heartily at sex jokes, one may at least say, that while he may live up to the conventions in this matter, it is certain that he regards the inhibitions as conventions, even though he give them lip-homage. No one finds much humor in the things he holds as really sacred, and if these are attacked in the joke he may laugh, but he is offended and angry at heart. Any man permits a joke on women in general, but he will not permit an obscene joke about his wife or his mother. Humor must not arouse the anger of the audience or the reader, and in this it resembles wrestling matches and friendly boxing, which are pleasant as attacks not seriously intended, but the blows must not exceed a certain play limit or war is declared.

To be entertained, to entertain, to escape from fatigue, monotony, inhibition, to seek excitement, to while away the time and thus to escape from failure, regret and sorrow are parts of the life and character of all. They who have nothing else but these activities in their lives are to be pitied, and they are unwise who allow themselves too little amusement and recreation.

But we have not spoken of pleasure as a whole, pleasure apart from entertainment, play and humor. The satisfaction of any physical desire is pleasant, so that to eat and drink and have sexual relations become great pleasure trends. There are some who live only for these pleasures, ranging from glutton to epicure, from the brutally passionate to the sexual connoisseur. Others whose appetites are hearty subordinate them to the main business of their lives, achievement in some form. There is a whole range of taste in pleasures of this kind that I do not even attempt to analyze at this point, even if it were possible for me to analyze it.

Pleasure in dress, in ceremonials, in all the ornamentation of life, forms part of the artistic impulses. The love of music is too lofty to be classed with the other pleasures. This is true of only a few people. For most of us music is an entertainment and is usually poorly endured if it constitutes the total entertainment. As part of the theater, of the movie, of dancing, it is "appreciated" by everybody. To most it stirs the emotions so deeply that its pleasure vanishes in fatigue if too long endured. The capacity to enjoy music, especially the capacity to express it, is one of the great variables of life. It is true that the poseurs in music and the arts generally seek superiority by pretending to a knowledge, interest and pleasure they do not really have, just as there are some who really try to enjoy what they feel they should enjoy. Nowhere is there quite so much pretense and humbug as in the field of the artistic tastes. Nowhere is the arbitrariness of taste so evident, and nowhere is the "expert" so likely to be a pretender. I say this in full recognition of the fact that science and religion have their modes and pretenses as well as art.

The "progress" of man is marked as much as anything by a change in "taste," change in what is considered mannerly, beautiful and pleasant. This progress is called refinement, although this term is also used in relation to ethics. Refinement in cooking leads to the art of the chef. Refinement in dress becomes developed into an intricate, ever-changing relation of clothes and age, sex, time of day, situation, etc., so that it is unrefined to wear clothes of certain texture and hues and refined to wear others. Refinement in manner regulates the tone of voice, the violence of gesticulation, the exhibition of emotions and the type of subjects discussed, as well as controlling a dozen and one other matters, from the way one enters a room to the way one leaves it. The savage is unrefined, say we, though he has his own standards of refinement. An American is a boor if he tucks his napkin in at the neck and uses bread to sop up the gravy on his plate, whereas Italians find it perfectly proper to do these things and find the bustle of the American life totally unrefined.

That refinement and developed taste are matters of convention and entirely relative is not a new thesis; it is an old accepted truth. What I wish to point out is this, that every development in refinement adds some new pleasure to the world but subtracts some old ones. He who develops his musical tastes from ragtime to the classics finds joys he knew not of, but is offended and disgusted whenever he visits friends, attends a movie or a theater. When people ate with their fingers there was little to be disgusted at in eating; when people need spotless linen and eight or ten forks, knives, and spoons for a meal, a single disarrangement, a spot on the linen, is intolerable. The higher one builds one's needs and tastes, the more opportunities for disgust, disappointment and discontent.

Most of the people of the world have never understood this. To the majority, acquisition, the multiplication of needs, desires and tastes constitute progress and seem to be the roads to happiness. Get rich, have horses, autos, beautiful things in the house, servants, go where you please and when you please,—this is happiness. The rich man knows it is not, and so does the wise man. Desires grow with each acquisition, the capacity for satisfaction diminishes with every gratification, novelty disappears and with the growth of taste little disharmonies offend deeply.

Some men have reacted in this way against gratification and satisfaction, against the building up of needs and tastes, and in every age we hear of the "simple life," the happy, contented life, where needs are few and things are "natural." The ascetic ideal of renunciation is the dominant note in Buddhism and Christianity; fly from the pleasures of this world, give up and renounce, for all is vanity and folly. To every struggler this seems true when the battle is hardest, when achievement seems futile and empty, and when he whispers to himself, "What is it all about, anyway?" To stop struggling, to desire only the plainest food, the plainest clothes, to live without the needless multiplication of refinements, to work at something essential for daily bread, to stop competing with one's neighbor in clothes, houses, ornaments, tastes,—it seems so pleasant and restful. But the competition gets keener, the struggle harder, tastes multiply, yesterday's luxury is to-day's need—to what end?

Will mankind ever accept a modified asceticism as its goal? I think it will be forced to, but it may be that the wish is father to the thought. Sometimes it seems as if the real crucifixion for every one of us is in our contending desires and tastes, in the artificial competing standards that are mislabeled refinement. To be finicky is to court anhedonia, and the joy of life is in robust tastes not easily offended and easily gratified.

Perhaps this is irrelevant in a chapter on play and recreation, but it is easily seen that much of play is a revolt against refinement and taste, just as much as humor is directed against them. In play we allow ourselves to shout, laugh aloud and to be unrefined; we welcome dirt and disorder; we forget clothes and manners; we are "natural," i. e., unrefined. The higher we build our tastes the more we need play. If such a thing as a "state of nature" could be reached, play and recreation in the adult sense would hardly more than exist.

CHAPTER XVI
RELIGIOUS CHARACTERS
DISHARMONY IN CHARACTER

I find in William James' "Varieties of Religious Experience", the following definition of religion: "Religion, therefore, as I shall ask you arbitrarily to take it, shall mean for us the feelings, acts and experiences of individuals in their solitude so far as they comprehend themselves to stand in relation to whatever they may consider the divine."

It seems to me the common man would as soon understand Einstein as this definition. In fact, the religious trends of the men and women in this world have many sources and are no more unified than their humor is. Whether all peoples, no matter how low in culture, have had religion cannot be settled by a study of the present inhabitants of the world, for every one of these, though savage, has tradition and some culture. Theoretically, for the one who accepts some form of evolution as true, at some time in man's history he has first asked himself some of the questions answered by religion.

For my part, as I read the anthropologists (whose answers to the question of the origin of religion I regard as the only valid ones, since they are the only ones without prejudice and with some regard for scientific method), it is the practical needs of man, his curiosity and his tendency to explain by human force, which are the first sources of the religions. How to get good crops, how to catch fish and game, how to win over enemies, how and whom to marry, what to do to be strong and successful as individual and group, found various answers in the taboo, the prayer, the ceremony and the priest, magician and scientist. Curiosity as to what was behind each phenomenon of nature and the tendency of man to personalize all force, as well as the awe and admiration aroused by the strong, wise and crafty contemporary and ancestor brought into the world the "old man-cult," ancestor- worship, gods and goddesses of ranging degrees and power, but very much like men and women except for power and longevity. Certain natural phenomena—death, sleep, trance, epileptic attack—all played their part, bringing about ideas of the soul, immortality, possession, etc. With culture and the growth of inhibition and knowledge and the use of art and symbols, the primitive beliefs modified their nature; the gods became one God, who was gradually stripped of his human desires, wishes, partialities and attributes until for the majority of the cultivated he becomes Nature, which in the end is a collection of laws in which one HOPES there is a unifying purpose. But the vast majority of the world, even in the so-called civilized countries, worship taboos, symbols, have a modified polytheistic belief or a personalized God, still attempt to persuade the Power in their own behalf, to act favorably to their own purposes and follow those who claim knowledge of the divine and inscrutable,—the priest, minister, rabbi, the man of God, in a phrase.

A part of religious feeling arises in civilized man, at least, from the feeling of awe in the presence of the vast forces of nature. Here science has contributed to religious feeling, for as one looks at the stars, his soul bows in worship mainly because the astronomer, the scientist, has told him that every twinkling point is a great sun surrounded by planets, and that the light from them must travel unimaginable millions of miles to reach him. As the world forces become impersonal they become more majestic, and a deeper feeling is evoked in their presence. Science aids true religion by increasing awe, by increasing knowledge.

A great factor in religion is the longing to compensate for death and suffering. Religion represents a reaction against fear, horror and humiliation. It is a cry of triumph in the face of what otherwise is disaster "I am not man, the worm, sick, old, doomed to die; I am the heir of the divine and will live forever, happy and blessed." Whether religious teaching is true or not, its great value lies in the happiness and surety of those who believe.

In its very highest sense the religious life is an effort to identify oneself with the largest purpose in the world. All cooperative purposes are thus religious, all competitive nonreligious. The selfish is therefore opposed to the altruistic purpose, the narrow to the broad. Good is the symbol for the purposes that seek the welfare of all: evil is the symbol of those who seek the welfare of a person or a group, regardless of the rest.

If this definition is correct, then every reformer is religious and every self-seeker, though he wear all the symbols of a religion and pray three times a day, is irreligious. I admit no man or woman to the fellowship of the religious unless in his heart he seeks some purpose that will lift the world out of discord and into harmony.

The power of the human being to believe in the face of opposed fact, inconsistency and unfavorable result is nowhere so well exemplified as in religion. I do not speak of the untold crimes and inhumanities done in the name of religion, of human sacrifice, persecution, religious war,—these are parts of a chapter in human history outside of the province of this book and almost too horrible to be contemplated. But men have believed (and do believe) that some among them knew what God wanted, that certain procedures, tricks and ceremonies conveyed sanctity and surety; that cosmic events like storms, droughts, eclipses and epidemics had personal human meanings, that Infinite Wisdom would be guided in action by the prayers of ignorance, self-seeking and hatred, etc., etc. The savage who believes that his medicine man's antics, paint and feathers will bring rain and fertile soil has his counterpart in the civilized man who believes that this or that ceremonial and professed belief insures salvation. Faith is beautiful in the abstract, but in the concrete it is often the origin of superstition and amazing folly. [80] However crudely intelligence and honest scientific effort may work, they soar in a heaven far above the abyss of credulity.

True religion in the sense I have used the word has faith in it, the faith that there is a purpose in the universe, though it seems impossible for us to discover it. In the personal character it seeks to establish altruistic feeling and conduct, though it does not rule out as unworthy self-feeling or seeking. It merely subordinates them. It does not deny the validity of pleasure, of the sensuous pleasures; it does not set its face against drinking, eating, sexual love, play and entertainment, but it urges a valid purpose as necessary for happiness and morality. It does not glorify faith as against reason, emotion as against intelligence; on the contrary, it holds that reason and intelligence are the governing factors in human life and only by use of them do we rise from the beast.

So the religious life of those we study will be of great importance to us. In the majority of cases we shall find that social heredity, tradition and backing will play the dominant role, in that most, in name at least, live and die in the faith in which they were born. We find those who identify form and ceremonial with religion (the majority), others who identify it with ethics and morality, and who can conceive no righteousness out of it. Then there is the strictly modern type of person to whom right conduct is held to have nothing to do with religious belief and who measures Christian, Jew, Mohammedan and agnostic by their acts and not at all by their dogma, and who thus relegates religion, in the ordinary use of the word, to a rather useless place in human life. Orthodoxy, piety, tolerance and skepticism represent attitudes towards organized religion: altruism, sympathy, good will, and fellowship are the measurements of the unorganized religion whose mission it is to find the purpose of life.

We have spoken throughout of man as a mosaic of character, and we must modify this statement. A mosaic is a static collection, whereas a man has character struggles, balance and overbalance. Really to know a man is to get at the proportionate power of his various trends, to understand his harmonies and disharmonies.

Character development is the story of the unification of the traits or characters. Disharmony, disproportion of traits and characters may be progressive and lead to disaster and mental disease, or a balance may be reached after a struggle and what we call reform takes place. Though our social life tends to narrow and repress character, it also tends to harmonize it by the preventing of excess development of certain traits. The social person is on the whole well balanced, though he may be mediocre. On the

---

[80] It would be amusing were it not sad to see how remarkably well some philosophers use their intelligence and logic to prove the invalidity of intelligence and logic. They praise emotion, instinct and "intuition" and such modes of knowing and acting, yet their works are closely argued, reasoned and appeal throughout to the intelligence of their readers for acceptance.

other hand, the non-social person usually tends to unbalance in the sense that he becomes odd and eccentric.

What are the chief disharmonies? I mean, of course, glaring disharmonies, for no one is of harmonious development, with intelligence, emotions, instincts, desires, purposes in cooperation with each other. This I propose to consider in more detail in the next chapter, on some character types, but it will be of use to sketch the great disharmonies.

Character is dynamic, and a fundamental disharmony, even if not noticeable early in life, may progress to the point of disruption of the personality. Thus an individual who is strongly egoistic in his purposes and aims may succeed if at the same time he is determined intelligent and shrewd. But let us suppose he has a son who is as strongly egoistic, is as determined, but lacks intelligence and shrewdness. Not becoming successful, this person ascribes his failure to others and develops ideas of persecution.

Again, a true poet is a person of keen sensibilities, but he must possess at the same time imaginative intelligence and the power of words. Let these be joined in proper proportions, and his verse becomes ours and we hail him as a poet. But let him lack the power of words, and though he sweat with a desire to write he is a failure or a hack poet, making up by industry what he lacks in beauty. Suppose there is a man deeply passionate, thrilled by the beauty of women and desiring them with a fierce ardor, and yet he has strong inhibitions, great purposes which hold him steady. Then throughout life he seems calm, chaste and controlled, and no one knows of the turmoil and battle within him. We may suppose that old age [81] or a sickness lowers his inhibiting qualities, and a startling change in conduct results, one that we can scarcely believe and which we are inclined to call a complete transformation of personality. In reality, a disharmony has occurred, some trend has been released, and conduct, which is a resultant, changes its direction.

Inhibition control, may develop later than it should, as I have already mentioned. At adolescence sex desire comes suddenly into play, but usually in one way or another there are checks upon its effects already established. But often there is not, and the boy or girl plunges into a sex life that brings them into violent conflict with themselves and society. Despite their efforts the non-ethical conduct continues; despite their tears and vows to reform they are swept by "temptation" into difficulty. Then suddenly or gradually, perhaps long after every one despairs of them, the inhibition appears, and they settle down to a controlled life. What has happened? We cannot say in anatomical terms, but from a psychological standpoint the function of inhibition, delayed in its appearance, finally comes on the scene. We see this delay in other phases of character; there is often delay in sex feeling, in the interest in work, in love of the beautiful, in control of anger, etc. Take the last mentioned: an irascible child grows into

---

[81] Sexual misdemeanor is not uncommon in old men who have hitherto been of hallowed reputation.

an irascible adolescent and even into a similar adult, flaring up under the least provocation, to the dismay and disgust of others and himself. "He can't control himself," so say others, and so thinks he. He vows reform, but nothing seems to help. Then like a miracle comes the longed-for inhibition; anger is still there when his will is crossed or his opinion scouted, but a firm hand is on it, and he maintains a calm he had despaired of reaching.

Man is a bundle of disharmonies, as the great Eli Metchnikoff pointed out, physically, psychologically and sociologically. When these disharmonies are within average limits we do not notice them; when they are greater in degree they bring about conduct that at once claims attention. Sometimes a disharmony is merely an excess development of some ability, in which case, if the ability is socially valuable, we have the talented person or the genius. This is often the case with the artistic abilities and also with the physical powers. If the disharmony involve an instinct, an emotion or certain phases of the intelligence, we are brought face to face with the abnormal.

There is, of course, disharmony through ordinary defect as in feeble-mindedness, as in absence of some essential emotion or instinct. These are hopeless situations and belong in the grim field of psychopathology. Often what seems to be a defect is a "sleeping" quality, and one that will awaken under appropriate circumstance. Conspicuously, maternal love is of this nature. One sees a girl who has no interest in children, considers them bores and nuisances, who marries with the hope she will be childless, and with the first baby becomes a passionately devoted mother, even fiercely maternal.

In the following pages I shall sketch some prominent character types. This has been done by such masters as Aristotle, Spinoza, Kant, La Bruyere, Stewart, Ribot, Mill, etc., but with a different purpose and starting point than mine.

Every great novelist is a professor of character depiction. Witness Scrooge, Pecksniff, Mark Tapley, Pickwick, Sam Weller and his father, created by Dickens; the four musketeers, especially D'Artagnon, of Dumas; Amelia and Rebecca Sharp, George, and the Major of Thackeray; Jane Austen's heroines and George Eliot's men and women; the narrators in the famous Canterbury Inn, the soldiers of Kipling, the Shylocks, Macbeths, Rosalinds and Falstaffs of the greatest dramatist; the thousand and one fictitious and yet real figures of literature.

The temperament studies by the psychologists and philosophers have been too broad and too classical to be of practical value. Sanguine and choleric temperament, the bilious, the nervous and the phlegmatic, the quick and the slow, all these are broad divisions, and no man really exemplifies them. What I propose to do is less ambitious, but perhaps more practical. I shall take a few of the qualities with which the previous pages have concerned themselves and show how they work out in individuals mainly sketched from life.

It will seem that perhaps a disproportionate number are pathological, but I wish to insist that there is no sharp line between the "normal" and "pathological" in character. In fact, normality is an abstract conception, an ideal never reached or seen, and each of us only approaches that ideal in greater or lesser degree. Moreover, certain deviations from the normal are useful, as the assemblage of qualities that make the genius or the reformer of certain types. Others are not useful, or at least not useful in the environment and age in which the deviated person finds himself. Undoubtedly the abnormal have helped found religions, for one who "hears" God and "sees" him as do many of the insane, if intelligent and eloquent at the same time, easily convinces others; but if such a person occurs in a group with well-established belief and resistant to the new, the insane hospital soon lodges the new apostle.

I shall not attempt to consider all the varied shades of harmony and disharmony, the extraordinary variety of types. There are as many varieties of persons as there are people, and the mathematical possibilities exceed computation. Those depicted are some of the outstanding types, in whom qualities and combinations of qualities can easily be seen at work.

CHAPTER XVII
SOME CHARACTER TYPES

There is one kind of energy discharger that we may call the hyperkinetic, controlled practical type. This group is characterized by great and constant activity, well controlled by purpose, with eagerness and enthusiasm manifested in each act but not excessively.

1. A. is one of these people. In school he specialized in athletics and was a fine all-round player in almost every sport. When he left high school to go to work he at once entered business. His employers soon found him to be a tireless worker, steady and purposeful in everything. In addition to carrying on his duties by day, A. studied nights, carefully choosing his subjects so that they related directly to his business. Despite the fact that his work was hard and his studies exacting, A. had energy enough left to join social organizations and to take a leading part in their affairs. He became quickly known as one of those busy people who always are ready to take on more work. Naturally this led to his becoming a leader, first in his social relations and second in his business. Always practical in his judgments and actions, A. fell in love with the daughter of a rich family and married her, with the full approval of her relatives, who were keen enough to see that his energy, power and control were destined for success.

The leading traits that A. manifests hinge around his high energy and control. He is honest and conventional, devoted to the ideals of his group and admires learning, but he is not in any sense a scholar. He is a poor speaker, in the ordinary sense of that term, but curiously effective, nevertheless, because his earnest energy and sturdy common sense win approval as "not a theorist." But mainly he wins because he is tireless in energy and enthusiasm and yet has yoked these qualities to ordinary purposes. The average man he meets understands him thoroughly, sympathizes with him completely and accepts him as a leader after his own heart.

So A. has become rich and respected. As times goes on, as he is brought more and more into contact with large affairs outside of business; as a trustee of hospitals and a director of charitable organizations, he broadens out but not into an "unsafe" attitude. He pities the unfortunate but is not truly sympathetic, in that it rarely occurs to him that success and failure are relative, that an accident might have shipwrecked his fortunes and that his good qualities are as innate as his complexion. For this man prides himself on his strong will and courage, whereas he merely has within him a fine engine in whose construction he had no part.

2. The hyperkinetic, controlled, impractical person. B. is, in the fundamentals of energy and control, singularly like A., but because of the nature of his interests and purposes their lives have completely diverged so that no one would ordinarily recognize the kinship in type. B. is and always

has been a worker, enthusiastic and enduring, and he has stuck to his last with a fidelity that is remarkable. He is very likable in the ordinary sense,—pleasant to look at, cheerful, ready to joke, laugh or to help the other fellow. Nevertheless, he has only a few friends and is a distinctly disappointed man at heart, because his interests are in the ordinary sense, impractical.

B. early became interested in physiology. From the very start he found in the workings of the human body a fascination that concentrated his efforts. Poor, he worked hard enough to obtain scholarships and fellowships in one university after another until finally he became a Ph. D. Here was a great error from the practical standpoint; for had he become an M. D., he would have had a profession that offered an independent financial future. But, in his zeal, he did not wish to take on the extended program of the physician, and he saw clearly that he might become a better scientist as a Ph. D. He became a teacher in one school after another, did a good deal of research work, but has not been fortunate enough to make any epoch-making discoveries. He is one of those splendid, painstaking, energetic men found in every university who turn out good pieces of work of which only a few know anything, and from which in the course of time some genius or lucky scientist culls a few facts upon which to build up a great theory or a new doctrine. He married one of his own students, a fine woman but unluckily not very strong, and so there fell on him many a domestic duty that a thousand extra dollars a year would have turned over to a maid.

Thus B. is an obscure but respected member of the faculty of a small university. He teaches well, though he dislikes it, and he is happy at the times when he works hard at some physiological problem. He loves his family and has vowed that his son will be a business man. He feels inferior as he contemplates his obscure existence, with its precarious financial state, its drudgery and most of all the gradual disappearance of his ideals. He is frank to himself alone, wishes he had made money, but is apt to sneer at the world of the "fat and successful" as less than his intellectual equal. He compares his own rewards with that of the successful man knowing less and with a narrower outlook.

Thus, through success, A. is broadening and becoming something of an idealist. B. is narrowing and through failure is losing his ideals. This is not an uncommon effect of success and failure. Where success leads to arrogance and conceit it narrows, but where the character withstands this result the increased experience and opportunity is of great value to character. Failure may embitter and thus narrow through envy and lost energy, but also it may strip away conceit and overestimation and thus lead to a richer insight into life.

3. The hyperkinetic, uncontrolled or shallow. This type, although quick and apparently energetic, is deficient in a fundamental of the personality, in the organizing energy. This deficiency may extend into all phases of the mental life or in only a few phases. Thus we see people whose thinking is rapid, energetic, but they cannot "stick" to one line of thought

long enough to reach a goal. Others are similarly situated in regard to purposes; they are enthusiastic, easily stirred into activity, but rarely do their purposes remain fixed long enough for success. As a rule this class is inconstant in affections, though warm and sympathetic. They gush but never organize their philanthropic efforts, so that they rarely do any real good. Often the most lovable of people, they are at the same time the despair of those who know them best.

M. is a woman who makes a fine first impression, is very pretty, with nice manners and a quick, flattering interest in every one she meets. She is usually classed as intelligent because she is vivacious, that is, her mind follows the trend of things quickly, and she marshals whatever she knows very readily. As one who knows her well says, "She shows all her goods the first time. You really do not know how slender her stock in trade is until you see the same goods and tricks every time you meet her." Needless to say her critic is a woman.

M. is interested in something new each week. The "new" usually fascinates her, and she becomes so extraordinarily busy that she hardly has time to eat or sleep. She is always put on committees if the organization heads do not know her, but if they do, she is carefully slated for something of no importance. After a short time her interest has shifted to something else. Thus she passes from work in behalf of blind babies to raising funds for a home for indigent actors; from energy spent in philanthropy to energy spent in learning the latest dances. Her enthusiasm never cools off, though its goal always changes.

Fortunately she is married to a rich man who views her with affection and a shrug of his shoulders. Her children know her; now and then, she becomes extraordinarily interested in their welfare, much to their disgust and rebellion, for they have long since sized her up.

She has often been on the verge of a love affair with some man who is professionally interested in something into which she has leaped for a short time. She raves about him, follows him, flatters and adores him, and then, before the poor fellow knows where he is at, she is out of love and off somewhere else. This mutability of affection has undoubtedly saved her from disaster.

Were she not rich, M. would be one of the social problems that the social workers cannot understand or handle, e. g., there is a type who never sticks to anything, not because he is bored quickly, or is inefficient, but because he is at the mercy of the new and irrelevant. Without sufficient means he throws up his job and tries to get the new work he longs to do. Sometimes he fails to get it, and then he becomes an unemployed problem.

This type of uncontrolled energy reaches its height in the manical or manic phase of the disease already described as manic depressive insanity. The "manic personality," which need not become insane, is characterized by high energy, vivacious emotions, rapid flow of thought and irrelevant associations.

4. The mesokinetic—medium or average in their energy (feeling and power)—run the range of the vast groups we call the average. This type is

spurred on by necessity, custom and habit to steady work and steady living. Possessed of practical wisdom, their world is narrow, their affections only called out for their kindred and immediate friends. Their interests are largely away from their work and as a rule do not include the past or future of the race. Usually conservative, they accept the moral standards as absolute and are quick to resent changes in custom. They follow leaders cheerfully, are capable of intense loyalty to that cause which they believe to stand for their interests. Yet each individual of the mass of men, though he never rises above mediocrity, presents to his intimates a grouping of qualities and peculiarities that gives him a distinct personality.

C. is one of those individuals whose mediocre energy has stood between him and so-called success. At present he is forty and occupies about the same position that he did at twenty. As a boy he was fond of play but never excelled in any sport and never occupied a place of leadership. He had the usual pugnacious code of boys, but because he was friendly and good-natured rarely got into a fight. He liked to read and was rather above the average in intelligence, but he never tackled the difficult reading, confining himself to the "interesting" novel and easy information. He left high school when he was sixteen and immediately on leaving he dropped all study. He entered an office as errand boy and was recognized as faithful and industrious, but he showed no especial initiative or energy. In the course of time he was promoted from one position to another until he became a shipper at the age of twenty. Since this time he has remained at this post without change, except that when he got married and on a few occasions afterward, when the cost of living rose, his salary was raised.

C. is married, and his wife often "nags" him because he does not get ahead. She tells him that he has no energy and fight in him, that if he would he could do better. Sometimes he takes refuge in the statement that he has no pull, that those who have been promoted over his head are favorites for some reason or another, and he rarely recognizes the superiority of his immediate superiors, though he is loyal enough to the boss. He lives in that "quiet despair" that Thoreau so aptly describes as the life of the average man, and he seeks escape from it in smoking, in belonging to a variety of fraternal organizations, in the movies and the detective story. He is a "good" father and husband, which means that he turns over all his earnings, is faithful and kind. Except that he admonishes and punishes his children when they are "bad," he takes no constructive share in their training and leaves that to the mother, the church and the school. He and his wife are attached to one another through habit and mutual need, but they have some time since outlived passion and intense affection. She has sized him up as a failure and knows herself doomed to struggle against poverty, and he knows that she understands him. This mutual "understanding" keeps them at arm's length except in the face of danger or disaster, when they cling to each other for comfort and support. This is the history of many a marriage that on its surface is quiet and peaceful.

The hypokinetic types. We cannot separate energy display from enthusiasm, courage, intelligence, persistent purpose, etc. If I have made myself clear in the preceding pages of this book, you will realize that no character of man works alone, but all feeling, thought and action is a resultant of forces. Nevertheless, there are those in whom the fire of life burns high and others in whom it burns low, and either group may be of totally different qualities otherwise.

There are people of low energy discharge, and these it seems to me are of two main kinds,—the one where nothing seems to arouse or create powerful motives and purposes, and the other in whom the main defect is a rapidly arising exhaustion. The first I call the simple hypokinetic group and the other the irritable hypokinetic group.

The simple hypokinetic person may be one of any grade of intelligence but more commonly is of low intelligence. In any school for the feeble-minded one finds the apathetic imbecile, who can be kept at work by goading and stimulation of one kind or another, who does not tire especially, but who never works beyond a low level of speed and enthusiasm.

5. A more interesting type is T. He may be called the intelligent hypokinetic, the high-grade failure. As a baby he learned to walk late, though he talked early and well. He played in a leisurely sort of way, running only when he had to and content as a rule to be in the house. He was not seclusive, seeming to enjoy the company of other children, but rarely made any efforts to seek them out. He was quick to learn but showed only a moderate curiosity, and he rarely made any investigations on his own account. It was noticed that he seldom asked "why" in the usual manner of intelligent children.

He did fairly well in school; he had a wonderful memory and seemed to see very quickly into intricate problems. It was always a great surprise of his teachers that he was so bright, as one said, in comparison to his standing. Once or twice a zealous teacher sought to stimulate him into more effort and study, but though he responded for a short time, gradually he slipped back into his own easy pace. He went through high school, and on the basis of a splendid memory and a keen intelligence, which by this time were easily recognized, he was sent to college. He took no part in athletics and little part in the communal college activities. He had so good a command of facts and with this so cynical a point of view that he became quite a college character and was pointed out as a fellow who could lead his class if he would. As a matter of fact, nothing could spur him to real competitive effort.

We may pass briefly over his life. After he left college, he drifted from one position to another. Usually in some hack literary line. Were it not for a small income he would have starved. After a few years he become very fat and gross looking, and then came a kindly pneumonia which carried him off.

We must not mistake the stolid for the hypokinetic. There was a classmate of mine in the medical school, a large, quiet fellow, D. M., who got by everything, as the boys said, by the skin of his teeth. He worked without enthusiasm or zeal, studied infrequently and managed to pass along to his second year, at about the bottom of the class. In that year we took up bacteriology, the "bug-bear" as one punster put it, of the school. Just what it was about the subject that aroused D. M. I never knew, but a remarkable transformation took place. The man changed over, studied hard, read outside literature and actually asked for the privilege of working in the laboratory Sundays and holidays so that he might learn more. When this was known to the rest of the class, there were bets placed that he would not "last," but quite to the surprise of everybody D. M. gained in momentum as he went along. As a matter of fact, his interest on the subject grew, and he is now a bacteriologist of good standing. In fact, his lack of interest in other matters has helped him, since he has no distracting tastes or pleasures.

Thus there are persons of specialized interest and energy, and it may well be that there is for most of the hypokinetic a line of work that would act to energize them. The problem, therefore, in each case is to find the latent ability and interest and to regard no case as really hopeless. I say this despite the fact that I believe some cases are hopeless. The pessimistic attitude on the part of parent or teacher kills effort; the optimistic attitude fosters energetic effort.

6. The irritable hypokinetic. Irritability [82] of a pathological type as a phase of lowered energy is well known to every physiologist and in the practical everyday world is seen in the tired and sick. There are people who from the very start of life show lowered endurance, who respond to certain stimuli in an excessive manner and are easily exhausted. This type the neurologist calls the congenital neurasthenic, and it may be we are dealing here with some defect in the elimination of fatigue products. This, however, is only a guess, and the disease factor, if there is any, is entirely unknown. I do not pretend that the person I am to describe is entirely representative of this group. Indeed, no dozen cases would show all the symptoms and peculiarities of the irritable hypokinetic group.

E. is a man at present thirty years of age. In person he is of average height, rather slender, with delicate features, somewhat bald, quick in action and speech. He flushes easily and thus often has high color, especially when fatigued or excited. This "vasomotor irritability," as the physicians call it, is quite common in this group of people, and in fact in all neurasthenia, whether acquired or congenital. Though I have described E. as belonging to the slender type of person, it is necessary to say that stout, rugged-looking people are often irritable and hypokinetic.

As a child E. "never could stand excitement or strain," as his mother says. What is meant is this: that he became overexcited under almost any circumstances and became profoundly fatigued afterwards. As we have seen, the intense diffusion of excitement throughout the whole body is a sign of the childish and inferior organism; as maturity approaches and

---

[82] One must take care not to mistake the irritability which is the characteristic of all living tissue for the irritability here considered.

throughout childhood excitability decreases and is better localized. When a noise is heard an infant jumps, and so do people like E., but the better controlled merely turn their head and eyes to see what the source of the noise may be. This lack of control of excitement extended in E.'s case to play, entertainment, novelty of any kind, crowds and especially to the disagreeable excitement of quarrels, fights, terrifying experiences, etc. Under anger he trembled, grew pale, and his shouts and screams were beyond control; under fear he became actually sick, vomited and showed a liability to syncope of an alarming kind. E. was not the selfish type of the neurasthenic; he was gentle and kind and ready to share with everybody, a lovable boy of an intensely sociable nature. Nevertheless, his high excitability and his quick fatigue made it necessary to shelter him, for any effort at toughening merely brought about a "breakdown."

Here we must reemphasize the fundamental importance of the fatigue reactions. The normal fatigue reaction is to feel weary, to desire rest and to be able to rest and sleep. The abnormal reaction, one directly opposed to the well-being of the individual, is to feel exhausted, to become restless and to find it difficult to sleep. There are children who thrive on excitement and exertion; they sleep sounder for it, they recuperate readily and gain in strength and endurance with every ordinary burden put upon them. There are others to whom anything but the least excitement and exertion acts as a poison, making them restless and exhausted. Not all children who show this perverse fatigue reaction grow up with it. It may be only a temporary phase of their lives, but while it lasts it is very troublesome.

In E.'s case the overexcitable hypokinetic stage lasted until about the ninth year, and then there was a great improvement, though he still was of the same general type. He became a fairly good runner for a short distance, learned to swim, though he stood the cold water poorly, was clever and graceful as a dancer and was quite popular. At sixteen he left school to enter business, because of the straitened means of his family. He entered into adolescent period later and suffered greatly from his sixteenth to nineteenth year from, fatigue, hypochondriacal fears, and had to have a good deal of medical attention at this time. Sex questions perplexed him, for he became quite passionate and at the same time had much moral repugnance to illicit relations. His sexual curiosity was intense, and he read all manner of books on the subject, went to the burlesque shows on the sly and almost became obsessed on sex matters.

At this stage he made only a mediocre showing in his business career, though his evident honesty secured him promotion to a clerk's position. After his nineteenth year he seemed to gain again in energy and endurance and was fairly well until his twenty-eighth year, though he had to nurse his endurance at all times, developed very regular habits of sleep, diet, etc., and in this manner got along. Once he had an opportunity to join an organization which would have paid him a better salary, but the hours were irregular, and it would have demanded much exertion and excitement, so he passed it by.

In 1917 he joined the army, partly because of patriotic motives, partly because he was convinced that army life might develop his endurance and energy. He was sent to an army post in the South and within two months of his entrance had "broken down." He was sleepless, restless, was irritable and "jumpy," had lost appetite and the feeling of endurance. Life seemed intolerable, though he had no desire to do away with himself, for he had no quarrel with life itself but was disgusted with his inferiority. He was hospitalized, but this did little good and he was afterwards discharged as medically unfit.

This, of course, hurt his pride, but essentially he was greatly relieved. He made but slow improvement until through the munificence of Uncle Sam he was given a new start in life through the Vocational Reeducation Board. Like many other city men, he has dreamed of the "chicken farm" as the ideal occupation free from too much work and yet lucrative. This, of course, is a mistaken notion, but while learning the work he is happy and is slowly regaining his energy. What time will bring forth no one can tell, but this is certain: throughout his life he will have to rely on good habits, carefully adjusted to his energy, in order to protect himself from the bankruptcy that so easily comes on him. A philosophy of life which will help to control his irritability is necessary, and the intelligent of the hypokinetic irritable acquire the habits and the philosophy necessary for their welfare.

Any neurologist could cite any number of such cases with varying traits of character, high intelligence or feeble-minded, controlled in morals or uncontrolled, happily or unhappily situated, whose central difficulty is an irritable and easily exhausted store of energy. They are easily excited and excitement burns them out; that is the long and short of their situation. Sex, love, hatred, anger, strain, fear in all its forms, illness,—all these and many other emotions and happenings may break them down. Such people, and those who care for them, must not make the mistake of thinking that rough handling, strenuosity, will cure what is apparently a fixed character.

There is an irritable, high-energy type—irritable hyperkinetic—that is well contrasted with the foregoing. This explosive personality works by fits and starts but does not wear out, merely, as it were, settles down to his ordinary pace when he rests up. He is like a six-day bicycle racer who plugs along but every now and then sprints like mad for a few laps and then comes back to a pace that would kill the average rider. I shall not trouble to cite such a case, but I can think of at least one man of good attainments who is of this explosive hyperkinetic type. He responds to every demand with a burst of energy, and his quota of ordinary activities is simply appalling.

Neglecting the further types of energy display for the simple reason that this quality shades off into every conceivable type and is also a part of every nature, we turn to the types of emotional mood display. With these it is necessary to consider excitability as well, and the most interesting beings are here our objects of study.

I wish first to emphasize my belief that where there is a great natural variation in excitability and emotionality in individuals, there is not nearly so much in races as we think, and that social heredity is tradition and cultural level plays the more important role in this. My friend and colleague, Dr. A. Warren Stearns, has made a study which shows that while the immigrant Italian is excitable and quick to anger and of revengeful reactions, his American-born descendent has so far controlled and changed this type of reaction that he does not especially figure in police records, in murders or assaults. My own studies of the second and especially the third generation Jew show there is an almost complete approach to the "American" type in emotional display, in what is known as poise. This third generation Jewish-American has dropped all the mannerisms of excitability in gesture and voice, and his adherence to good form includes that attitude of nonchalant humor so characteristic of the American.

1. The generally excitable, overemotional type. This type is more common in the Latin, Hebrew and Celtic races. In some respects it corresponds to the hypokinetic irritable, but it is not necessarily hypokinetic. The artistic type of person, so called, is of this group, but is, of course, talented as well. Talent need not be present, and there are persons of no artistic ability whatever who show a generalized, excitable-emotional temperament. All young children show the main traits of this type, and there is something essentially simple about all these folk, no matter how civilized or sophisticated they get to be.

A. L., a woman of fifty, belongs to this group. She is a Jewess and now a widow. All of her life her character and temperament have been the same, and though her experiences have been varied she has not in any essential altered. This last is rather characteristic of the group, for experience has but little effect on their emotional reactions.

A. L. cries very easily and readily, but her tears are easily dried and her joy is grotesquely childlike. She is readily frightened, worries without restraint and finds a melancholy satisfaction in the worst. At the same time, her fears do not persist and are easily dissipated by encouragement or good fortune. She is readily angered and "raises a row" with great facility and without restraint. For this reason her relatives and friends become panic-stricken when she becomes angry, for they know that she does not hesitate to make an embarrassing scene. In the efforts to conciliate her they are apt to give her her own way, as a result of which she is the proverbial spoiled child, capitalizing her weakness.

Our Jewess uses her emotions for effect, which means that she has become theatrical. Though there is reality in her emotional display, time and the advantages she has gained have brought enough finish and restraint to her manifestations to gain the designation artistic. True, it is a crude artistry, for intelligence does not sufficiently guide it, and her art is used sometimes indiscriminately and inopportunely. As she grows older the value of her tears is less, and she is becoming that prime nuisance, the elderly scold.

Among the emotional types well recognized by the neurologist is that known as the cyclothymic. In the individuals of this group there is a periodicity to mood (rather than to emotions). There is a definitely pathological trend to the cyclothymic, and in its most marked form one sees the recurring depressions and excitement of Manic Depressive Insanity.

Aside from these pathological forms, there are persons who show curious periodic changes in mood. They become depressed for no especial reason, are "blue" for day after day and then quickly return to their normal. Sometimes these blue spells alternate with periods of exaltation and happiness, but in my experience this is far less common than periodic blue spells, a kind of recurrent anhedonia.

L. D. is ordinarily what is known as a vivacious person. Bright, talkative, keen in her discriminations, she has all her life been at the mercy of strange alterations in mood, alterations which come and go without what seems to others adequate reason.

As a child L. D. was sick a great deal. She showed an unusual susceptibility to infection, and it was not until she was nine years of age that she attended school regularly. Her illnesses made it impossible to discipline her, and so she has always been a bit "spoiled," though her kind and generous nature makes her a charming person. But more important than the fact that she could not be disciplined is the lowering of energy that these sicknesses produced, a lowering marked mainly by a liability to fatigue and depression.

Let there come a sickness, and this woman's stock of hopeful mood goes and there results a loss of interest in life, a loss of zest and joyousness.

A digression,—and a return to the theme of the first chapter of this book. The dependence of the mental life on bodily structure, equally true in the both sexes, is exquisitely demonstrated in woman. In many women there occurs an extraordinary increase of sex desire just before the menstrual period and in some to the point where it causes great internal conflict. Others show moderate depression and even confusion at this time, and to the majority of women some mood and thought change is taken for granted. At the menopause mental difficulties to the point of insanity are witnessed, and in some cases the change is permanent. Back of mood is the entire organic life of the organism, and back of the nature of our thoughts and deeds is mood.

A peculiarity of fatigue is remarkably well shown by this person. When she is tired or convalescent a depressing thought sticks, becomes an obsession, a fixed idea, to the plague of her life. Thus when she was nursing her first baby the night feedings exhausted her. One night, half asleep and half awake, with the vigorous little animal pulling away at her breast, she watched the pulsing fontanelle on the top of the baby's head, and the thought came to her how dreadfully easy it would be to injure the brain beneath. Her heart pounced in fear, she almost fainted at the thought, and yet it "stuck" and came back to her with each random association. I need not detail how the idea recurred a dozen times a day and brought the fear that she was going insane. She stopped nursing the baby at night, got a good rest, and the idea disappeared. She was "able to shake off" when rested that which was a hideous obsession when fatigued.

Indeed, one might speak of persons of this type as hypothymic as well as cyclothymic. The hypothymic are those whose stock of courage and hope is easily exhausted, who become easily discouraged. They are borrowers of energy and vigor, they need sturdier folk around them; often they are said to be sensitive, and while this is sometimes true, it is more often the case that they are more affected. That is, two persons may notice the same thing or suffer the same sickness, but the so-called sensitive has a reserve of courage and energy that disappears, whereas the other has enough left in stock so that he does not feel any change.

The extraordinary complexity of human character is well illustrated by C. D. She is hypothymic or cyclothymic to the little affairs of life and to the minor illnesses. Yet when her family fortunes were greatly imperilled by a financial crisis, she stood up against the strain far better than did her husband, a man sturdy and buoyant in most of the affairs of life. His ego was more concerned with financial fortune than was hers, and against this ill she was the philosopher and not he.

We may well contrast L. D. with her husband. He belongs to the sturdy in emotions and morals,—the stable. Dark days and bright days, sickness and health, fatigue and rest seem to impair his courage, hope and general cheerfulness of mood but little. He has a high organic balance and a well-built-up philosophy. I started to say of him that he is an optimist, but this is not true. He is cheerful, but he does not sing, "Tra la la, all the things that are, are good." He says, "There are bad things, but I must carry on and fight the good fight." His is a philosophy of courage and endurance, but not of optimistic twaddle. He is too wide-brained to speak of life as "all good" when he knows of inherited disease, cruelty, preventable poverty, gross neglect and unmerited misfortune. Yet he lends hope and comfort to the afflicted, and he has an unvarying comfort for his cyclothymic mate.

He has built up his ego around a business, one in which there was sunk not only his own fortune but that of a host of friends. When this was so threatened as to seem inevitably lost, his ego was deeply wounded, he lost courage and hope and then needed the strength of his wife. This she gave, and when the tide of affairs turned, his own courage was ready and unimpaired. We are like trees,—the hard, strong, knotty parts of our fiber are distributed in irregular fashion, and he who seems strongest has a weak place somewhere. Attack that, and his resistance, courage and hope disappear.

While there are the types of mood and emotional make-up, there are curious monothymic types, people who habitually tend to react with one emotion or mood.

The fear type. It must again be emphasized that we cannot separate emotion, mood, instinct, intelligence in our analysis. And so we shall speak of individuals of this or that type when what we mean is that they reacted habitually and remarkably in one direction. Thus with the man F., who has quick imagination, and whose ability to forecast is inextricably mixed with a liability to fear. It is true that some do not fear because they do not foresee, and that placidity and calmness are less often due to courage than to lack of imagination.

F. feared animals excessively as a child and injury to himself as a boy, so that he played few rough games. To a large extent his parents fostered this fear in him by carefully guarding and watching him, by putting him through that neurasthenic regimen so brilliantly described by Arthur Guiterman in his story of the aseptic pup. Yet he had a brother as carefully brought up as himself who became a rough-and-tumble lad, with as little likelihood to fear as any boy. So that we may only assume that F.'s training fostered fear in him; it did not cause it.

At the age of thirteen the fear of death entered F.'s life, the occasion being the death of an uncle. The mourning, the quick fleeting sight of the dead man in the black box, the interment of the once vigorous, joyous man in the earth struck terror into the heart of the boy. From that time much of his life was controlled by his struggles with the fear of death, and his history is his reaction to that fear. At fourteen he astonished his free-thinking family by becoming a devout Christian, by praying, attending church regularly and by becoming so moral in his conduct as to warrant the belief that there was something wrong with him. Indeed, had a psychiatrist examined him at this time, there is no doubt he would have diagnosed his condition as a beginning Dementia Precox. But he was not; he simply was compensating for his fear of death.

At sixteen he entered an academy where he was forced to go into athletics. The fear of injury and death plagued him so that he broke down, but this breakdown did not last long, and he reentered athletics and did fairly well. Indeed, in order to break himself of fear, he became outwardly a rather daring gymnast, hoping that what he had so often read of the sickly and puny becoming strong and vigorous through training would be true of him. As soon as he reached a stage in school where compulsory training was dropped, he discontinued athletics, with much inward relief. In fact, pride, fear of being considered a coward, was mainly responsible for his efforts in this direction.

In college he fell under the influence of Omar Khayam and the epicurean reaction to death. He feverishly entered pleasure and swung easily from religious fervor to a complete agnosticism. He became a first-nighter, knew all the chorus girls it was possible for him to become acquainted with, learned to drink but never learned to enjoy it. In fact, after each sensual indulgence his reaction against himself led him to a despair which might have terminated in suicide were it not that he feared death more than the reproaches of his conscience. Then he fell under the influence of a group of men and women in his college town, philanthropists and social reformers, whose enthusiasm and energy seemed to him miraculous, and as he grew to know them he realized with a something like ecstasy and yet governed by intelligence, that in such work was a compensation for death that might satisfy both his emotions and his intelligence. Again to the surprise of his parents, and in the face of their prediction that he would soon "tire" of this fad, he entered into their activities and proved himself a devoted worker. Too devoted, for now and then he needs medical attention, and it was in one of these "neurasthenic" periods that I met him. I learned that the spur that kept him going, that made him energetic, was the fear that death would overtake him before he achieved anything worth while; that he hated to die and was appalled by the thought of death, but that he could forget all this in work of a socially useful kind.

F. might almost stand for mankind in his reactions to death. He seemed to me almost too good to be true as a demonstration of a pet thesis of mine, namely, that the fear of death is behind an enormous amount of men's deeds and beliefs. His reaction was of the compensatory type, where the fear arouses counter-emotions, counter-activities. F.'s is a noble response to fear, just as the cowardly reaction is the ignoble response.

I shall not depict the coward. There are some in whose lives the fear of death, injury, illness or loss is in constant operation to prevent activity, to lower energy and effort. One finds the coward very commonly in the clinics for nervous diseases, and in some cases the formidable term of psychasthenia is merely camouflage for the more direct English word. There is a type of the timid, who will not stand up for their rights, who receive meekly, as if it were their due, the buffets of fortune. This type is well exemplified in F. B., who passes through life cheated by every rogue and walked on by any strong-willed person that comes along. As a boy he was bullied by nearly all his playmates, did the chores, was selected for the "booh" parts in games and never dared resent it, though he was fully conscious that he was being put upon. When he went to work in a factory he was the one selected for all those practical jokes in which minor cruelty manifests itself. His parents also bullied him, so that he was compelled to turn over most of his earnings to them and was allowed to keep so little that he was shabby, half-starved and without any of the luxuries for which even his timid soul longed.

F. B. was mortally afraid of girls; they seemed to him to be terrible and beautiful creatures, very scornful and awe-inspiring. They made him feel inferior in a way that sent him edging from their presence, and though he sometimes surged with passion he avoided any contact with them.

As a good workman he received good pay, for he chanced, by the merest luck, to fall into the hands of a kind employer, who profited by his kindness, for F. B. gave more than a dollar of value for each dollar he received. Timid, he gave to the employer a great loyalty, which was in part based on his awe of any aggressive personality.

In society this man was tongue-tied, embarrassed and overawed by the well-dressed and prosperous-looking. His sense of inferiority was in no way compensated for, and to avoid pain he became a sort of recluse, doing his work and returning to his shell, so to speak, each night.

When he was thirty-six his mother died, his father having died earlier. This left him rather well to do, for his thrifty parents had well utilized his earnings. At once a thoughtful woman of his acquaintance, distantly related by marriage, set out to capture him, and by forcing the issue led him to the altar. Needless to say, she ruled the household, and F. B.'s only consolation lay in the crop of children that soon appeared in the house, for timidity is no barrier to parenthood. This consolation rather tends to disappear as the children grow older, for they become his masters. Such men as F. B. have a collar around their necks to which any one may fit a chain.

Does F. B. rejoice in inferiority, in the masochistic sense spoken of before? Is his humility a sign of inversion, in the Freudian sense, a sort of homosexuality? Possibly, and there are very crude and coarse phrases of the common man indicating a sexual feeling in all victory and defeat. But I am inclined to call this a sort of monothymia, a mood of fear and negative self- feeling coloring all the reactions.

I have previously cited the case of the man obsessed by fear in all the relations of life,—shrinking, self-acknowledged inferiority—who lost it with "a few drinks under my belt." "Dutch courage" drove from many a man the inferiority and the fear that plagued his soul. True, it drove him into a worse situation, but for a few moments he tasted something of the life that heroes and the great have. If we can ever find something that will not degrade as it exalts, all the world will rush to use it.

Of the monothymic types the choleric or angry are about as common as those predisposed to fear. The anger emotion is aroused by a thwarting of the instincts and purposes, and in the main the strongly egoistic are those most given to explosive or chronic anger. The angry feeling, however, must be controlled, else failure or social dislike awaits the choleric. When a man wins success he frequently allows himself the luxury of indulging his anger because he feels his power cannot be challenged. The Duchess in "Alice's Adventures in Wonderland," with her choleric "off with his head" whenever any one contradicted her, is a caricature, and a very apt one, of this type of person. We think of the bull-necked Henry the Eighth—"bluff King Hal"—as the choleric type, though here we also assume a certain cyclothymia, great good nature alternating with fierce anger.

I have in mind G. as a type of the angry person. G. cannot bear to have any one contradict him. Either he swallows his resentment, if he is in the presence of one he cannot afford to antagonize, or else he starts to abuse the victim verbally. He is sarcastic or violent according to circumstances; rarely is he pleasant in manner or speech. Though he is honest and said to be well-meaning, his ego explodes in the presence of other self-assertive egos. When a man truckles to him he is angry at his insincerity; when the other disputes his statements, or even offers other views, he finds himself confronted by one who has taken deep offense. As a result G. has no real friends, and this has added fuel to his anger. Often he has made up his mind to "control" himself, to keep down his scorn and rage, but rarely has he been able to maintain a proper attitude for any length of time.

In the last analysis a high self-valuation is part of the chronic choleric make-up, a conceit of overweening proportions. The man who realizes his own proneness to err, and who keeps in mind the relative unimportance of his aims and powers, is not apt to explode in the face of opposition or contradiction. G. is as a rule absolutely sure of his belief, tastes and importance, though he is crude in knowledge, coarse in tastes and of no particular importance except to himself. He is the "I am Sir Oracle; when I ope my lips let no dog bark."

Anger is often associated with brutality or deeds of violence. There is cold-blooded brutality, but by far the most of it has anger behind it. I know one man who in his youth was hot-tempered, i. e., quick to anger and quick to repent, a charming man who gradually learned control and passed into late middle life serene and amiable.

One day he was driving his car when it became obstructed by two young rowdies driving another car. With him was his wife. When he expostulated with the men, one of them turned with a sneer and said something insulting at which the other laughed. The next thing my friend knew he was in the other car, striking heavy blows at the pair (he is a very powerful man.), and it was only the opportune arrival of a policeman that prevented a murder.

"Whatever came over me I hardly understand," said he afterwards sadly. "I used to have rages like that as a boy, but I have been very well controlled for over thirty years. I was a raging demon for a while, and it appalls me to think that in me there lurks such a devil of anger."

Akin to anger, akin to fear, is suspicion. There is a sullen non-social personality type whose reactions are characterized by suspicion. He never willingly gives his trust to any one, and when he hands over his destinies to any one, as all must do now and then, he is consumed with dread, doubt and latent hostility.

Every one is familiar with men like H. He is full of distrust for his fellow men. Himself a man of low ideals, he ascribes to every one the same attitude. "What's in it for you?" is his first thought concerning anybody with whom he deals.

He has a little store and eyes each customer who comes in as if they come to rob him. As a result his trade is largely emergency, transient trade, those who come because they have nowhere else to go or else do not know him. The salesmen, who supply the articles he sells have long since cut him off their list for desirable goods, and his only callers are those salesmen who are working up new lines and are under orders to try every one. H. has moments and days when he believes the whole world is against him, and on such occasions he locks his store and refuses to see any one. But at his best he cannot yield his ego to full free intercourse with others. It seems as though there were a hard shell surrounding him, and the world as it flowed around never brought love and trust through to him.

H. is not insane in the ordinary sense, but he is one of those paranoid persons we spoke of previously. Turn to L., a true case of mental disease, a paranoid whose career strangely resembles some of the great historic paranoids, for it must be remembered that man has been imposed upon by those who deceived themselves, who fully believed the strange and incredible things they succeeded in making credible to others.

The fantastic paranoid is made up of the same materials as the rest of us, except that his ego feeling is without insight, and his suspicion grows and grows until it reaches the delusion of persecution. L. was a bright boy, always conceited and given to non-social acts. Thus he never would play with the other boys unless he were given the leading role, and he could not bear to hear others praised or to praise them! Parenthetically the role that jealousy plays in the conduct of men and women needs exposition, and I recommend that some Ph. D. merit his degree by a thesis on this subject. When he was a little older he got the notion that hats were bad for the hair, and being proud of his own thick black mop, he went without a hat for over a year, despite the tears and protestations of his family and the ridicule of his friends. There is no one so ready to die for a cause, good or bad, as the paranoid.

He entered the medical school, and to this day there is none of his classmates who has forgotten him. Proud, even haughty, with only one or two intimates, he studied hard and did very good work. Now and then he astonished the class by taking direct issue with some professor, disputing a theory or a fact with the air of an authority and proposing some other idea, logically developed but foolishly based, as if his training were sufficient. It is characteristic of all paranoid philosophy and schemes that they despise real experimentation, that they start with some postulate that has no basis in work done and go on with a minute hyper-logic that deceives the unsophisticated.

Though L. was "bright," there were better men in his class, and they received the honors. L. was deeply offended at this and claimed to his own friends that the professors were down on him, especially a certain professor of medicine, who, so L. intimated, was afraid that L.'s theories would displace his own and so was interested to keep him down. This feeling was intensified when he came up for the examinations to a certain famous hospital and was turned down. The real reason for this failure was his unpopularity with his fellow students, for they let it be known to the examiners that L. would undoubtedly be hard to get along with, and it was part of the policy of the hospital to consider the personality of an applicant as well as his ability.

L. obtained a hospital place in a small city and did very good work, and though his peculiarities were noticed they excited only a hidden current of amused criticism, while his abilities aroused a good deal of praise. Stimulated by this, he started practice in the same city as a surgeon and quickly rose to the leading position. His indefatigable industry, his absolute self- confidence and his skill gave him prestige almost at once. His conceit rose to the highest degree, and his mannerisms commenced to become offensive to others. He came into collision with the local medical society because he openly criticized the older men in practice as "ignoramuses, asses, charlatans, etc.," and indeed was sued by one of them in the courts. The suit was won by the plaintiff, the award was five thousand dollars and L. entered an appeal.

From this on his career turned. In order to contest the case, and because he began to believe that the courts and lawyers were in league against him, he studied law and was admitted to the bar. He had meanwhile married a rich woman who was wholly taken in by his keen logical exposition of his "wrongs," his imposing manner of speech and action; and perhaps she really fell in love with the able, aggressive and handsome man. She financed his law school studies, for it was necessary for him to give up most of his practice meanwhile.

As soon as he could appear before the Bar he did so in his own behalf, for this case had now reached the proportions where it had spread out into half a dozen cases. He refused to pay his lawyers, and they sued. One of them dropped the statement that L. was "crazy," and he brought a suit against the lawyer. Moreover, he began to believe, because of the adverse judgments, that the courts were against him, and he wrote article after article in the radical journals on the corruptness of the courts and entered a strenuous campaign to provide for the public election and recall of judges.

These activities brought him in close relations with a group of unbalanced people operating under the high-sounding name League of Freedom. These people, led by a man, J., eagerly welcomed L., largely because his wife was still financing his ventures. Here comes a curious fact, and one prominent in the history of man, for this group, led by two unbalanced men, actually engineered a real reform, for they brought about a codification of the laws of their State, a simple codification that made it possible to know what the laws on any matter really are. This may be stated: the average balanced person is apt to weigh consequences to himself, but the paranoid does not; and so, when accident or circumstances [83] enlist him in a good cause, he is a fighter without fear and is enormously valuable.

This success brought L.'s paranoia to the pinnacle of unreason. He attacked the courts boldly, openly and publicly accused the judges of corruption, said they were in conspiracy with the Bar and the medical societies to do him up, added to this list of his enemies the Irish and the Catholic Church, because the prosecuting attorney in one county and the judge in that court were Irish and Catholic, and then turned against his wife because she now began to doubt his sanity. He brought suits in every superior court in the State, and at the time he was committed to an Insane Hospital he had forty trials on, had innumerable manuscripts of his contemplated reforms, in which were included the doing away with Insane Hospitals, the examination of all persons in the State for venereal disease and their cure by a new remedy of his own, the reform of the judiciary, etc., etc. He accused his wife of infidelity, felt that he was being followed by spies and police, claimed that dictagraphs were installed everywhere to spy

---

[83] See Lombroso's "Man of Genius" for many such cases.

on him and had a classical delusional state. He was committed, but later he escaped from the hospital and is now at large. The State officials are making no effort to find him, mainly because they are glad to get rid of him.

While the cases like L. are not common, the "mildly" paranoid personality is common. Everywhere one finds the man or woman whose abilities are not recognized, who is discriminated against, who finds an enemy in every one who does not kotow and who interprets as hostile every action not directly conciliating or friendly. In every group of people there is one whose paranoid temperament must be reckoned with, who is distrustful, conceited and disruptive. Often they are high-minded, perhaps devoted to an ideal, and if they convince others of their wrongs they increase the social disharmonies by creating new social wars, large or small according to their influence, intelligence and other circumstances.

The type of the trusting need not be here illustrated by any case history. Dickens has given us an immortal figure in the genial, generous and impulsive Mr. Pickwick, and Cervantes satirized knighthood by depicting the trusting, credulous Don Quixote. We laugh at these figures, but we love them; they preserve for us the sweetness of childhood and hurt only themselves and their own. Trust in one's fellows is not common, because the world is organized on egoism more than on fellowship. Where fellowship becomes a code, as in the relations of men associated together for some great purpose, then a noble trust appears.

So I pass over those whose mood runs all one way the hopeful, the despondent, the pessimist and the optimist—to other types. We shall then consider the two great directions of interest, introspection and extrospection, and those whose lives are characterized by one or the other direction.

1. The introspective personality is no more of a unit than any other type. Intelligence, energy and a host of other matters play their part in the sum total of the character here as elsewhere.

H. I. is what might be called the intellectual introspective personality. From the very earliest days he became interested in himself as a thinker. "How do my words mean anything?" he asked of his perplexed father at the investigative age of five. "Where do my thoughts go to when I do not think them?" was the problem he floored a learned uncle with a year later. This type of curiosity is not uncommon in children; in fact, it is the conventionality and laziness of the elders that stops children in their study of the fundamentals. H. was not stopped, for the zeal of his interest was heightened as time went on.

He played with other boys but early found their conclusions and discussions primitive. He became an ardent bookworm, reading incessantly or rather at such times when his parents permitted, for they were simple folk who were rather alarmed at their boy's interests and zeal. No noticeable difference from other boys was noted aside from precocity in study, yet even at the age of ten life was running in two great currents for this boy. The one current was the outer world with its ever varied happenings, the other was the inner world of thoughts and moods, deeply, fascinatingly interesting. It seemed to H. I. that there were "two I's, one of which sat just over my head and looking down on the other I, watching its strivings, its emotions, its thoughts with a detached and yet palpitating interest. When I watched the other boys at play I wondered whether they too had this dual existence, whether they chewed the cud of life over and over again as I did."

Came puberty with the great sex passions. The vibrating life within him suddenly became tinged with new interests. One day at a party a vixen of a girl threw herself boldly in his arms and tried to push him into a chair. The bodily contact and the swift bodily reaction threw him into a panic, for the passion that was aroused was so powerful that he seemed to himself stripped of all thought and reflection and impelled to actions against which he rebelled. For he was fully acquainted, at second hand, with sex; he knew boys and girls who had made excursions into its most intimate practices and despised them.

This episode gave his introspective trends a new direction. From now on sex was the theme his fancy embroidered. Curiously enough, he became more austere than ever, shunned girls and especially the heroine of his adventure, and even avoided the company of boys who spoke habitually and "vulgarly" of sex. His mind built up sex phantasies, sex adventures in which he was the hero and in which girls he knew and those he imagined were the heroines, but at the same time, standing aloof as it were, another part of him seemed to watch his own reactions until "I nearly went crazy." He became obsessed by a feeling of unreality and adopted a Berkleyan philosophy of idealism: nothing seemed to exist except his own consciousness, and that seemed of doubtful existence. He took long walks by himself, read philosophy and science with avidity, yet turned by preference to these dreams of sex adventure, palpitating, alluring, and yet so unreal to his critical self. To others he was merely a bit moody and detached, though friendly and kind.

He went to college, and his interest in sex became secondary almost immediately. His student days were passed at Harvard at a time when Royce, Palmer, Santayanna, and James ruled in its philosophy, and H. I. became fascinated by these men and their subject. His mind was again drawn into introspection, but in an organized manner. He asked himself continually, "What are the purposes of life; why do we love; does man will or is he an automaton who watches the hands go around and thinks he moves them?" Where before his feeling of unreality was largely emotional, now it received an intellectual sanction, and he swung from hither to yon in a never-ending cycle. He became wearied beyond measure by his thoughts; he envied the beasts of the field, the laborer in the ditch and all to whom life and living were realities not in the least to be examined and questioned. Deliberately he decided to shift his interests,—to buy an automobile and learn about it; to play cards; to have his love affair; to taste emotion and pleasure and to seek no intellectual sanction for them.

He disappeared from college for a year and came back tanned, ruddy and at rest. He had found a capacity for interest and emotion outside of himself. He had experienced phases of life about which he would not talk at first, but in later years he admitted that he had been a "man of the world." He regretted much that had happened, but on the whole he rejoiced in an equanimity, in a capacity for objective interest, that he had never had before. His introspective trend was still very strong, but it lent subtlety and wisdom to his life, rather than weakness. Now and then he became harassed by a feeling of unreality, by a questioning skepticism that nullified happiness, and he felt himself divided by his intellect. These he shook off by dropping his work, by hunting, fishing and accepting simple goals of activity. Later on he married, and became a scholar of some note. I think he now relishes life as well as any really thoughtful man of middle life can.

There is a personality type, the emotional introspective, whose interest in life is directed toward their own sensations and emotions. They do not view people or things as having a value in themselves and for themselves; they deliberately view them as sources of a personal pleasurable sensation. I do not mean the crude egoist who asks of anything or anybody, "What good is it (or he) for me?" but I mean that connoisseur in emotions, casually blase and bored, who seeks new sensations. This is an introspective deviation of a serious kind, for the connoisseur in emotions rarely is happy and usually is most deeply miserable. Bourget in his remarkable psychological novel, "A Love Crime," has admirably drawn one of these characters. The exquisite Armand, seeking pleasure constantly, is divided into the sensualist who seduces and ruins and the introspectionist who watches the proceeding with disgust and disillusion. It is not an outraged conscience that is at work but the inability to feel without analyzing the feeling "Ah, for a single passion that might apply my entire sensibility to another being, like wet paper against a window pane." This is the eternal tragedy of sophistication,—that there results an anhedonia in large part manifested by a restless introspection. The mind is drawn away from the outside world, and everything is seen out of proportion.

The hypochondriac directs his attention to his health and is in part a monothymic of the fear type. Moliere's "Le Malade Imaginaire" is a classical study of this person, and I do not, presume to better it. Modern popularizing of disease has distinctly increased the numbers of the hypochondriacs, or at any rate has made their fears more scientific. Brain tumor, gastric ulcer, appendicitis, tuberculosis, heart disease, cancer, syphilis,—often have I seen a hypochondriac run the gamut of all these deadly diseases and still retain his health. The faddy habits they form are the sustenance of those who start the varied forms of vegetarianism, chewing cults, fresh-air fiends, wet-grass fanatics, back-to-nature societies, and the mild lunacies of our (and every) age.

One such hypochondriac, J., after suffering from every disease in the advertising pages of the daily newspapers, developed a system of habits that finally became a disease in itself. He rose at 6.30 each morning, stood naked in the middle of the room, took six deep breaths, rolled around on the floor and kicked his arms and legs about for fifteen minutes, took a drink of cold water, had a shower bath and a rub-down, shaved, attended to "certain bodily functions" (his term, not mine), ate a breakfast consisting of gluten bread, two slices, one and one-half glasses of milk, a soft-boiled egg (three and one-half minutes) and an orange; walked to work, taking exactly twenty minutes to do it; opened the windows wide in his office (fighting with the other clerks who preferred comfort to fresh air), ate a health luncheon at noon consisting of Postum, nuts, health bread, and two squares of milk chocolate; walked home at six, taking exactly 20 minutes to do it; washed, lay on the couch fifteen minutes with mind fixed on infinity (a Hindoo trick, so he heard), ate dinner, which never varied much from rice, cream, potatoes, milk and, heritage of saner days, a small piece of pie! All the day he watched each pain and ache, noted whether he belched or spit more than usual, and at night went to sleep at 10.30. Needless to say he had no friends, was known as "that nut" and really broke down from too arduous an introspective existence.

The term self-denial has been used from earliest times to indicate what we have called inhibition. But self-denial is fundamentally a wrong term, since it implies that the self is that which lusts and shirks, and that which controls desire and holds the individual to a consistent and ethical line of conduct is not the self. In fact, the self is based on inhibition and control, and when there is failure in these regards there is self-failure.

Interesting is the under-inhibited person. I mean by this term the one who consistently and in most relationship shows an inability to control the primitive instincts, impulses and desires. J. F. may stand as a type that becomes the "black sheep" and in many cases the "criminal." He comes of what is known as a "good family," which in his case means that the parents are well-to-do, of good reputation and rather above the average in intelligence. The brothers and sisters have all done well, are settled in their ways and are not to be distinguished from the people of their social set in manners or morals.

It was impossible to discipline J. As a very young child he resisted his mother's efforts to train him into tidiness or restraint. He stole whatever he desired, and though he was alternately punished and pleaded with, though he seemed to desire to please his parents, he continued to steal whenever there was opportunity. At six he entered a neighbor's house, and while there took a purse that was lying on a table, rifled it of its contents and disappeared for nearly a day, when he was found in a down-town district, having gorged himself with candy and cake. From then on his peculations increased, and his conduct became the scandal of his family, for he stole even from the maids employed in the house, as well as from guests. In each case the stealing was apparently motivated to give a good time to himself and also to certain chums he made here and there in the city. He would lie to evade punishment, but finally would yield, confess his guilt, express deepest repentance and accept his punishment with the sincerity of one fully conscious of deserving it.

In school he did poorly. He was bright enough. In fact, he was somewhat above the average in memory and comprehension and may be described as keen, but it was difficult for him to keep his attention consistently on any subject, and the discipline of school irked him. He ran away several times to avoid school, and each time, until he was about fourteen, came back after a few days,—bedraggled, hungry and repentant. The freedom of the streets appealed to him as offering a life varied enough to suit his nature, and with excitement and adventure always in the air. So he mingled with all kinds of boys and men and at the age of fourteen shocked his parents by being arrested as one of a gang that was engaged in robbing drunken men in the slum quarters of the city. It took all kinds of influence to get him released on probation, but this was accomplished and then the boy disappeared from home.

He was gone three years and despite all search had completely disappeared. His people had given up all hope of seeing him again (although certain members of his family were not at all saddened by the prospect) when they received a communication from the police of a distant city with a photograph of the boy, asking if it was true that he was their son. It seems that J. had drifted from place to place, now working as newsboy, stable hand, errand boy, messenger, theater-usher, until he had reached this city. There he was wandering on the streets, hungry and ragged, when a philanthropic old gentleman noticed him. J. has the good fortune to be very innocent looking, and no matter what his crimes, his face might belong to a cherub. A friend once stated that if J. appeared at Heaven's gate, St. Peter would surely take him to be an angel come back from a stroll and let him in. The philanthropist stopped, the boy and inquired into his history. J. told him a very affecting story of being an orphan whom a cruel guardian had robbed of his heritage and exaggerated his sufferings until the indignant old fellow threatened to have the police prosecute his betrayer. With a show of great magnanimity, J. refused to disclose his real name, and the philanthropist took him home. He had him clothed and fed, and then, taken by the boy's engaging manners and bright ways, decided to educate and adopt him. He was dissuaded from the latter by a friend, but he sent J. to a private school of good grade. To the surprise of the old man, J. was continually getting into mischief, and finally he was accused of stealing. Unable to believe the school authorities, the old gentleman took the boy home and quizzed him. He gave an unsatisfactory account of himself and that night disappeared with a considerable sum of money. The police were notified, and a week later he was found in a house of the type—so euphemistically called—of "ill fame." There he was spending the money lavishly on the inmates and was indulging his every desire. One of the women, a police stool-pigeon, identified him as the boy who was wanted by the law, and he was arrested.

Despite the efforts of the parents and the philanthropist, the boy was given a prison sentence and is still serving it. Characteristic of this group of personalities are these traits: (1) an impatience with the arduous, an incapacity or unwillingness to wait for results in the ordinary way; (2) a decided dread of monotony, a longing for excitement; (3) an inability to form permanent purposes and to inhibit the distracting desires; (4) a desire to win others' good opinion and sympathy,—therefore he always lavished his money on those whom that kind of "good fellowship" wins and told pathetic stories to those whose sentimentality made them easy victims; (5) a weak kind of egoism, seeking easy ways to pleasure and position, restless under discipline, always repentant after wrong-doing, fluent in speech but lacking the courage to face the difficulties of life.

This under-inhibited type may suddenly reform and apparently entirely emerge from difficulties. I have in mind a conspicuous case, a young woman now happily married and the mother of fine children. When she was thirteen or fourteen the petty pilferings of her childhood took on a serious character. She began to steal from the person of strangers and from the homes of friends. She romanced in the most convincing fashion, told strangers the most remarkable stories, usually of such a nature as to make her interesting and an object of sympathy, but which tended to blacken the reputation of her family. She lost place after place at work, was sent to a hospital to become a nurse and demoralized her associates by her lies and her thefts. She was a very sweet girl in every other way, kindly, generous, self-sacrificing, studious even, and her character-contradiction made people reluctant to believe she was not insane. She was discharged from the hospital, stayed at home for a few months,—and then came the miracle. She obtained a place in a large business house and worked there for seven years or up till the time of her marriage. She was steadily promoted and was accounted the most reliable and honest employee of the establishment. She handled money and goods, was absolutely truthful and her earnest efficiency was noteworthy. Her private life was in complete harmony with this business career. She helped her parents, who are poor, dressed modestly, studied nights and yet showed the same fondness for dancing and good times that the normal girl does. She met a promising young business man who fell immediately in love with this demure looking young woman, and they were later married. Once I asked her how the reform came about. "I don't know myself," she answered frankly. "I never was happy—when I was the other way. I always vowed reform, but when there was money around I'd think and think about it until it was mine. Then I'd spend it in a silly way to get rid of it fast. I craved good things, and you know how poor we were. Then I lied just to have people like me and pity me, even though I called myself a fool while doing it. Often, often I tried to reform and for a week or two would be real good. Then perhaps I'd see some money, and I'd try to think of something else. But that money would come to my mind, and I'd get hot and dizzy thinking about it. Perhaps I'd say, 'I'll just look at it,' and finally I'd go and take it—and feel so relieved and spend it. After I left the hospital it seemed to me that I could never smile again. I cried all night long; I wanted to die. I could see one girl who thought I was so good and nice, and her face as she looked at me when I left! Her eyes were wide open, and her mouth was so stern, and she looked as if she wanted to speak but she turned around and walked

214

away. One day I woke up after a restless night at home, and it seemed to me that I had strength, that something had turned around in my nature, and since that day I have never even wanted to steal. I haven't had to try to be good; it came as natural as eating and sleeping."

The sexually under-inhibited are those whose sex control is deficient. This may be either from over-passionate nature, bad example, deficient mentality, vanity and desire for good times, as in certain girls, etc. To discuss these types would be to write another book, and so I forbear. But this I wish to emphasize: that neither age, sex protestation of indifference and control, occupation or social status, alters the fact that the history of the sex feelings, impulses and struggles is essential to a knowledge of character. Without detailing sex types, these are some that are important.

1. The uninhibited impulsive, passionate (the bulk of the prostitutes).

2. The controlled, passionate. Very common.

3. The frigid. Not so rare as believed.

4. The extremely passionate (nymphomania, satyriasis). Rare. Always in trouble.

5. The sensualist, a deliberate seeker of sex pleasure, often indulging in perversion. Common type.

6. The perverted types,—autoerotic (masturbator), homosexual, masochists, sadists, fetishist, etc. More common than the ordinary person dreams.

7. The periodic, to whom sex life is incidental to certain periods and situations. Common among women, less common among men.

8. The sublimators, whose sexual activity has somehow been harnessed to other great activities. Fairly frequent among these who either through choice or necessity are to remain continent.

9. The anhedonic or exhausted. Found in the sensualists and often reacted to by the formation of religious and ethical codes, which eliminate sex,—Tolstoy, the hermits, certain Russian sects, etc.

There is under-inhibition of a good kind. There are generous-hearted people always ready to give of themselves to anything or anybody that needs help. Often "fooled" by the unworthy, they resolve to be calm, judicial and selfish, and then,—their generous social natures over-ride caution, and again they plunge into kindness and philanthropy.

F. L. is one of these. As child, boy and young man he was free-hearted to an extraordinary degree. Ragamuffin, stray dog or cat, tramp, down and outer of every kind or description, these enlisted his sympathy and help despite the expostulation and remonstrance of a series of conventional good people, his mother and father, his best friends and his outraged wife. The latter never knew, she used to say, what he would bring home for dinner. "He always forgot to bring home the steak, but he never forgot to lug along some derelict." More than once he was robbed, often he was imposed upon. Once he met an interesting vagabond who spoke several languages, quoted the Bible with ease and accuracy, and so fired the heart of our simple man that he bought him clothes and brought him home to stay. His wife threw up her hands in despair. "But, my dear," said F. L., "he's a scholar who has fallen on evil days." "Ah," she answered, "I fear it will be an evil day for us when you took him home." She had a good chance to say, "I told you so," when the rogue eloped with the best of their silver.

Not only is F. L. impulsive and uninhibited in his generosity, but his "pitch in and help" quality is about as well manifested in other matters. If he sees a man or boy struggling with a load, he immediately forgets that he is over fifty and well dressed and steps right in to help. He saw an ash and garbage man—this is his wife's star story—struggling to lift a much befouled can into his wagon. F. L. left his wife and some friends without a word and with a cheery word threw the can into the wagon. Unfortunately some of the contents splashed, and F. L. suffered both in dignity and appearance as a consequence. He had to go home by back alleys and had to endure the mirth of his friends for a long time. But it did not change his reactions in the least, although he was really vexed with himself and endeavored to be conventional and self-controlled for a while. The point is that F. L. attempts inhibition of generous impulses and fails as ignominiously as a drunkard struggling with the desire to drink.

Of course he is of the salt of the earth. Upon such uninhibited fellowship feeling as his rests the ethical progress of the world. A dozen inventors contribute less to their fellow men than does he. For their contributions may be used to destroy or enslave their fellows, and it is a commonplace that science has outstripped morals. But his contributions spread kindly feeling and the notion of the brotherhood of man.

The over-inhibited, those whose every impulse and desire is subjected to a scrutiny and a blocking, often come to the attention of the neuropsychiatrist. But there are many "normal" people who fall into this group, and whose conduct throughout life is marked by a scrupulosity that is painful to behold. The over-inhibition may take specific directions, as in the thrifty who check their desires in the wish to save money, or the industrious who hold up their pleasures and recreations in the fear that they are wasting time. A sub-group of the over-inhibited I call the over-conscientious, and it is one of these whose history is epitomized here.

K. has always had "ingrowing scruples," as his exasperated mother once said. As a small child he never obeyed the impulse to take a piece of cake without looking around to see if his mother and father approved. He would not play unreservedly, in the whole-hearted impulsive way of children, but always held back in his enjoyment as if he feared that perhaps he was not doing just right. When he started to go to school his fear of doing the wrong thing made him appear rather slow, though in reality he was bright. The other children called him a "sissy," mistaking his conscientiousness for cowardice. This grieved him very much, and his father undertook to educate him in "rough" ways, in fighting and wrestling. He succeeded in this to the extent that K. learned to fight when he believed that he was being wronged, but he never seemed to learn the aggressiveness necessary to get even a fair share of his rights. His mother, a similar type, rather encouraged him in this virtue, much to the disgust of the father.

Not to spend too long a time over K.'s history, we may pass quickly over his school years until he entered college. He was a "grind" if there ever was one, studying day and night. He had developed well physically and because of his hard work stood near the top of his class. He took no "pleasures" of any kind,—that is, he played no cards, went to no dances, never took in a show and of course was strictly moral. It seems that the main factor that held him back was the notion he had imbibed early in his career that pleasure itself was somehow not worthy, that an ideal of work made a sort of sin of wasting time. Whenever he indulged himself by rest or relaxation, even in so innocent a way as to go to a ball game, there was in the back of his mind the idea, "I might have been studying this or that, or working on such a subject; I am wasting time," and the pleasure would go. By nature K. was sociable and friendly and was well liked, but he avoided friendships and social life because of the unpleasant reproaches of his work conscience and the rigor of his work inhibitions. He grew tired, developed a neurasthenic set of symptoms, and thus I first came in contact with him. Once he understood the nature of his trouble, which I labeled for him as a "hypertrophied work conscience," he set himself the task of learning to enjoy, of throwing off inhibition, of innocent self-indulgence, and my strong point that he would work the better for pleasure took his fancy at once. He succeeded in part in his efforts, but of course will always debate over the right and wrong of each step in his life.

This one example of a high type of the over-inhibited must do for the group. There is a related type who in ordinary speech find it "difficult to make up their minds,"—in other words, are unable to choose. Bleuler has used the term ambivalent, thus comparing these individuals to a chemical element having two bonds and impelled to unite with two substances. The ambivalent personalities are always brought to a place where they yearn for two opposing kinds of action or they fear to choose one affinity of action as against the other. They are in the position of the unfortunate swain who sang, "How happy I could be with either, were t'other dear charmer away."

M. is one of these helpless ambivalent folk, always running to others for advice and perplexed to a frenzy by the choices of life. "What shall I do?" is his prime question, largely because he fears to commit himself to any line of action. Once a man chooses, he shuts a great many doors of opportunity and gambles with Fate that he has chosen right. M. knows this and lacks self- confidence, i.e., the belief that he will choose for the best or be able to carry it through. He lacks the gambling spirit, the willingness to put his destiny to fortune. Often M. deliberates or rather oscillates for so long a time that the matter is taken from his hands. Thus, when he fell in love, the fear of being refused, of making a mistake, prevented him from action, and the young woman accepted another, less ambivalent suitor.

M. is in business with his father and is entirely a subordinate, because he cannot choose. He carries out orders well, is very amiable and gentle, is liked and at the same time held in a mild contempt. He has physical courage but has not the hardihood of soul to take on responsibility for choosing. Sometimes he gets good ideas, but never dares to put them into execution and shifts that to others.

He hates himself for this weakness in an essential phase of personality but is gradually accepting himself as an inferior person, despite intelligence, training and social connection.

Yet his sister is exactly the opposite type. She makes decisions with great promptness, never hesitates, is "cocksure" and aggressive. If M. is ambivalent, his sister B. M. is univalent. Choice is an easy matter to her, though she is not impulsive. She rapidly deliberates. She never has made any serious errors in judgment, but if she makes a mistake she shrugs her shoulders and says, "It's all in the game." Thus she is a leader in her set, for if some difficulty is encountered, her mind is quickly at work and prompt with a solution. If she is not brilliant, and she is not, she collects the plans of her associates and chooses and modifies until she is ready with her own plan. Her father sighs as he watches her and regrets that she is not a man. It does not occur to him or any of his family, including herself, that she might do a man's work in the business world.

In pathological cases the inability to choose becomes so marked as to make it impossible for the patient to choose any line of conduct. "To do or not to do" extends into every relationship and every situation. The patient cannot choose as to his dress or his meals; cannot decide whether to stay in or go out, finds it difficult to choose to cross the street or to open a door; is thrown into a pendulum of yea and nay about speaking, etc. This psychasthenic state, the folie du doute of the French, is accompanied by fear, restlessness and an oppressive feeling of unreality. The records of every neurologist contain many such cases, most of whom recover, but a few go on to severe incurable mental disease.

I pass on, without regard for logic or completeness, to a personality type that we may call the anhedonic or simpler a restless, not easily satisfied, easily disgusted group. Some of these are cyclothymic, over-emotional, often monothymic but I am discussing them from the standpoint of their satisfaction with life and its experiences. The ordinary label of "finicky" well expresses the type, but of course it neglects the basic psychology. This I have discussed elsewhere in this book and will here describe two cases, one a congenital type and the other acquired.

T. was born dissatisfied, so his mother avers. As a baby he was "a difficult feeding case" because the very slightest cause, the least change in the milk, upset him, a fact attested to by vigorous crying. Babies have a variability in desire and satisfaction quite as much as their elders.

Apparently T. thrived, despite his start, for as a child he was sturdy looking. Nevertheless, in toys, games, treats, etc., he was hard to please and easy to displease. He turned up his nose if a toy were not perfection, and he had to have his food prepared according to specification or his appetite vanished. Moreover, he had a very limited range of things he liked, and as time went on he extended that list but little. He was very choice in his clothes—not at all a regular boy—and quite disgusted with dirt and disorder. "A little old maid" somebody called him, having in mind of course the traditional maiden lady.

As T. grew his capacity for pleasure-feeling did not increase. On the contrary his attention to the details necessary for his pleasure made of him one of those finicky connoisseurs who, though never really pleased with anything, get a sort of pleasure in pointing out the crudity of other people's tastes and pleasures. This attitude of superiority is the one compensation the finicky have, and since they are often fluent of speech and tend to write and lecture, they impose their notions of good and bad upon others, who seek to escape being "common." In T.'s case his attitude toward food, clothes, companions, sports and work created a tense disharmony in his family, and one of his brothers labeled him "The Kill-joy." Secretly envious of other people's simple enjoyment, T. made strenuous efforts at times to overcome his repugnances and to enlarge the scope of his pleasures, but because this forfeited for him the superiority he had reached as a very "refined" person, he never persisted in this process.

When he was twenty he found himself the theater of many conflicts. He was weary of life, yet lusted for experiences that his hyperestheticism would not permit him to take. Sex seemed too crude, and the girls of his age were "silly." Yet their lure and his own internal tensions dragged him to one place after another, hoping that he would find the perfect woman, able to understand him. At last he did find her, so he thought, in the person of a young woman of twenty-five, a consummate mistress of the arts of femininity. She sized him up at once, played on his vanity, extolled his fine tastes and never exposed a single crudity of her own, until she brought him to the point where his passion for her, his conviction that he had found "the perfect woman," led him to propose marriage. Then came the blow: she laughed at him, called him a silly boy, gave him a lecture as to what constituted a fine man, extolling crudity, vigor and virility as the prime virtues.

His world was shattered, and its shadowy pleasures gone. At first his parents were inclined to believe that this was a good lesson, that T. would learn from this adventure and become a more hardy young man. Instead he became sleepless, restless and without desire for food or drink; he shunned men and women alike; he stared hollow-eyed at a world full of noise and motion but without meaning or joy. Deep was this anhedonia, and all exhortations to "brace up and be a man" failed. Diversion, travel and all the usual medical consultations and attentions did no good.

One day he announced to his family that he was all right, that soon he would be well. He seemed cheerful, talked with some animation and dressed himself with unusual care. His parents rejoiced, but one of his brothers did not like what he called a "gleam" in T.'s eyes. So he followed him, in a skillful manner. T. walked around for a while, then found his way to a bridge crossing a swift deep river. He took off his coat, but before he could mount the rail his watchful brother was upon him. He made no struggle and consented to come back home. In his coat was a letter stating that he saw no use in living, that he was not taking his life because of disappointment in love but because he felt that he never could enjoy what others found pleasurable, and that he was an anomaly, a curse to himself and others.

He was sent away to a sanatorium but left it and came home. He began to eat and drink again, found he could sleep at night (the sleepless night had filled him with despair) and soon swung back into his "normal" state. He passes throughout life a spectator of the joys of others, wondering why his grip on content and desire is so slender, but also he thinks himself of a finer clay than his fellows.

As a complement to this case let me cite that of the ex-soldier S. He reached the age of twenty-two with a very creditable history. Born of middle-class parents he went through high school and ranked in the upper third of his class for scholarship. His physique was good; he was a joyous, popular young fellow; and wherever he went was pointed out as the clean young American so representative of our country. That means he worked hard as assistant executive in a production plant, was ambitious to get ahead, took special courses to fit himself, read a good deal about "success" and how to reach it, dressed well, liked his fellow men and more than liked women, enjoyed sports, a good time, the theaters, slept well, ate well and surged with the passions and longings of his youth. Had any one said to him, "What is there to live for?" he would have had no answer ready merely because it would have never occurred to him that any one could really ask so foolish a question.

Came the war. Full of the ardor of patriotism and the longing for the great experience, he enlisted. He took the "hardships" of camp life, the long hikes, the daily drills, the food dished out in tins, as a lark, and his hearty fellowship identified him with the army, with its profanity, its rough friendliness, its grumbling but quick obedience and its intense purpose to "show 'em what the American can do." He went overseas and learned that French patriotism, like the American brand, did not prevent profiteering, and that enlistment in a common cause does not allay or abate racial prejudices and antagonisms. This, however, did not prey on his mind, for he took his Americanism as superior without argument and was not especially disappointed because of French customs and morals. He took part in several battles, made night attacks, bayonetted his first man with a horror that however disappeared under the glory of victory.

One day as he and a few comrades were in a front line trench, "Jerry" placed a high explosive "plump in the middle of it." When S. recovered consciousness, he found himself half covered with dirt and debris of all kinds, and when he crawled out and brushed himself off, he saw that of all his comrades he alone survived, and that they were mangled and mutilated in a most gruesome way. "Pieces of my friends everywhere," is his terse account. He lay in the trench, not daring to move for hours, the bitterest thoughts assailing him,—anger, hatred and disgust for war, the Germans, his own countrymen; and he even cursed God. When he did this he shuddered at his blasphemy, became remorseful and prayed for forgiveness. A little later he crawled out of the trench and back to where he was picked up by the medical corps and taken to a hospital. He was examined, nothing wrong was found and he was sent back to duty.

From that episode dates as typical an anhedonia as I have ever seen. Gradually he became sleepless and woke each day more tired than he went to bed. The food displeased him, and he grumbled over what were formerly trifles. He wearied easily, and nothing seemed to move him to enthusiasm or desire. He gave up friendship after friendship, because the friends annoyed him by their noise and boisterousness. He dreaded the roar of the guns and the shriek of shells with what amounted to physical agony. He brooded alone, and though not melancholy in the positive insane sense, was melancholy in the disappearance of desire, joy, energy, interest and enthusiasm.

Fortunately the armistice came at this time. S. was examined and discharged as well because he made no complaints, for he was anxious to get home. This was his one great desire. At home, with a nice bed to sleep in, good food to eat and the pleasant faces of his own people, his "nerves" would yield, he had no doubt. But he was mistaken; this was not the case. He became no better, and though he tried his old "job," he found that he could not find the energy, enthusiasm or concentration necessary for success. He was then referred to the United States Public Health Service, where I saw him, and he became my patient.

My first problem was to restore the power of sleeping. This I succeeded in doing by means that were entirely "physical." With that accomplished, the man became hopeful of further results, and this enabled one to bring about a desire for food, again by physical means, medicine, in short. The problem of awaking S.'s interest simmered down to that of finding an outlet for his ambition. The Federal Vocational Board granted him the right to take up a business course in a college. Though he found the study hard at first, he was encouraged to keep on and told to expect little of himself at first. This is an important point, for if a man holds himself to a high standard under conditions such as those of S., then failure brings a discouragement that upsets the treatment. At any rate this method of readjustment, with its reliance on medicines to bring sleep and appetite and on training to bring hope and relief from introspection, worked splendidly.

The fact is that no abstruse complicated psychological analysis was necessary here or in most cases. A man is "jarred" from light-hearted health to a grim discouraged state. This discouragement brings with it sleeplessness and loss of appetite, and there gradually develops a series of habits which lower endurance and energy. The habit elements in this condition are not enough recognized, and also the fact that most of the disability is physical in its development though psychological at the start. That is, A. had a severe emotional reaction to a horrible experience; this brought about insomnia and disordered nutrition, and these, by lowering the endurance and ability, brought to being a vicious circle of fatigue and depression, in which fatigue caused depression and depression increased fatigue. The treatment must be directed at first to the physical factors, and with these conquered the acquired forms of anhedonia usually yield readily.

It would be interesting to consider other types related to the anhedonic personality. The complainer, the whiner, the nag, all these are basically people who are hard to satisfy. The artistic temperament (found rather frequently in the non-artistic) is hyperesthetic, uncontrolled, irritably egoistic and demands homage and service from others which exceeds the merit of the individual; in other words, there is added to the anhedonic element an unreasonableness that is peculiarly exasperating. I pass these interesting people by and turn to the opposite of the anhedonic group, the group that is hearty in tastes and appetites, easily pleased as a rule and often crude in their relish of life. There are two main divisions of these hearty simple people,—those who are untrained and relatively uneducated, and whose simplicity may disappear under cultivation, and another type—cultivated, educated, wise—who still retain unspoiled appetite and hearty enjoyment.

Briefly let me introduce Dr. O., an athlete in his youth and always a lover of the great outdoors.

O. is Homeric in the simplicity of his tastes. A house is a place in which to sleep, clothes are to keep one warm, food is to eat and the manner of its service is an indifferent matter. He enjoys with almost huge pleasure good things to eat and good things to drink, but as he puts it, "I am as much at home with corned beef and cabbage as I am with any epicurean chef d'oeuvre. I like the feel of silk next my body, but cotton pleases me as much." He is clean and bathes regularly, but has no repulsion against dirt and disorder. At home, among the utmost refinements of our present-day life, he prefers the rough bare essentials of existence. To him beauty is not exotic, but everywhere present, and he sees it in a workman clad in overalls and breaking stone quite as much as in a carefully harmonized landscape. He has no pose about the beauty of nature as against the beauty of man's creations, and he thinks that a puffing freight engine, dragging a load of cars up a grade, is as much a thing to enthuse about as a graceful deer sniffing the scent of the hunter in some pine grove.

Imbued with a zeal for living and a desire for experience, O. has not been as successful as one more cautious and less impetuous might have been. He loves his profession so well that he would rather spend a day on an interesting case in the ward of some hospital than to treat half a dozen rich patients in his consulting room. His purpose is indeed unified; he seeks to learn and to impart, but the making of money seems to him a necessary irrelevance, almost an impertinent intrusion upon the real purposes of life. He is eager to know people, he shows a naive curiosity about them, an interest that flatters and charms. All the phenomena of life—esoteric, commonplace, queer and conventional—are grist to his mill.

His sexual life has not differed greatly from that of other men. In his early youth his passions outran his inhibitions, and he tasted of this type of experience with the same gusto with which he delved into books. As he reached early manhood he fell in love and pledged himself to chastity. Though he fell out of love soon his pledge remained in full force, and though he cursed himself as a fool he held himself aloof from sex adventure. When he was twenty-seven he again fell in love, had an impetuous and charming courtship and married. He loves his wife, and there is in their intimacy a buoyant yet controlled passion which values love for its own sake. He enters into his duties as father with the same zeal and appetite that characterizes his every activity.

O. is no mystic, proclaiming his unity with all existence, in the fashion of Walt Whitman. Rather he is a man with a huge capacity for pleasure, not easily disgusted or annoyed, with desires that reach in every direction yet with controlled purpose to guide his life. As he passes into middle age he finds his pleasures narrowing, as all men do, and he finds his appetites and tastes are becoming more restricted. This is because his purpose becomes more dominant, his habits are more imperious, his energy less exuberant. In thought O. is almost a pessimist because his knowledge of life, his intelligence and his sympathy make it difficult to understand the need of suffering, of disease and of conflict. But in emotion he still remains an optimist, glad to be alive at any price and rejoicing in the life of all things.

Apropos of this contradiction between thought and mood, it is sometimes found reversed. There are those whose philosophy is optimistic, who will not see aught but good in the world, yet whose facial expression and actions exhibit an essential melancholy.

In every category of character there are specialists, individuals whose main reactions are built around one great trait. Thus there are those whose egoism takes the form of pride in family, or in personal beauty, or some intellectual capacity, or in being independent of others, who worship self-reliance or self-importance. There are the individuals whose social instincts express themselves in loquacity, in a talkativeness that is the main joy of their lives, though not at all the joy of other lives. A fascinating series of personalities in this respect come to my mind—L. B., who talks at people, never with them, since he seems to take no note of their replies; T. K., who seems to regard conversation as largely a means of demonstrating her superiority, for she picks her subjects with the care a general selects his battlefield; F., who is a born pedagogue and seeks to instruct whoever listens to him, whose conversation is a lecture and a monologue; R. O., the reticent, says little but that pertinent and relevant, cynical and shrewd; and R. V., who says little and that with timidity and error. So there are specialists in caution and "common sense," self-controlled, never rash, calculating, cool and egotistic, narrow and successful. Every one knows this type, as every one knows the "fool," with his poor judgment, his unwise confidence in himself and others, his lack of restraint. There is the tactful man, conciliating, pliant, seeking his purposes through the good will of others which he obtains by "oil" and agreeableness, and there is the aggressive man, preferring to fight, energetic, at times rash, apt to be domineering, and crashing on to victory or defeat according to the caliber of his opponents and the nature of the circumstances.

Those whose ego feeling is high, whose desire for superiority matches up well with their feeling of superiority are often called the conceited. Really they are conceited only if they show their feelings, as, for example, does W. Wherever he goes W. seeks to occupy the center of the stage, brags of his achievements and his fine qualities. "I am the kind" is his prefix to his bragging. W. thinks that everything he does or says is interesting to others, and even that his illnesses are fascinating to others. If he has a cold he takes a remarkable pride in detailing every pain and ache and every degree of temperature, as if the experience were remarkable and somehow creditable. But W. is very jealous of other's achievements and is bored to death except when he can talk or perform.

W. does not know how to camouflage his egoism, but F. does. Fully convinced of his own superiority and with a strong urge at all times to demonstrate this, he "knows enough" to camouflage, to disguise and modify its manifestations. In this way he manages to be popular, just as W. is decidedly unpopular, and many mistake him for modest. When he wishes to put over his own opinion he prefaces his statements by "they say," and though whatever organization he enters he wishes to lead, he manages to give the impression that he is reluctant to take a prominent part. A man of ability and good judgment, the narrow range of F.'s sympathies, his lack of sincere cordial feeling, is hidden by a really artistic assumption of altruism that deceives all save those who through long acquaintance know his real character. One sees through W. on first meeting, he wears no mask or disguise; but F. defies detection, though their natures are not radically different except in wisdom and tact.

Half and more of the actions, poses and speech of men and women is to demonstrate superiority or to avoid inferiority. There are some who feel inwardly inferior, yet disguise this feeling successfully. This feeling of inferiority may arise from purely accidental matters, such as appearance, deformity, tone of voice, etc., and the individual may either hide, become seclusive or else brazen it out, so to speak.

A famous Boston physician was a splendid example of a brusque, overbearing mask used to hide a shrinking, timid, subjectively inferior personality. Always very near-sighted and unattractive, he was essentially shy and modest but decided or felt that this was a rough world and the way to get ahead was to be rough. Towards the weak and sick he was kindness itself—gentle, sympathetic and patient—but towards his colleagues he was a boor. Distant, haughty, quick to demand all the consideration due him, he was noted far and wide for the caustic way he attacked others for their opinions and beliefs and the respect he required for his own. The general opinion of physicians was that he was a conceited, arrogant, aristocratic man, and he was avoided except for his medical opinion, which was usually very sound. Those admitted to the sanctum of this man's real self knew him to be really modest and self-deprecatory, anxious to do right and almost obsessed by the belief that he knew but little compared to others.

One day there walked into my office a lady, head of a large enterprise, who had been pointed out to me some time previously as the very personification of self-assurance and superiority. A dignified woman of middle age, whose reserve and correct manners impressed one at once; she bore out in career and casual conversation this impression of one whose confidence and belief in herself were not misplaced, in other words, a harmoniously developed egotist. What she came to consult me about, was—her feeling of inferiority!

All of her life, said she, she had been overawed by others. As a girl her mother ruled her, and her younger sister, more charming and more vivacious, was the pet of the family. Brought up in a strict church, she developed a firmness of speech and conduct that inhibited the frankness and friendliness of her social contacts. Because of this, and her overserious attitudes generally, girls of her own age rather avoided her, and she became painfully self-conscious in their company as well as in the company of men. She wanted to "let go" but could not, and in time felt that there was something lacking in her, that people laughed at her behind her back and that no one really liked her. Her reaction to this was to determine that she would not show her real feelings, that she would deal with the world on a basis of "business only" and cut out friendship from her life. Her intelligence and her devotion to her work brought her success, and she would have gone her way without regard for her "inferiority complex" had not chance thrown in her way a young woman colleague who saw through her elder's pose and became her friend. My patient drank in this friendship with an avidity the greater for her long loneliness, and she was very happy until the younger woman fell in love with a man and began to neglect her colleague.

This broke Miss B.'s spirit. "Had I not known friendship I might have gone on, but now I feel that every one must see what a fool I am and what a fool I have been. I am more shy than ever, I feel as if every one were really stronger than I am, and that some day everybody will see through my pose,—and then where will I be?"

Hide-and-go-seek is one of the great games of adults as well as of children. We hide our own defects and seek the defects of others in order to avoid inferiority and to feel competitive superiority. But there is a deep contradiction in our natures: we seek to display ourselves as we are to those who we feel love us, and we hide our real self from the enemy or the stranger. The protective marking of birds and insects "amateurish compared to the protective marking we apply to ourselves.

I forbear from depicting further character types. People are not as easily classified as automobiles, and the combinations possible exceed computation. Character growth, in each individual human being, is a growth in likeness to others and a growth in unlikeness, as well. As we move from childhood to youth, and thence to middle and old age, qualities appear and recede, and the personality passes along to unity and harmony or else there is disintegration. He who believes as I do that the Grecian sage was immortally right when he enjoined man to know himself will agree that though understanding character is a difficult discipline it is the principal science of life. We are only starting such a science; we need to approach our subject with candor and without prejudice. Though our subject brings us in direct contact with the deepest of problems, the meaning of life, the nature of the Ego and the source of consciousness, these we must ignore as out of our knowledge. Limiting ourselves to a humble effort to know our fellow men and our own selves, we shall find that our efforts not only add to our knowledge but add unmeasurably to our sympathy with and our love for our fellows.